"In his new book, *Inspire!*, Lance Secretan distinguishes a new paradigm for heartfelt leadership that will transform the way you show up in every area of your life. Whether you are seeking to become a more effective parent, partner, teacher, professional, or friend, *Inspire!* will show you how to reconnect to your creative juices, your love, your passion, and your joy. Prepare to be moved, touched and transformed by Lance's radical ideas."
   Debbie Ford, Author, *The Right Questions*

"With one foot firmly rooted in the material world, and the other just as firmly in the sacred, this heartfelt book is a shining manifesto of what is possible when leaders draw on the deepest cores of personal power and authenticity. It's not for the faint-of-heart, though. What Lance Secretan is after is nothing less than unleashing the volcanic power of the human spirit."
   Gregg Levoy, Author, *Callings: Finding and Following an Authentic Life*

"Lance Secretan believes everyone is blessed with good qualities that make each one of us special. He provides a road map to help you discover who you are, what your purpose is, and how to realize your potential, while, at the same time, energizing and empowering others to do the same."
   Lillian Vernon, Founder, Lillian Vernon Corporation

"The greatest contribution today's business leader can make is to affirm their belief in the sanctity of the human soul, and truly learn how to *Inspire!* We have an opportunity and a responsibility to help return our companies and our society to Higher Ground, and through this process regain our connection with each other. Lance Secretan's compelling new book illuminates the path for us."
   Phil Jacques, President and CEO, Axiom Technologies

"Every issue is made up of tangible and intangible factors. Most of us understand tangibles and miss the intangibles. Lance has given body to key intangible factors which drive all the rest to become substance."
   Don Watt, Founder, DW+Partners Inc.

"Lance Secretan is a proven leader who has been out in front and knows how to inspire. *Inspire!* will give you all the tools you need to gain the courage and confidence to deliver up honor in your own organizations and will help you chart your own course to successfully get to the Higher Ground."
   Mike Abrashoff, Founder and CEO, Grassroots Leadership; Author *It's Your Ship: Management Techniques from the Best Damn Ship in the Navy*

"Secretan is right. Great leaders *inspire* people to find and pursue their own highest purpose. Today's ethics crises remind corporate executives of their higher leadership responsibilities. This book can help re-focus corporate missions and goals on fulfilling long-term social contracts."
   Hazel Henderson, Author, *Building a Win-Win World* and *Beyond Globalization*

"Our work with Lance and his associates was an enlightening process that has led to remarkable results. Our senior team has matured to a high state of awareness of the needs of others and functions in a more cohesive and truthful manner. The journey mapped by Lance and his associates has been an honest and inspiring one that is the beginning of an organizational cultural transformation that has served to awaken the entire organization to provide a higher level of service to all whom it touches."
   Ian Sinclair, Former Associate Vice President, Corporate Planning, Credit Valley Hospital

"Lance Secretan's *Inspire!* is a must-read for every leader who wants to create a culture of service and operational excellence that will endure. Engaging the heart and soul of employees is at the very core of success."
   Quint Studer, CEO, Studer Group, Author, *Hardwiring Excellence*

"*Inspire!* reveals that when the heart and soul work in harmony, the foundation of successful leadership is laid. This book offers the keys to outstanding organizational performance through honoring and serving people. Indeed, it is creating a new culture at Centura where our associates serve passionately and effectively, inspired by leaders who nurture their souls."
   Joseph R. Swedish, President and CEO, Centura Health, Denver, CO

"Growth's biggest enemy—fear—can easily be removed through Higher Ground Leadership. Once again, Lance shows the way with his brilliant thinking and, more importantly, the real-life successes of clients who are applying these breakthrough ideas."
   David Chilton, Author, *The Wealthy Barber*

!nspire!

What Great Leaders Do

Lance Secretan

WILEY

John Wiley & Sons, Inc.

Published by John Wiley & Sons, Inc., Hoboken, New Jersey.
Published simultaneously in Canada.

For general information on our other products and services, or technical support, please contact our Customer Care Department within the United States at 800-762-2974, outside the United States at 317-572-3993 or fax 317-572-4002.

Wiley also publishes its books in a variety of electronic formats. Some content that appears in print may not be available in electronic books. For more information about Wiley products, visit our web site at www.wiley.com.

This book has been manufactured from a high-yield thermomechanical pulp, using less trees per ton of paper than traditional chemical pulping methods, resulting in a lighter stock that wields a better bulk/weight ratio. A totally chlorine-free process using oxygen and hydrogen-peroxide is applied to whiten the paper.

Library of Congress Cataloging-in-Publication Data:

Secretan, Lance H. K.
    Inspire! : what great leaders do / Lance Secretan.
        p. cm.
    "Published simultaneously in Canada."
    ISBN 0-471-64882-5 (cloth : alk. paper)
    1. Leadership. I. Title.
HD57.7 .S43 2004
658.4′092—dc22

                                        2003023867

Printed in the United States of America.

10 9 8 7 6 5 4 3 2 1

To You.
You are the ones we have been waiting for.

Credits:

When you work you are a flute through
whose heart the whispering of the hours
turns to music.
Which of you would be a reed, dumb and silent,
When all else sings together in unison?

Always you have been told that work is
a curse and labor a misfortune.
But I say to you that when you work you fulfill
a part of earth's furthest dream, assigned to you
when the dream was born,
And in keeping yourself with labor you
are in truth loving life,
And to love life's labor is to be intimate
with life's innermost secret.

From *The Prophet* by Kahlil Gibran

Contents

Contents

Lance Secretan's:

Destiny:

To help create a more sustainable and loving planet.

Personal Cause:

To inspire others to honor the sacredness in all relationships.

Corporate Cause:

To change the world by reawakening spirit and values in the workplace.

Calling:

To lead and serve through my writing, teaching, and speaking.

Foreword

Inspire! What Great Leaders Do is a very important book. Lance Secretan's ideas have changed our lives and our organizations and the lives of tens of thousands of our employees. These ideas have touched the lives of millions of people whom we serve every day. This book could change *your* life—and your organization, too.

We are the leaders of some of North America's largest and most successful healthcare systems. Healthcare is the largest employer in America and Canada—employing one in eight people. Fifteen percent of the U.S. gross national product is spent on healthcare.

For years, we have looked to industrial and commercial organizations for our role models in leadership. The public and community sectors have not been appreciated in the same way. This is changing. Healthcare is perhaps the most complex sector of the economy. In healthcare, leaders guide, coach, and mentor tens of thousands of employees, negotiate with thousands of suppliers, regulators, independent contractors, security, and safety institutions. We oversee police, fire, ambulance, helicopter, and drug control services. We build enormously complex buildings and infrastructure. We operate degree-granting colleges, laboratories, and research centers, bring babies into this world, care for those leaving it, and heal those in between. We employ diagnostic equipment that is some of the most expensive and sophisticated in the world. We work closely with national security, military, law, and drug enforcement agencies; foreign governments; academic and research institutions; and foundations and charitable organizations. In effect, we are running a vast medical community—a sprawling and immense hotel, complete with complex, internally managed catering needs, power and energy systems, water, security, maintenance, insurance, and fire services—not to mention a wide array of life-and-death medical interventions and services. All of this is done in collaboration with physicians, who are among the best educated and most intelligent people, and who are, for the most part, independent practitioners, not employees. Thus, old story tactics of intimidation and fear do not work—the leader must rely on influence and inspiration. The CEO of a healthcare system has, in effect, a more complex responsibility than a city mayor, in one of the most regulated, legally challenged, and critical industries in the world. It can be argued that if one can learn to lead and inspire in these contexts, one can lead and inspire anywhere.

This book is important because it describes a philosophy called *Higher Ground Leadership* that has been widely used in healthcare and, as a result, has contributed to widespread personal transformation among healthcare workers and their leaders, service providers, and vendors and has thus helped to inspire an industry that is not only reinventing itself, but is also setting the agenda for leadership and corporate governance in the decades ahead.

The principles of Higher Ground Leadership have helped our organizations reduce staff turnover by as much as 66 percent, double levels of employee morale and patient and customer satisfaction, increase the clinical outcomes of many procedures, implement Six Sigma programs successfully, thus contributing to dramatic cost savings and waste elimination, cut the time taken to prepare operating rooms by 50 percent and dramatically increase their throughput, increase profits by 1,000 percent and eliminate layoffs and the use of outsourced labor. Higher Ground Leadership touches the whole human, not just the working human, so it has helped to heal marriages, improve relationships between parents and children, among others, contributed to addiction cessation, strengthened values and beliefs, and raised personal performance. Most importantly, it has contributed to personal fulfillment, meaning, and inspiration and, therefore, organizational performance and reputation. One practitioner stated simply that, after the birth of her children, Higher Ground Leadership was the most important experience in her life.

This is a book for our times and our success. Our society has been so caught up in reacting to change, making a strong bottom line, reducing our workforce, and running from one magic bullet to another that we have lost sight of the very essence of what makes great organizations—its people—and understanding what inspires (not motivates) the hearts and souls of people. People want to be led, and they will follow an inspired and committed leader. Inspiring through love, caring, compassion, and hope is what gets to the heart and soul of who we all are. However, this has too often been seen as the "touchy-feely stuff" that gets in the way of the hard-core, tough-action leaders we have been reading about for the past 10 to 15 years. What we have also been reading about is the lack of integrity, trust, commitment, and loyalty that our organizations now face. Why? It is because we have been ignoring the "soft stuff" that draws people in, gives them a purpose, inspires, and fulfills them. It is what helps them to make a difference and keeps them doing and being all they can be for their friends and loved ones and for the organizations in which they work. This book touches the core of what we believe and feel is the essence of success. It is reaffirming and gratifying to see a book that talks to the human side of business and provides fresh ideas on how we as leaders need to spend the majority of our time doing the "soft stuff"—which is, actually, the "hard stuff."

We urge you to consider the wisdom contained in this book. Read it with an open heart—to read it and reap. It contains the secrets of our success, and perhaps yours.

PAM BILBREY
Baptist Health Care, Pensacola, FL

BOB BURGIN
Mission Hospitals, Asheville, NC

JOE CALVARUSO
Mount Carmel Health System, Columbus, OH

ROBERT A. COLVIN
Memorial Health, Savannah, GA

VAL HALAMANDARIS
National Association of Homecare and Hospice, Washington, DC

JIM PAQUETTE
Providence Health, Kansas City, KS

RICK PEARCE
Riverside Health System, Newport News, VA

SCOTT REGAN
Memorial Health, Savannah, GA

MARK SCOTT
Formerly Mid-Columbia Medical Center, The Dalles, OR

KATHLEEN SELLICK
University of Washington Medical Center, Seattle, WA

MICHAEL SLUBOWSKI
Trinity Health, Novi, MI

AL STUBBLEFIELD
Baptist Health Care, Pensacola, FL

JOSEPH R. SWEDISH
Centura Health, Denver, CO

JOLENE TORNABENI
Inova Health System, Falls Church, VA

KEN WHITE
Trillium Health Center, Mississauga, ON, Canada

Acknowledgments

Thank you to all our clients and Higher Ground Leadership Retreat participants, for this is a book about their experiences and teachings. I thank them for being courageous, trusting, and for letting us guide them in radical ways, and for their inspiration—it is a gift to the heart to see so many people inspiring others and changing the world for the better. I am grateful for the privilege of sharing these inspiring journeys and for the encouragement they have all given during the writing of this book. In particular, Joe Calvaruso and Joseph Swedish are bold pioneers of Higher Ground Leadership. Between them, more than 20,000 employees benefit from their daily inspiration—and so do I.

Friends and clients alike have influenced and critiqued my work over many years, and I am enormously grateful for what I have learned from them and for their encouragement and support. To name a few: Mike Abrashoff, David Alexander, Colleen Barrett, Pam Bilbrey, Jim Blanchard, Ken Blanchard, Bob Burgin, Deb Canales, Ed Carlson, Sam Caster, David Chilton, Deepak Chopra, Robert A. Colvin, Moe and Tricia Dixon, John Dornan, Karen Edelman, Riane Eisler, Debbie Ford, Margot Franssen, Faye Gargiulo, Bill George, Peter Giammalvo, Seth Godin, Jim Goodnight, Val Halamandaris, Carl Hammerschlag, Charles Handy, Hazel Henderson, Gary Holdren, Catherine Ryan Hyde, Phil Jacques, Laurie Kennedy, Gregg Levoy, Sally Lewis, Bill Litton, Scott Livengood, Andrew Lothian (Senior and Junior), Jeff Malone, Caroline Martin, Ted Matthews, Janet Moore, Miles Nadal, Jim Paquette, Rick Pearce, Ian Percy, Bob Pike, Bill Pollard, Charlene Proctor, Scott Regan, Heather Reisman, Joseph Roberts, Rob Ryder, Gerry Schwartz, Mark Scott, Kathleen Sellick, Tim Shriver, Mary Ann Signorelli, Ian Sinclair, Knox Singleton, Michael Slubowski, Hugh Smythe, Julie Snyder, Al Stubblefield, Quint Studer, Jeffrey Swartz, Don Tapscott, Jolene Tornabeni, Brian Tracy, Pat Vanini, Lillian Vernon, Annette Verschuren, Ken White, Marianne Williamson, and Don Ziraldo.

Thank you to my inspiring colleagues at the Secretan Center, especially Rae Brown (Keeper of the Soulspace), Tricia Field (Provider of Resources and

Knowledge), Linda Goodenough (Director of Reality), John Pollock (our former Director of Unlimited Possibilities), T. Kay Rix (Chief Focus Officer), and Tammy Sullivan (Manager of WOW), as well as Sarah Grimmer and the team at Cattails Multimedia.

Thanks to our brilliant worldwide faculty for their marvelous ideas, criticism, and insights; their wisdom, skill, and mastery with clients, and their editorial and research support. They include Kathy Bass, Erin Caldwell, Diane Hoover, Marie Knapp, Helen Morley, Susan Nind, Janice Parviainen, Carol Seglins, Ruth Webber, Catherine Wood, and Deborah Zins.

The team at the Leigh Bureau has been a constant source of support, insight, and inspiration, particularly Bill Leigh, Ron Szymanski, and Wes Neff. Maureen Drexel, Laurie Harting, Matt Holt, Tamara Hummel, Michelle Patterson, and Deborah Schindlar have been an encouraging and inspiring team at John Wiley & Sons.

Thanks to Don Watt for his beautiful cover design and to Simone Gabbay, who has, once again, worked so seamlessly with me to order my straying syntax and perplexing prose.

My wife, Tricia (Moccasin Walker), is a continuing source of inspiration for everything I do in life. She is magic, she nurtures my soul, and she makes my life complete. This book contains much of her wisdom, practical input, loving criticism, and brilliant suggestions. She is my Higher Ground Leader.

Meditation of a New Story Leader

So many meetings get off on the wrong foot, and the energy among the group becomes strained. Beginning your meeting with a meditation can positively influence the tone, direction, and outcome of your discussions. Centering leads to high performance. Let's use meditation to center ourselves as we begin this book, too.

As we are gathered together as colleagues, let us be truly together—as one.

(Silence—reflect for a moment)

Let us pay attention to our breathing.

(Silence)

Let us center in our bodies and our minds.

(Silence)

Let us calm our bodies and our minds.

(Silence)

Let us go within.

(Silence)

Let us put a half-smile on our faces and cause it to flow to every corner of our beings.

(Silence)

Let us reflect on the Source of each of us, our colleagues, and everything in the universe.

(Silence)

Let us remember that we are all living beings, brothers and sisters, nourished by the same Source of life.

(Silence)

Let us resolve to cease being a cause of suffering to each other at work and throughout life.

(Silence)

From the Source, let us fill our hearts with love and compassion—toward each other and all living things.

(Silence)

Let us resolve to live and work in a way that does not harm our planet—and instead heals it.

(Silence)

Let us resolve to live and work in a way that harms no other living beings—and instead affirms and supports them.

(Silence)

With humility, and the recognition of the sacredness of life, let us pray for and practice loving-kindness.

(Silence)

Let us share sacred space together on Higher Ground.

Introduction

One of the greatest needs of the human spirit is to be inspired and to inspire. Inspiration is the oxygen of the soul. Inspiration comes from love, not fear—we cannot be inspired if we are not loving and loved. Yet, it is a paradox of our times that we are more afraid and less inspired than ever before.

Recently, I spent the day on the 56th floor of a building in Chicago. At the end of the day, I called my wife. "I have just had a fantastic day," I told her. "I have been in a wonderful meeting on the 56th floor of a skyscraper in Chicago. It was a glorious, blue-sky day, and I could see for miles—the Navy pier, Lincoln Park Zoo, sailboats on Lake Michigan, Comiskey Park, Wrigley Field—it was beautiful." My wife paused for a minute and then said, "I'm glad you waited until this evening to tell me this—the U.S. Department of Homeland Security called for a Code Orange today, and I've been worried about you." A few years ago, she would probably have said, "Oh! How wonderful! How far could you see? How did it feel to be up so high?" There has been a fundamental shift in how we view life—people filtering their experiences through new lenses of fear.

> Keep your fears to yourself, but share your inspiration with others.
>
> Robert Louis Stevenson

This growing level of fear that has characterized our lives in recent years has led to an epidemic loss of personal inspiration and a widespread sense of personal sadness—fear is the shadow of love and the enemy of inspiration. Fear has seeped into the lives of all of us. Whether we admit it or not, these are times in which fear stalks and grips us, distracting our attention from tasks and people and, therefore, reducing our mastery and effectiveness as humans. We are afraid of health risks, personal safety, inadequate financial security on retirement, job loss, institutions, government, radicalism, dying, racialism, isolation, violence—and the list of fears is endless. Being inspired and optimistic is one thing; trying to inspire or be inspired from a place of fear is another thing altogether.

From Out There to In Here

We live in paradoxical times. We are afraid of the world and the dangers it holds, but optimistic that we have the inner resources to weather these storms. We have lost a measure of confidence in our institutions, our government, self-centered capitalism, quick fixes, and easy answers, but we have a growing hope that there is more than these things. Leading and parenting becomes more difficult as we discover that followers and children know more about most things than we do — just reflect on who the Information Technology manager is in your family. We are more grounded and spiritually mature, yet less confident about a brave new world. Citing their findings in a survey of 38,000 respondents worldwide, the Pew Research Center for the People and the Press concluded, "In most countries surveyed, people rate the quality of their own lives much higher than the state of their nation; and their rating of national conditions is more positive than their assessment of the state of the world."[1] This prompted Rushworth Kidder, director of the Institute for Global Ethics, to observe, "Translation: Things aren't so good, but I'm doing better than my country, which is doing better than the world. The point: That there's less and less I can trust out there, and more and more need to fall back upon my own resources."[2]

We are beginning to realize that "out there" may not be as secure as we thought, nor does it seem to hold all the answers we assumed it did. "In here," it seems, for people all over the world, may contain more wisdom and meaning than anything "out there." Old story leaders, still clinging with assurance to the models and theories that worked so well for them in the past, continue to look for answers "out there." New Story Leaders, seeing a leadership paradigm better suited for an earlier time that no longer exists, search for wisdom "in here." The former is fear based, the latter is inspired by love.

From this we can conclude that we have two choices: playing not to lose, a fear-based way of living; or playing to win, an attitude that overcomes fear with love.

A leader who does not inspire is like a river without water.

Every follower yearns to be inspired by his or her leader. Indeed, every person yearns to be inspired by every other person. When we fail to do so, we diminish each other and sadden our souls. Thus, the role of each of us is to inspire. Inspiration is a subject that engages us in every aspect of our lives — not just in some compartments of it.

So I set out on a journey of discovery:

- Why are we short of great contemporary examples of people who inspire us?
- Why are we unable to discern and practice a durable theory of inspiration?

Looking back over history, we can all see that this has not always been so—the history of every culture is rich with examples of inspiring people. As I began to research the great inspirers throughout history, learning about their characteristics and searching for clues about their unique gifts, I found a common theme. The most inspiring people in history had a clear inner knowing about their:

- Destiny (*Why* I am here on Earth).
- Cause (How I will *be* while I am here—what I will stand for).
- Calling (What I will *do* and how I will use my talents and gifts to serve).

I call this combination the "Why-Be-Do" (Figure I.1).

The most inspiring people in history all knew these things, although they probably did not use my terminology. From over 10 years of research, I distilled a series of sacred insights that evolved into a model, based on the wisdom of these great people. The essence of their greatness as inspirers and leaders was about *being* as well as doing—how they *lived* inspiring lives and therefore inspired others and themselves, rather than learning "a method" of inspiring.

These insights inspired me to form a body of work that I call *Higher Ground Leadership* that has since been taught to thousands of people around the world by hundreds of teachers. It forms the heart of this book.

Higher Ground Leadership is the term we are using to describe a breakthrough leadership practice based on the proven behaviors of these great leaders that questions, deepens, and enriches conventional leadership thinking (which I call "the old story") with wisdom based on ancient teachings that have been adapted to our times (which I call "the New Story").

Some years ago, I was about to make a speech to a large audience of senior leaders. During the barbecue that preceded the event, one of the participants asked me what I was going to talk about. I said, "I am going to say that we should all love each other and tell the truth, but I am going to take an hour-and-a-half to

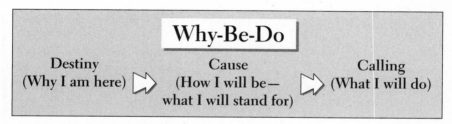

Figure I.1   Destiny, Cause, and Calling—Why-Be-Do.

say it! It is the same message I have written in all my books, too, because there isn't anything more to say. It has all been said before by people worthier than I am—but I will state it in a modern idiom." The New Story of leadership is Higher Ground Leadership—a way of being and leading that is rooted in these two fundamental, if not new, ideas: *We should love one another and tell the truth.*

When we peel away the outer theories and the models postulated by so many writers, theorists, and students of leadership, one thing remains at the essence of the practice of great leadership—*inspiration.* What do great leaders do? They inspire. What does a parent do to encourage brilliance, growth, and values in their children? We could say they lead them—but if we look closer, what they are really doing is inspiring them. Perhaps our study of leadership has caused us to focus too much energy on the less relevant aspects of leadership—the mechanics instead of the essence—the sunset data rather than the joy, beauty, and experience of the sunset. After all, leadership is something we *live ourselves,* rather than *do to others.*

The ideas of Higher Ground Leadership proposed in this book go beyond the popular theories of leadership widely practiced in modern organizations and in society. It is a body of work that is built on a clearer understanding of inspiration, how it works, how we can learn to inspire others and ourselves.

Before we look at this radically different approach, we review current thinking and theory about the psychology of relationships, the reasons why we experience so much discomfort with the popular models as they are practiced today, why we find it so hard to change from the old story to the New Story, despite incontrovertible evidence that we should do so, and the major forces that are converging in such a momentous way to cause us to rethink old story practices.

In my search for something more profound than the usual personality-based ideas about inspiration and leadership and my research into the lives of scores of the most inspiring people in history, as well as many contemporary ones, I found clear evidence that all of these great people:

- Had extraordinary clarity about their Destiny, Cause, and Calling;
- Aligned these fully in their lives;
- Knew how to serve and bring out the best in others; and
- Had a gift for being inspired themselves.

These were shared characteristics among all of those I studied, that I will describe in this book, together with the seven steps I have identified (in these great leaders) so that you can learn how to become more inspired and, in turn, inspire others more.

This is a book that will help to regenerate your life, redefine your dreams, and infuse new passion into your very existence. Our capacity to inspire others depends on our own sense of meaning, purpose, and fulfillment. When we are truly *on purpose* in our lives, our energy translates into an inspiring experience for ourselves—and therefore for others.

> **!**
> Life is change.
> Growth is optional.
> Choose wisely.
> Karen Kaiser Clark
> **!**

This book is also about regaining our voice, becoming courageous enough to be authentic again—becoming re-inspired and remembering how to inspire others—as teachers, professionals, parents, executives, friends—anywhere where others will flourish if they are inspired.

I hope that these pages will re-invigorate what it means for you to be inspiring—at home or at work—and that as you travel on this journey of discovery with me, a fresh understanding of the *Why*, *Be*, and *Do* of your life will unfold for you. Together we will share concepts, engage in reflection, and meditate. The purpose of our journey together is to explore and discern the process learned by all those who arouse greatness in others—past and present. You will learn the process that will reveal the *real* purpose of your life, *why* you are here, *what* you are meant to do while you are here, *how* you will do it, *how* you will serve, *how* you will invite others to fully participate with you, and *how* you can inspire them and therefore yourself. Thus, your capacity to be inspired will eclipse your fears, as well as the fears of others, enabling them to be inspired by you.

There are many opportunities for us to become more inspired, but the workplace may offer the richest soil to till. When the late country singer Johnny Paycheck was asked about the appeal of his inspirational worker's anthem, *Take This Job and Shove It*, he observed, "Well, I think it is what everybody would like to say to their boss but can't. They can use the song and play it in jest, but way down, deep inside, they mean it."[3]

There is no shortage of data showing the lack of inspiration at work. A 2003 study by Towers Perrin/Gang and Gang,[4] showed that three-quarters of those surveyed felt negatively toward their work and, of these, 28 percent were actively looking to find employment elsewhere, and, perhaps most disturbing of all, 28 percent of those most "intensely negative" planned to continue being unhappy right where they were! Gallup's U.S. Employee Engagement Index, which has been completed by more than 87,000 divisions or work units within corporations and approximately 1.5 million employees, shows that 28 percent of employees are engaged (equivalent to being inspired and emotionally attached to the organization), 55 percent are disengaged, and 17 percent are *actively disengaged*. This

means that 72 percent of America's employees are either emotionally disconnected from their work, or, even worse, actively working to undermine the organization for which they work.[5]

What can we do to move ourselves and others from a place of fear to a place
of love, from scarcity to abundance, from motivation to inspiration, and thus create inspiring environments that provide hope and encourage high performance?
In *Inspire!* we explore the circumstances that have led to our present intense
hunger for inspiration—more intense, I believe, than ever before in history—discover better ways to lead others, to inspire and ennoble them and their souls
through learning to respect the sacredness in them and in everything.

Confusing Motivation with Inspiration

Motivation, which is based on fear, comes from the personality. Inspiration,
which is based on love, comes from the soul. People often ask me to define the
soul. I cannot do it. Many others have tried. Alain wrote, "The soul is that which
denies the body. For example, that which refuses to run when the body trembles,
to strike when the body is angry, to drink when the body is thirsty," and George
Santayana said, "The soul is the voice of the body's interests." But these remain
elusive concepts. Perhaps the soul is best defined by its ineffable effect: Thomas
Carlyle thought that "the soul gives unity to what it looks at with love," and Ralph
Waldo Emerson believed that "the soul's emphasis is always right."

You probably share my difficulty in defining the soul, the greatest of all concepts. But this I know: The soul is bigger than any single corporation, government,
community, family, healthcare facility, law enforcement, religious, or learning institution. No single organization is big enough for the soul. Of one thing we can be
sure: Our soul is infinite and part of the largest universe we can imagine—and
then some.

How can we define the soul? Most theories of leadership revolve around the
ego and the personality. The central idea of contemporary leadership theory is
that successfully manipulating, exploiting, and controlling the behavior of other
people is a set of teachable concepts. Many of the nearly 60,000 books on leadership listed on Amazon.com attest to this thinking. But the secret of leaders who
inspire is that they have grown so that they can comfortably integrate both personality and the ego.

What if we could inspire others by appealing to something within them that
is far greater than the personality or the ego? What if we could excite something
emotional or intuitive that is at the very essence of our humanness? What would
we call this if we could find it, work with it, and engage it? I think we would call

this ineffable thing the *soul*—the holiness and sacredness within us that is larger than anything we can imagine in the narrow definition of personality or ego—something that is the mystical, magical, and extraordinary essence that is the life force in each of us.

While our personalities may be excited, stimulated, motivated, or intimidated—this can never be enough. We all need and want more, and that more is to be found in a very deep place. Most of us never connect at that level. But what if we could? What if our leadership talents and understanding were such that every relationship honored this special place—the soul—and engaged it, excited it, honored it, and nourished it? We all have a sense, each of us in our own ways, of what is really meant here. It is something bigger, something that embraces meaning and fulfillment, something that we experience far too rarely in our lives. All of us can name those sacred moments—for many of us, too few and far between—when we felt so engaged, so inspired, and so filled with spirit, that we were certain we had made a soulful connection. These extraordinary moments almost always pass too quickly. But what if we could sustain them? What if we could revisit them? What if we knew how to reach those places in each of us, anytime we wished? Then we would have the power to inspire the soul. Mechthild von Magdeburg, the thirteenth-century mystic and visionary, said, "The soul is made of love and must ever strive to return to love. Therefore, it can never find rest or happiness in other things. It must lose itself in love. By its very nature it must seek God, who is love." We cannot inspire unless we have let go of our fears.*

Inspiration occurs in all of life, but is measured in different ways from motivation. Inspiration is as natural to humans as motivation, and both are an essential part of our whole. Motivation is the yang; inspiration is the yin. The source of motivation can be found in the personality; the source of inspiration is to be found in the soul.

Inspired people become enthused. The word *enthuse* derives from the Greek root words meaning to be inspired and being possessed by the divine, *en* and *Theos*. So, enthusiasm means "one with the energy of God." Thus, inspiration and enthusiasm are conditions desired by all of us. Individuals and teams who are inspired and enthused are operating on a different plane than the rest of us, and they know it and cherish it. People frequently move from well-paying positions where they are highly motivated to lesser-paying positions where they are inspired. The new reality (although there is nothing really new about it, we have just been slow on the uptake) is that people want to work in inspiring organizations, for inspiring leaders, in inspiring industries and careers, doing work that inspires customers and suppliers and each other. *Anything less than this is just a*

---

* Please visit http://www.secretan.com/inspire to experience a multimedia version of this section entitled *Leading from the Soul*.

> If you don't live it, it won't come out of your horn.
>
> Charlie Parker

job. Indeed, this is true throughout our lives—we want to be married to inspiring people, have inspiring friends and children, and live an inspired life.

What compelled followers to dedicate themselves with such passion to the visions of Christ, Buddha, Gandhi, Confucius, Martin Luther King Jr., Mother Teresa, Jefferson, Washington, and Nelson Mandela? They were inspired more than motivated. We know that Martin Luther King Jr. did not say, "I have a strategic plan!" And Mother Teresa did not have a quality program—she didn't need one. As we unravel the mysteries of these subtle but significant nuances in leadership and relationship style, we find that inspiration underpinned the philosophy of every great leader.

We tend to assume that our role is to motivate others to achieve something. Yet the greatest leaders in history seldom thought this way—none of these leaders principally focused on getting other people to "do things." They were trying to practice a way of *being* and thus inspire—not motivate—people to change and enhance themselves and the world.

We can design incentive programs that will motivate; we can even motivate with fear. This is a common practice among many old story leaders because motivation exploits different levels of power—the power of one person to punish or reward another. Motivation is therefore a valuable currency that the old story leader keeps in his toolkit. For the motivator, it is a "technique," a means for altering the behavior of others, a means of exploiting, controlling, and manipulating them. It is a self-focused practice, too. When we attempt to motivate others, we intend to cause behavior in them that achieves something *we* want. When we attempt to motivate, we are not usually intending to serve others in their best interests. At its best, motivation is an attempt to serve others in *our* best interests. It is this transparently selfish intent that causes cynicism instead of inspiration.

> I used to think that running an organization was equivalent to conducting a symphony orchestra. But I don't think that's quite it; it's more like jazz. There is more improvisation.
>
> Warren Bennis

Many people achieve great mastery of the technology of the personality. With careful study and the routine practice of modified behavior, they become experts in personal relationships. They are able to "manage" and "exploit" relationships brilliantly. They have great charm and visible grace and endear themselves to those with whom they connect. But this practice has its limits. The more we practice, the better we become experts in "personality"—but that is all. We can only go so far using the personality alone, for the technology of personality leads us eventually to a cul-de-sac. What is needed at this stage in our development is a journey down a different path: We need to turn our attention to the soul, engaging others at the level of the soul, relating with them from our soul to theirs, without managing or manipulating anything and without any conscious modification. For many, this is a very different way to be.

We have been confusing motivation with inspiration. The dictionary tells us that to motivate is "to provide a motive; to induce, incite, impel." We hire "motivational speakers" at conferences to "rev up the troops" and buy motivational posters, mugs, plaques, T-shirts, and greeting cards. Unfortunately, our levels of cynicism have reached epic proportions because we understand the technology of motivation, and we sometimes experience the hypocrisy of it. *Forbes* magazine reflected this sense of cynicism by proposing these tongue-in-cheek suggestions:

> Maybe a poster for the boss's wall: "Thanks for all the overtime. I haven't seen my kids in years." Or a plaque: "This award is presented to [name of boss] for forcing me to make a BIG deference." For the factotum just forced out: A preprinted greeting card that says, "Here's to the day when the board does to you what you just did to me."[6]

Motivation is something we "do" to someone; inspiration is something that is the result of a soulful relationship. Anyone who has had the privilege of working with a great mentor in their lives knows and appreciates the difference. The mentor is not in it for themselves; they are offering a gift to you, an act of love and service. Their generosity of spirit and their gift of learning is what inspires—them and you. Motivation comes from a place of self-concern—"I want to change your behavior with a reward or incentive, so that, if you meet the targets or goals I set for you, I will meet my own needs and goals." Inspiration, on the other hand, comes from a place of love and service, with no strings attached—"I love you and wish to serve and teach you and help you to grow." When we motivate, we serve ourselves first; when we inspire, we serve others first.

When we are motivated, our emotions and behavior are determined by external powers. When we are inspired, our emotions and behaviors are determined by powers from within. Many people have become adept at manipulating the personality—motivating others—but we have much to learn about inspiring the souls of others. Few people can even bring themselves to talk this kind of language publicly, fearing that they may appear too "warm and fuzzy." Yet after our need to love and be loved, inspiration is the key priority of individuals and organizations. Where people may be motivated to achieve, avarice and self-indulgence are the energies that propel them. The energy that propels inspiration is love. Motivation is self-focused; inspiration is other-focused. Motivation serves me; inspiration serves you. The difference in organizations, teams, and families is palpable. Inspired people arouse the hearts of others, and thus inspire the world.

Inspiration is strikingly different from motivation. The word is derived from the Latin root *spirare* meaning "spirit," to breathe, to give life—the breath of God. *Webster's Dictionary* defines inspiration as "breathing in, as in air to the lungs; to infuse with an encouraging or exalting influence; to animate; stimulation by a divinity, a genius, an idea or a passion; a divine influence upon human beings." It is not difficult to see the difference between being motivated and the blissful experience of being inspired. Motivation is a relationship between personalities; inspiration is a relationship between souls.

Inspiration does not depend on power relationships. On the contrary, when we are inspired, we are truly empowered. To inspire others, we must create an environment in which people sense a power beyond another human, a higher power, a divine influence that wells up from deep within, causing them to be infused with the breath of God. In other words, we must become as effective at engaging the energy of the soul (inspiration) as we have become at engaging the energy of the personality (motivation).

Moving from Tired to Inspired

Because we are so absorbed with perfecting the techniques of motivation, we feel compelled to "drive" everything. We overuse the word "driven." We want to be values-driven, customer-driven, mission-driven, market-driven, technology-driven, solutions-driven, and self-driven. Perhaps this is why so many people are driven to drink, driven insane, or driven to distraction? Are Zen masters "driven"? Were Christ, Lao-Tzu, Confucius, Buddha, or Mother Teresa "driven"? Is being driven part of the problem rather than part of the solution? What would it look like if we were customer-inspired? Or market-inspired? Or values-inspired? Or family-inspired? Wouldn't anyone rather be inspired than driven? There is a greater sacredness and inner beauty associated with inspiration, the breath of God, compared to the manic style of the old story leader that causes us to be driven—and thus drained. *We yearn to move from feeling tired to inspired.*

Inspiration is that moment when we access the ineffable experience of the spirit inside us. It is our muse, our creative juice, our love and passion and joy bursting from our heart in a tide of beautiful energy. Inspiration is an inner knowing that transcends any external motivation. Inspiration is a different class of experience from motivation.

The purpose of this book is to change and inspire your life, to slow the personality down long enough for the soul to be heard, to help you ask important questions, thus creating the opportunity for your soul to become an equal life-partner with your personality. Carl Jung observed that the birth of the self is always a defeat for the ego. I hope that in this book, I can help you to ask yourself the right questions and provide you with some examples, stories of those who have found and are living their Destiny, Cause, and Calling—their "Why-Be-Do"—and have learned an expanded way of being inspiring and being inspired, and offer a process for reflection and some tools to help you refresh your awareness of how you want to *be* in this world.

The last and by far the most difficult part is how you choose to act on the discoveries you make. However, if you reflect honestly and deeply to mine the riches that are buried among your most precious inner resources—you may just change your life.

And your life, when lived to its full potential, will become another miracle.

In our organization, we have a question that we often ask each other: "What are you teaching when you are not speaking?" Inspiring others is more about who you are deep inside than what you have copied from others. Knowing who we each are, and using the wisdom in these discoveries, is how we inspire others. Every communication between humans and other living things is an opportunity to inspire. We are on this planet for a short time—this in itself is an inspiration. It is important that we do nothing that spoils this magic or violates this divine trust. If notable military leaders can inspire their followers to forfeit their lives in acts of extreme human sacrifice, violence, and folly, then we must strive to inspire others to even more noble aspirations through love and grace.

> Live as if you were to die tomorrow. Learn as if you were to live forever.
>
> Mahatma Gandhi

Leaders are coaches. Great coaches inspire. A coach develops an ongoing partnership that inspires others toward improved performance and greater quality and fulfillment in their personal and professional lives. All great athletes have coaches—they would not be great without them—and greatness in life is no different. Coaches listen, observe, and advise others based on their own experience and wisdom. They honor and support the sacredness, creativity, and resourcefulness of those they coach. Coaching is an act of love and service. Great coaches—and great leaders—identify fears, erase them with love, and therefore inspire—and that is what this book is all about.

1

Stuck in the old story

Who Is Required to Inspire?

We *all* need to be inspired and to inspire others. We are called to inspire in almost every aspect and stage of our lives—it is an essential ingredient of every part of the human experience. Inspiration builds relationships, forms friendships, changes thinking and philosophies, gives birth to new ideas, and shapes lives and hearts. As children, we inspire—at school, in sports, in our pastimes, and in our friendships. As we grow and become parents, we are invited to assume new responsibilities, and we are called on to inspire at home, in our places of worship, in our corporations, in our communities, and in our countries. Inspiration changes the world.

Let's start with my definition of leadership that will guide us throughout this book:

> *Leadership is a serving relationship with others that inspires their growth and makes the world a better place.*

This definition excludes such leaders as Hitler, Stalin, Attila the Hun, Mussolini, Machiavelli, and Genghis Khan—they did not make the world a better place, an essential characteristic of a Higher Ground Leader.

So often, leadership is rehearsed. We read books by former corporate leaders. We learn "techniques" and "the tricks of the trade": how to dress, how to make a speech, how to command attention. Through all this, the soul waits patiently while the personality indulges itself. This is why leadership often gets such bad press: It is practiced as a function instead of as the result of noble, powerful, and passionately held values. The truth is, nothing happens without the presence of inspiring leadership. But because the soul waits patiently, it often remains

> Never undertake anything for which you wouldn't have the courage to ask the blessing of Heaven.
>
> G. C. Lichtenberg

unheard—suspended. Meanwhile, the personality engages in "doing." Eventually, the personality becomes aware of the soul and chooses—or is sometimes forced—to listen to it. This is when we change from "acting" to "being"—perhaps the most important change in our lives.

This is the difference between old story leadership and New Story Leadership—the difference between working from the personality alone on the one hand, and aligning the personality *and* the soul on the other—*the difference between doing and being*, the difference between being unconscious and becoming *conscious*. It is the difference between *talking* about Higher Ground Leadership and *being* a Higher Ground Leader.

Table 1.1 on page 3 compares the essential differences between old story and New Story thinking.

To engage the soul, we must ask questions that go beyond the personality or the ego, such as, "What are we communicating when we are not using words?" and we must be rigorous when we ask ourselves if we are pleased with the answers. Asking subtle, soul-centered questions like these is a sign that the soul has been stirred, that we are becoming conscious and ready to inspire others from a place of inner wisdom, authenticity, and integrity, rather than from a rehearsed, rote-learned, or copied approach to leadership and inspiring others that lacks substance and roots.

> You can tell whether a man is clever by his answers. You can tell whether a man is wise by his questions.
>
> Naguib Mahfouz

Inspiration is not a formula or a model—it must come from a natural and deep place. NBC news anchor Tom Brokaw describes former President Richard Nixon's unsuccessful attempts to inspire an employee during a presidential motorcade, when one of the motorcycle escorts crashed and broke his leg. The injured man was lying 10 yards from Nixon and someone said, "The guy has worked three years for you—comfort him. So Richard Nixon walked over and looked at the injured man and said, 'Do you enjoy your job?'"[1]

Inspiration comes from inside, from a deep place we call *authenticity*. It is a way of *being*.

How might we touch the world if we engaged the soul, becoming *fully conscious leaders*, totally awake and aware of our Destiny, Cause, and Calling—our sacred purpose for being in *this* universe at *this* time?

TABLE 1.1
The old story and the New Story Compared

	Old Story Leaders Believe	New Story Leaders Believe
Leadership	Warriors make the best leaders. Our values are shaped and defined by our religious and political leaders. Rational thinking and focused logic are the hallmarks of great leadership.	Servant-leadership is overhauling the entire notion of leadership. Organizations have become the greatest force for positive social change on Earth. Empathy and being connected to our feelings and the feelings of others are the key to inspiring others.
Values	Our values are determined by what we can legitimately get away with.	Values systems must always enhance the well-being of others and the planet.
The End of Competition	We compete in a fear-based, "dog-eat-dog" world, in which only the fittest survive.	The end of competition is at hand. We are an interdependent whole.
The Cause	People and organizations become great when guided by superior mission, vision, and values statements.	A great Cause is a magnet for passion.
The New Customer	The purpose of an organization is to create profit by identifying customers and meeting their needs. The "Brand" is built by investing in marketing, advertising, and positioning.	The purpose of an organization is to create profit by inspiring people who inspire others and build great organizations. The "Brand" is built from the inside out—how we relate to others and the planet becomes our "Voice."
Harmony	Personal and work life is separate. Personal and work life must be in balance.	The lines between work and personal life are disappearing. Our lives are becoming whole, seamless, and integrated.
The Calling	The best career is one that will provide the greatest financial prospects.	By practicing our true Calling, not a career, and guiding others to do the same, we ensure that we do not die with our music still inside us.

(continued)

TABLE 1.1 *(Continued)*

	Old Story Leaders Believe	New Story Leaders Believe
Soulspace	Work environments should be secular and efficient.	Our well-being depends on the quality of the physical environment in which we undertake our work—Soulspace.
Technology	The purpose of technology is to automate the mundane.	The purpose of technology is to connect the souls of the planet together.
Learning	The most important fringe benefits are health insurance and retirement plans.	The most important fringe benefits are life-long learning and wisdom, which guarantee health insurance and secure retirement.
Inspiration	Motivation drives high performance.	Motivation is based on fear. Inspiration is based on love. Therefore, the human heart thrives on inspiration.

Before looking at how we become inspired and inspire others, let us review the major changes in context that are requiring us to re-frame our thinking, what has brought us to our current views and practices on this subject, and the fundamental shifts in our thinking that are required if we are to become transformed and able to transform others.

The Powerful Energies of Change

Seismic changes are reshaping the social landscape, making the role of leading and inspiring more complex than ever before.

The first change is the growth in public awareness, self-responsibility, and accountability. Patients know more about their own health today than their physicians did two decades ago; they often know more than their specialist medical advisors. When *Fortune* magazine ran a cover article about prostate cancer, it was Andy Grove, then chairman of Intel Corp., not a cancer specialist, who made the cover. Inside were 11 pages describing Grove's illness, his research, his research techniques, and how he made his treatment decisions. For additional insights, reporters turned to other prostate cancer victims, including Norman Schwarzkopf and Michael Milken.

We live in an age where everyone is an expert on all popular subjects, and some are experts on the arcane. Because people have experienced the fallibility of professionals and the systems in which they practice, they have concluded that it is in their best self-interest to reclaim responsibility for their own lives through self-education and advocacy. They have found a cornucopia of data in journals, popular science, and medical reports, specialist associations, radio, television, movies and theater, nonmainstream advisors, and the Internet, where a wealth of instant information is available. Our access to education and information has never been greater, and this search for and acceptance of personal accountability is being repeated in every facet of our lives. As a result, we are all now mini-specialists in a wide range of areas, including healthcare, education, politics, religion, the environment, and work. This means that any leadership role, whether at home as parents, or at work as executives, is complicated by the fact that we are leading people who know more than ever before, and usually more than we do. Leading and inspiring an expert is different from leading a learner. The New Story Leader understands and has mastered this challenge.

The second major energy of change is the growth of "leadership fatigue"—we have become tired of the leader-as-motivator stereotype. In the workplace, there has been a dramatic growth in the understanding of the dynamics and practice of leadership. Wide access into boardrooms, corporate decision-making processes, and the inner workings of organizations has begun to describe leadership in plain language for nonleaders. Our entertainment media teaches leadership (the good and the bad) and demystifies it for audiences of every age, every day.

In the past, almost everyone, from tin-pot dictators to schoolyard bullies, not to mention old story CEOs and religious and political leaders, learned the technology of "power-based leadership"—a fear-based leadership that seeks to manipulate, control, and dominate followers.

The Annual Global CEO Survey conducted by PricewaterhouseCoopers in conjunction with the World Economic Forum found 1,161 CEOs from 33 countries sharing a growing concern about how the public perceives corporations.[2] The golden glow of corporate leadership has recently been tarnished, and while it is in all our best interests to burnish the reputation and practice of corporate leadership, the reality is that, for a while at least, we are destined to lead an increasingly cynical group of followers.

As a result, the old story, power-driven leader now has to contend with skeptical and sometimes unresponsive followers, weary of leadership jargon and techniques. They have heard it all before—the "rah-rah" urgings, the slogans and T-shirts, the hype of conferences, and the internal public relations programs. This has made them a jaded audience for leaders—and they therefore fail to inspire.

The third significant change is the dramatic and universal search for greater meaning in our lives that is sweeping the world. Rushworth Kidder, commenting on the Pew Research cited later in this chapter, wrote that there is

> a growing vortex of distrust in professional expertise. As gurus of various stripes encounter high-profile peril and moral mayhem—from medicine to academics, from auditing to the church, from athletics to investment advice—the public has still more reason to turn inward and rely less on others. But if we're thrown back on our own devices, what is there at the core to rely on? Americans have no long traditions of metaphysical discourse. The pragmatic individualism that settled the frontier left little room for an intense French introspection or a brooding Russian philosophizing. It's hard enough to get the average Yankee to comment on the meaning of things, never mind the meaningfulness of meaning.[3]

> Your vision will become clear when you can look into your heart. Who looks outside, dreams; who looks inside, awakens.
>
> Carl Gustav Jung

Yet, difficult and wrenching though we may be finding it, we are becoming both more introspective and philosophical. A growing number of people are embracing the notion that we are spiritual beings with spiritual needs, not just personalities with ego needs.

A word here about terminology: *Religion* is a system of beliefs and practices shared by a community of people—a doctrine. These beliefs and practices nurture and encourage a relationship with a particular deity, provide moral guidance, and give meaning of life. *Spirituality*, on the other hand, is the way we live out our deepest beliefs, values, and convictions in our daily life. It is the way we live out our search for peace and meaning. Some people call this "lived religion." Religions are one way in which spirituality can be expressed. They are systems of beliefs and practices that have become recognizable as a particular tradition, but spirituality is not synonymous with religion, and spirituality can be expressed and developed in many ways apart from religion. And just as there are religious people who are not spiritual, there are also spiritual people who are not religious.

> Here is the test to find whether your mission on Earth is finished: If you're alive, it isn't.
>
> Richard Bach

Our everyday choices reveal glimpses of our spirituality by pointing toward what we value most in life and what ethical principles we follow. The old story of power-based leadership appealed to the personality. But people crave nourishment for their hearts and souls. They are yearning to be inspired through relationships with people who are aware of and care for their spiritual needs. They want to connect from the heart.

The great excitement of our times is the growing number of people who are awakening from their deep sleep to the realization that they are experiencing an acute spiritual hunger, an inner sense of restlessness, and a desire for a greater sense of purpose in their lives. As a force that leads to radical change, no power in the universe is greater than a soul seeking to satisfy its spiritual hunger. The greatest idea in the study of community building and human relationships that will shape the future is the awareness that leaders must tune in to the wisdom and spirit of their followers.

> ❗
>
> The question is not whether we will die, but how we will live.
>
> Joan Borysenko
>
> ❗

Asking the Right Questions

Since so many people are asking if there is more to life, we need to ask ourselves if we are ready to consciously offer more—are we inspired and do we inspire others? To get at the essence of how we inspire ourselves and others, we must first be clear about who we are, why we are here, and what we plan to do in our short time on Earth. It is from this crucible of self-knowing that we fashion the gold of inspiring relationships.

Perhaps you have, at some time or other, wondered what your life was all about. For many people, the purpose of life is simply to be born, go to school, grow up, be happy, get a job, get married, buy a house, have children, retire, and then die. Millions of people do these things every day—all with varying levels of success. But *why* do we do these things? And what distinguishes any of us from the rest of the teeming millions shackled to the relentless assembly line of life? Could we *be* more than this? As the great skiing legend Warren Miller said, "Don't take life seriously, because you can't come out of it alive."

Perhaps you may have wondered:

- Have I made the most of the life I have lived (and is there time to claim the one I haven't?) as I turn the pages of my life's calendar, observing the mystery of my biography?
- Is there more to my life than increasing market share, beating the competition, achieving the budget, meeting deadlines, dominating the marketplace, increasing shareholder wealth, adding shareholder value, and becoming the lowest-cost producer?

- How did I get to be doing the work I am doing, working for the company I work for, living with the person I live with, in the particular town I live in, being the person that I am, behaving the way I do?
- Why have I pursued the career that I have?
- Could my life be enriched with greater fulfillment and deeper meaning?
- Have I been living my life *too small*?
- What is my purpose on Earth?
- What will my legacy be?

Reflect for a moment on these questions. If you keep a personal journal, please use it to make some notes if you feel this might be helpful.

When we begin to ask the really important questions that matter in our personal universe, we connect—often for the very first time in our lives—with our true potential, because this creates the opportunity for us to achieve the fuller maturity that will enable us to grow. Until then, the surface questions about life offer no more than idle chatter for the mind that has yet to become fully conscious. Life is not just about acquiring things or achieving performance goals. In fact, it isn't about goals at all—it is about *being in the moment*. It is about evolving our full spiritual potential—becoming what we were always meant to be.

But before we can know the answers to those questions—the eternal questions about the meaning of life, we must first do some profound inner work—Soulwork. This requires us to go deep. It requires us to ask reflective, sometimes even disturbing, questions, and then decide whether or not we wish to listen to the answers. In 1903, Rainer Maria Rilke wrote in his *Letters to a Young Poet*:

> . . . have patience with everything unresolved in your heart and try to love the questions themselves as if they were locked rooms or books written in a very foreign language. Don't search for the answers, which could not be given to you now, because you would not be able to live them. And the point is to live everything. Live the questions now. Perhaps then, someday far in the future, you will gradually, without even noticing it, live your way into the answer.[4]

During a university course taught by Albert Einstein, a student pointed out to the great teacher that the questions were the same as the previous semester. Einstein kindly but firmly replied, "That may be, but the *answers* are different this time."

The Legacy of the Higher Ground Leader

One of the questions posed earlier asks: What will your legacy be? Leadership can be the achievement of the mundane, or it can be the achievement and creation of a noble legacy. It can be the achievement of a material legacy—Wal-Mart, Starbucks, Microsoft, Amazon.com, IBM, and other great institutions, for instance, have changed forever the way the world works because of the vision of individuals who saw the greater picture. But it can be an even greater achievement than this—it can be the achievement of a spiritual legacy—the Internet, Disney, Medtronic, Centura Health, Mount Carmel Health System. It is not about whether one is better or worse than the other, but about the order of magnitude of the legacy being created.

> Be daring, be different, be impractical, be anything that will assert integrity of purpose and imaginative vision against the play-it-safers, the creatures of the commonplace, the slaves of the ordinary.
>
> Sir Cecil Beaton

Higher Ground Leaders are New Story Leaders whose personal lives and capacity to inspire others are guided by their Destiny, Cause, and Calling and who create a legacy built on the CASTLE Principles (described in Chapter 12) and therefore change the way the world works, make it a better place, and positively impact the way people do things, how they live their lives, and how they fulfill their dreams. In the end, therefore, it is about creating a noble legacy that people will admire for generations. It is about creating a legacy where the legacy builder and the associated family, community, or institution glows warmly in our minds and hearts, filling our thoughts with ideas that seem both larger-than-life and a confirmation of the magic of life.

Why It's So Difficult to Change

There is a growing sense of anxious anticipation at home and at work, of impending change—the shadow of apprehension, disenchantment, and betrayal conflicts with the light of hope, opportunity, and new beginnings. These are confusing times. They are exciting times. The old story leader, the fierce and brave warrior who takes no prisoners, is ideologically bankrupt, but we are in that awkward place of leaving the old and moving to the new—the transition to the New Story Leader who loves others and tells the truth. We know we need to change, we hear the exhortations, but we are experiencing extreme difficulty doing it. Even when presented with a seemingly endless array of logical arguments and data that should convince us to change, we still don't. There are four reasons why this happens:

1. *Paradigms:* Ever since the publication of Thomas Kuhn's *The Structure of Scientific Revolutions* in 1962, the notion of the paradigm has been a popular concept.[5] Academics graduate within the framework of a specific discipline, complete with rules, assumptions, beliefs, and strictly prescribed ways to make decisions. This becomes our operating paradigm—a box—and if we step out of the box, we will not graduate. Once what our teachers deem to be *the* operating paradigm has been internalized in our minds, all other paradigms appear as wrong, flawed, or silly. Thus equipped, our new paradigm becomes our intellectual operating software, and we become convinced that ours is the *only* right, sensible, and objective way of doing things. Our paradigm is the very water in which we swim, and to be asked to leave this warm and comfortable environment is not only unthinkable, but perhaps even dangerous. We do not ask questions from inside the box—the box *is* the answer. If they are not of our paradigm, the rest of the world is wrong. Our habits thus become ingrained, and our ability to be original or inquiring dies. Many theorists believe that the essentials of personality formation are completed by the age of six, and if this is so, our personal paradigms may be fixed much earlier in our lives than we are prepared to accept. When we act like six-year-olds, this may be the level of personal development at which some of us have maxed out!

> **!**
> Common sense is the collection of prejudices acquired by age eighteen.
> Albert Einstein

2. *Ego and intellectual arrogance:* Thus, equipped with the sureness of our paradigm, we prepare ourselves to rigorously defend the certainty that we are right. For example, from within the box of the leader-as-warrior paradigm, we feel especially threatened by concepts like the soul or love or truth. This is because warrior-leaders regard themselves as the Darwinian survivors of the organizational evolutionary struggle—if we are on top of the corporate food chain, this argument goes, then who is anyone else (and by inference, lesser) to challenge this? A certain intellectual smugness results, and like-minded thinkers close ranks to support each other. Thus, to question the wisdom of the warrior-leader paradigm is to risk seeming "odd" or out-of-step with mainstream thinking, and to do so carries political risks that threaten the ego.

3. *The copyfrog effect:* We remain part of the silent, and therefore invisible, majority, knowing deep inside that we are living a lie, but afraid to step out and say so. An old, but false, urban legend helps to illustrate what can happen to us if we fail to be courageous by challenging the status quo, or the perceived attitudes and opinions of others. According to the legend, if you drop a frog into a pot of hot water, it will quickly jump out, but if you drop the frog in a pot of cold water and gradually increase the temperature, the frog will not react and will eventually cook to death. You might expect that the frog would say, "Hey! Something is wrong here, let's check this out — in fact, let's check out of this pot!" But the frog is either too embarrassed to say anything or doesn't notice the changing environment until it's too late. Like the frog, we are often too busy and too distracted to analyze situations objectively and thoroughly, or to pay attention to the changing ideas and conditions around us with open minds. Our failure to do so results, at best, in missed opportunities, and at worst, in our demise. Thus, we remain on the trailing edge rather than the leading edge of innovation, effectiveness, performance, and relationships. Another metaphorical animal is the copycat: someone who copies the words or behavior of another. Join these two critters together and we have a *copyfrog* — someone who is afraid to speak up for fear of ridicule or feeling alone, or appearing not to be a team player, even though many others may feel the same way, and are also afraid to speak out. The result is that we copy the perceived (but not the real) beliefs of others — we copy others who are copying us. The *copyfrog effect* causes us to perpetuate, and inadvertently endorse, the existing paradigm because, though it is being questioned silently by everyone else, it outwardly appears to us as though we are the only ones doing so — what Leslie Perlow has called the "vicious spiral of silence."[6] With this misunderstanding, a paradox occurs: We march in lockstep, supporting an obsolete or unpopular paradigm with which we don't agree. This is how unpopular wars begin.

> We would rather be ruined than changed;
>
> We would rather die in our dread
>
> Than climb the cross of the moment
>
> And let our illusions die.
>
> W. H. Auden

4. *The conflicting values of society:* We all claim that to love one another and to tell the truth is the right way to live our lives, and many of us claim that this is how we actually do live our lives. All of the great religions and faith-based philosophies direct us to do so, and the majority of us claim to follow

a religion or an ancient wisdom and its attendant beliefs. But these spiritual values hardly have a voice in "the real world" of our political, social, and economic practice. While our spiritual values encourage us to be generous, truthful, loving, compassionate, and caring, our quest for the "American Dream" or "personal success" may be more guided by the pursuit of wealth, reputation, or power. Thus, we find our personal values in direct competition with the values of society. While we profess to believe that we should be kind to our competitors and generous to our political opponents, the very terms *competitor* and *opponent* make these empty aspirations. Thus, we are condemned to living inauthentic lives—at home and at work. We know what to do, but we have lost our voice and our courage.

Projection

Being trapped in the box of a paradigm explains one of the reasons why we find it so hard to change. Our tendency to "project" is another reason. We need courage to begin our journey, and courage to get past the mistaken belief that if we lay down our swords and armor, setting aside violence and aggression as leaders, that others "won't get it" or "aren't ready to hear the New Story language." The copy-frog effect is very often the result of our projection.

We are all role models for others, and for this reason we have a responsibility to inspire others by showing them how we practice our courage and by modeling the behavior we want to see in others by speaking our truth. We often disguise our words because we believe that people are not ready to hear the language of the spirit. But Higher Ground Leaders model courage by using the language that comes from their hearts, regardless of how it may initially be judged by others. In time, followers catch up with the vision expressed in a great Destiny or Cause, but none of this can happen without the courageous-hearted leader. The greatest Higher Ground Leaders of all time were unequivocal. Buddha did not disguise his language in order to avoid offending his audiences by using camouflage words like "caring" and "helpful," when he really meant compassionate, loving, and graceful. This is a test of our personal courage—if we can't even bring ourselves to say the words, how can we teach the ideas? If we fudge the language, we are probably less enlightened, less authentic, than those we seek to inspire and teach. We are supposed to set the example, and we can do this best by raising the bar. It is to us that others are looking for guidance and for the new frontier. It is ours to establish.

When we see behavior in others that fails to inspire us, it is often the result of our own projection. The term *projection* describes our feelings and thoughts when we project onto others certain hidden, denied, or "shadow" actions or characteristics of our own personality. When we project, we attribute certain personal traits or feelings to someone else to protect our own ego from accepting the reality that we own the very same traits or feelings—that they reside and flourish in our own shadow. It is especially likely to occur when we lack insight into our own impulses and traits. For example, if we feel inadequate in some way, we may inadvertently project those feelings onto others and therefore cause them to feel inadequate. All this wells up from our shadow and is sometimes seen by others as our less-inspiring self. We may not even be aware of it, but it is how others may see us, and therefore, for them, *it is who we are*. The behavior we dislike or find uninspiring in others is very often the behavior that exists in our shadow and which we project onto others, and this becomes their experience of us. If we are having trouble getting along with others, we may project this behavior onto them, and this may cause others to have difficulty in getting along with us. We project too when, based on our own experience of life, we attribute behaviors to others because it is exactly how we would behave in the same circumstances, and we assume that others are like us and would therefore do the same. How else could we see the world but through the lenses of our own lived experience? But because this behavior is generated from our shadow, we are very often unaware of it. When our shadow is directing and prompting our feelings and our dialogue, our egos can become tripped, and this can cause us to savage the emotions of others. When we let this happen, we can initiate emotional damage to those we love, those who are our best friends, and those who are the most important sources of inspiration in our lives. Projecting onto others, then, is one of the main causes of our inability to change. It is also one of the main reasons we lack inspiration in our lives. Yet, knowing this, we also know that the opposite can be true as well, because understanding what resides in our shadow can yield enormous learning and personal growth.

> The sky does not misunderstand. The sky does not judge. The sky, very simply, is.
>
> Richard Bach

Psychologists frequently portray projection in a negative way. For example, it is said that people who have a latent tendency to disloyalty may not acknowledge this consciously, but it may show in their readiness to suspect others of potential disloyalty, or a potential adulterer may accuse his wife of infidelity. If

> I've had many problems in my life—most of which never happened.
>
> Mark Twain

we are exceptionally frugal, greedy, or selfish, we may project our own lack of generosity onto others, because we assume they are the same as we are. Or we may believe that we are inadequate and therefore project onto others a similar lack of abundance and sufficiency.

What magic might unfold if we used the concept of projection as an ally—if our projections were positive? If uninspiring behavior in others is often the result of our projecting our own uninspiring behavior onto them, what greatness could we achieve by inviting inspiring behavior from others, by projecting our own *inspiring* behavior onto them? Projection does not always need to be negative—we have the power to live in the light instead of the shadow, by identifying our behavior, naming it, and making conscious decisions to change it, and therefore changing the behavior of others.

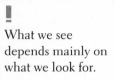

What we see depends mainly on what we look for.

Sir John Lubbock

The growing edge of our life is engaged with continual learning about our shadow, so that we can bring it into the light. Once it is in the light, it can be named, and once we can name it, we can change the behavior that arises from it. Changing our behavior based on our awareness of our own shadow, painful though this can be at times, is the first step toward becoming someone who always inspires others and to becoming someone who is open to change. Projection causes us to judge and be critical of others. By recognizing the dysfunctional nature of such behavior and then modifying our reactions accordingly, we reduce our propensity to judge or criticize, and we therefore become more inspiring people. People yearn to be loved this way—without judgment or criticism. The more we learn about our tendency to project our behavior onto others, the more we become aware of the need to tame it and

A loving person lives in a loving world. A hostile person lives in a hostile world. Everyone you meet is your mirror.

Ken Keyes, Jr.

integrate it, and the more we grow. And this we do by connecting soul-to-soul as often, or even more so, than ego-to-ego.

For many years, we have been living with an old story paradigm that has fooled us into believing that the workplace is an inappropriate setting for emotions, spiritual language, or beliefs that demonstrate a profound respect and caring for humans and that the marketplace is a dog-eat-dog world. Even this is a slur—and another example of projection—most dogs don't eat other dogs. Often, this is a classic case of projection: The things we say that others are not yet ready for, are the things that *we* are not yet ready for. When we say that others are not ready for a leader who loves others and tells the truth, we may mean that *we are not yet ready* to love others and tell the truth. When we say that we must eat or be eaten in the competitive market, we may mean that we believe the world will devour us if we don't devour others first. Thus, by projecting this way, we may be creating the very outcomes we fear, and by doing so, we may think we are protecting our egos, when in reality, we are imprisoning our souls. When we do our inner work, we may discover that it is *we* who are not yet ready, not they. What we are looking for, we need to look with. The truth is that most of us have been intimidated by a cynical and secular society and an excess of political correctness that has forced us to hide our true feelings and needs. It is the most natural urge in the universe for the spirit within to yearn for retrieval, to reclaim the lost spiritual dimensions of our work and home lives. Indeed, it is the essential juice of life and to deny it is contrary to our very essence. What ails us is the result of this denial and suppression. The resulting flow of toxic energy in the workplace, for instance, alienates us even more from each other and from our work—and it saddens the soul and perpetuates the old story of leadership.

> Everything that irritates us about others can lead us to an understanding of ourselves.
>
> Carl Gustav Jung

Our challenge is that we have all succumbed to so many years of intimidation that we fear going first—the *copyfrog effect*. But deep in our hearts, we are all looking at each other and wondering, "Who will take the first step? Who will be the brave one? Who will lead? Who will say the words I want to say?" As soon as we see someone else displaying compassion, love, truthfulness, and grace, the floodgates open, everyone pours through the breach and embraces the leader for their courage and authenticity. This is the role of the Higher Ground Leader.

Moving from the old story to the New Story

Why old story Approaches Have Become Obsolete

We are experiencing a leadership paradox of staggering proportions: Leaders struggle to find ways to increase organizational effectiveness in times of wrenching change, while those they lead are disconnecting from them in growing numbers. Parents and teachers struggle to make sense of the attitudes and behaviors they see represented in the young people they now lead. As leaders strive harder to motivate and influence their followers and communities, this disaffection increases.

In 2001, Richard Brown, CEO of EDS, decreed that the thousands of employees being terminated under his watch should have their severance pay cut from a maximum of 26 weeks to four. But none of this frugality borne by departing employees could stem a staggering 2002 market-value decline of $24 billion, which prompted the board to terminate Brown. Brown's 20-page contract, however, stipulated that only outright dishonesty or "willful repeated violations of his obligations" would constitute "cause"—so he was terminated without cause, thus enabling him to collect $37 million in severance payments. As Michael Jordan, Brown's successor, said later in what seems like a rather understated remark, "people-care has suffered."[1]

The loss of priceless talent that occurs when *people-care* suffers and relationships deteriorate can be catastrophic. One of our clients—and this is very typical—surveys the reasons that employees leave: The number one reason stated by 40 percent of departing employees is friction with their immediate supervisor.

> If Moses had been a committee, the Israelites would still be in Egypt.
>
> J. B. Hughes

When people-care suffers because we are inattentive to the dreams of employees, tragic loss of talent occurs. According to Columbia University business professor Amar Bidhé, 70 percent of *Inc.* magazine's *Inc. 500* were started by entrepreneurs whose original idea came to them while they were working for other employers. Bidhé points out that this is not a new trend—the 17-year-old printer's apprentice Benjamin Franklin is one early example.[2]

Remember the old joke? Question: What's the difference between a chain gang and a corporation? Answer: On a chain gang, you get to work outside.

Why do so many people feel this way?

Perhaps the reason is that we have become more committed to results than to people. One of the world's most respected management theorists wrote in the *Harvard Business Review,* "Organizations need to remember that their ultimate goal is performance, not employee satisfaction and morale."[3] If we continue to teach this kind of thinking, we will lose sight altogether of the most important idea for any organization: Organizations are meant to serve people, not the other way around.

> !
> Until you value yourself, you won't value your time. Until you value your time, you will not do anything with it.
>
> M. Scott Peck
> !

What are the consequences of pursuing results at the expense of people? A sad and alarming one is the ruthless replacement of mature and wise followers with younger ones who are paid less and are free of family responsibilities and ready to work 90-hour weeks. Baby boomers, most of whom are now over 50, will hardly feel inspired by leaders who affront their souls by discriminating against wisdom in this way. In January 2003, California's state retirement system, CalPERS, was ordered to pay an estimated $250 million, the largest in history, to settle the claims of 1,700 firefighters, police, and other law officers who had their disability benefits unfairly reduced based on their age.[4] Bethlehem Steel is just one in a long list of steel companies that defaulted on pension obligations by abandoning their commitments to 95,000 former employees following a filing for Chapter 11 bankruptcy.

Remember the sergeant in the TV series *Hill Street Blues* who finished each police briefing with the words, "Be careful out there"? This is good advice for those over 40 in a world where reducing costs, increasing profits, achieving budget, and boosting results can sometimes be more important to old story leaders than people.

Employees already understand the goals of management and how to achieve them. They know what is necessary to improve productivity, quality, and customer satisfaction. What they want to know is:

- Do leaders care?
- Are our leaders compassionate?
- Are people more important than metrics?
- Is my career secure?
- How can I achieve greater meaning and fulfillment from my work?
- Am I being told the truth?
- Is this an organization with integrity?
- Do our leaders respect me and treat me as a spiritual being rather than just a means of production?
- Does my contribution matter?
- Are my gifts seen?

When followers are convinced that their leaders value these needs through their behavior and genuine concern for their spiritual wellness, followers will do everything it takes to help their leaders succeed. They will do this because they know that their leaders wish to serve them, not as functions or labels, but as spiritual beings.

Old story leadership models spring from the cult of personality and celebrity, thus shaping much of the corporate culture of our time. Though subject to many variations and interpretations, the model that old story leaders follow consists of four steps:

1. *Develop a shared vision and mission.* Old story leaders craft a shared vision together with their leadership team—as a sort of *bonding* exercise. This results in the widely practiced ritual of forming a committee to define organizational aspirations. When Winston Churchill observed: "A camel is a horse designed by a committee," he must have been thinking about committees that design lame mission statements.

2. *Orchestrate the buy-in to the vision.* Once the vision and mission statements are created and approved by all of the stakeholders, the old story

> Most of what we call management consists of making it difficult for people to get their jobs done.
>
> Peter Drucker

leaders hit the road to drum up support for them. This dog-and-pony-show, familiar to all corporate denizens, becomes the vehicle for gathering disciples—for rousing employees, unions, customers, shareholders, and suppliers to buy into the new vision and mission. If followers discover that the message is simply old wine in new bottles, their sense of disenchantment deepens and they become further alienated from their leaders.

3. *Develop a strategy to achieve the vision.* The next task for old story leaders is to develop the strategic plan that will move the organization toward the (now shared) new vision. This entails a broad-ranging collaboration among disparate departments and functions. The goal of this process is to ensure that everyone feels empowered through his or her contribution. The underlying theory is that if people help to design the new vision, they will own it, and if this process succeeds, it will achieve the most powerful buy-in.

4. *Motivate employees and implement the strategy.* Last, the old story leaders assemble the team that will implement the strategy. Their job now is to motivate the employees to achieve the strategy that will lead to the new vision.

This is a mechanical model based on an old story concept of leadership that seeks to manipulate, control, and exploit the personality. But it ignores the one thing people yearn to nourish—their spirit.

The Distance between the Elite and the Street

In the world of the old story leader, there is a growing gulf between the leaders' perception of the world of work and that of followers. One measure of these two solitudes can be found in the statistics of hours worked in America. According to the U.S. Department of Labor survey of business establishments, the average workweek shrank from 39 hours in the 1950s and early 1960s to 35 hours in the 1990s. Tell that to just about any employee today, and they will think you just got off a spaceship.[5] Their disbelieving impressions are supported by the surveys of Lou Harris & Associates. From 1973 to 1980, the number of hours spent working, as broadly defined, rose from 41 to 47 hours. It then rose slowly to 51 hours in 1994, dropped back to 50 in 1998, and remained there until 2002, when the number of hours worked eased back to previous highs of 47.[6] Researchers have found that managers simply don't know how hard their employees are working, believing that the old watermark of 35 or 40 hours still prevails. The truth is that many old story leaders have no idea how many hours employees invest of their own time, including time on their computers at home.

Not only are many managers detached from the realities of employee life, but also, as noted earlier, many employees are not thrilled with their work experience. A survey by Kepner-Tregoe Inc. of Princeton, New Jersey, asked how employees felt their organization was managed—like a symphony orchestra, a medieval kingdom, or a three-ring circus. A kingdom or a circus was chosen by 59 percent of supervisors and 72 percent of employees.[7]

The same study reported 38 percent of managers and 47 percent of employees were dissatisfied with their jobs. Such disconnects between leaders and followers are dangerous—for the relationship between them, for organizational effectiveness, and for families and communities. This was confirmed in another Kepner-Tregoe survey, which reported that 61 percent of managers and 65 percent of employees frequently discuss leaving their current employer. At a *Forbes* Women's Summit, I asked attendees, all high-achieving female executives and entrepreneurs, "Have you thought of leaving your job in the last six months?" Using remote keypads to anonymously key in their responses, 82 percent indicated they had. These are some of the most successful women in North America—how would your employees answer the same question? How would you? Old story leaders are putting at risk the spiritual and emotional well-being of the souls in their organizations, as well as their intellectual capital, if they ignore these danger signals.

In so many aspects of communicating with others, we focus on our perception of reality and what will achieve our own material ends, seldom considering the needs of the souls with whom we are partnering—our employees, customers, suppliers, colleagues, friends, families, and communities. When we ask leaders to define leadership and then ask their employees the same question, the difference in their answers is astonishing. It is the difference between the elite and the street. Leaders say that the hallmarks of great leadership include having a clear vision, defining strategic goals, being decisive, winning in the marketplace, dominating the competition, hiring brilliant people, and motivating them. Ask their followers the same question, and hardly any of the leaders' criteria are included. Instead, they say they want their leaders to be great mentors and teachers, to be fair and respectful of people and the planet, to act with integrity and practice high standards of values, to be good listeners, to show compassion, and to communicate well.

It is an illusion that the goals of personality will lift the hearts of others. The goals of personality are important, but they don't amount to the bigger picture or the meaning of life, which is what we are all searching for. As Bill George, the former CEO of Medtronic, pointed out, "Shareholder value is a hollow notion as the sole source of employee motivation. If you do business that way, you end up like ITT." This comment comes from the New Story Leader who led a company making 50 percent of the world's pacemakers and many other implantable medical devices. Half of Medtronic's revenues come from products introduced in the past 12 months—and the company's total return to shareholders has averaged about 34 percent over the past decade. Every employee receives a bronze medallion inscribed with the company's Cause: "To alleviate pain, restore health, extend life"—an inspiring rallying call if ever there was one. The company revels in unabashedly emotional and, therefore, inspiring activities such as holding a party each year to which patients, their families, and doctors are flown in to share their stories with employees about how Medtronic's products saved their lives. It is not that the return to shareholders is unimportant; it is just not *the most important thing*, and it alone cannot inspire.

How did such a great discrepancy occur between the leaders' and followers' descriptions of leadership? If followers are the customers for what leaders are offering, how could the gap between offering and need be so wide? If we were to misread the needs of consumers to the same degree, we would have a marketing catastrophe on our hands. Do we have a leadership catastrophe on our hands?

The real purpose of the New Story Leader is to serve the needs of others—especially followers. Thus, the principal purpose of the leader is to act as the main source of inspiration, personal development, support, and guidance for the principal customers of the leader—those who are followers. Otherwise, the role of the leader becomes superfluous since most followers know more about their work, goals, technologies, desired outcomes, and professional expertise than anyone who may be *leading* them. Followers are the *customers* of the New Story Leader, and New Story Leaders strive to meet or exceed the outer *and* inner needs of followers.

> The first responsibility of a leader is to define reality. The last is to say thank you. In between, the leader is a servant.
>
> Max De Pree

The Higher Ground Leader is a servant-leader. This is a leader who says, "I am your leader. How can I serve you?"

Recently I spoke to a group of managers. My speech was sandwiched between motivational messages and media clips from the corporate president outlining new sales targets, incentive programs, and bonus plans designed to achieve greater levels of output and profit. As the conference closed, I signed books for audience members. After everyone had left, the president turned to me and asked, "Why do people surround you like this, asking questions and having you sign their books?" I said that it happens that way every time. "Why?" she asked. I asked her permission to be frank and she agreed. "Most of your time was spent talking about *your* needs," I explained. "Most of mine was spent talking about *theirs*. People are yearning to hear that others genuinely care about their needs as much as they do. When we show that we care about them, that we understand our role as servant-leaders, then they will exceed our sales targets."

The perfect relationship between the New Story Leader and the follower exists when what the follower needs is what the New Story Leader most wants to give.

The old story leader—The Warrior

Speaking to an audience of business leaders recently, I was surprised to find the entire Asian region management team dressed in black army fatigues, combat boots and berets, and "guarded" by staff dressed in fatigues and black balaclava helmets. The *Mission Impossible* theme blared from speakers, underscoring the challenge of repeating the prior year's growth of 70 percent. I scanned the program. The lunch invitation read, "1200: Eat lunch or be eaten."

I found my host and alerted him that I feared my message might conflict with his, perhaps undermining the company's strategy or throwing off their meeting agenda. He told me not to worry. I walked to the podium and gamely started my speech by making references to "peaceful warriors," a popular term, but one that I view as suspect because it is an oxymoron. Was Buddha a peaceful warrior?

> Our scientific power has outrun our spiritual power. We have guided missiles and misguided men.
>
> Martin Luther King Jr.

As I progressed, I knew that I could not present a discussion on the importance of truth-telling without being honest myself. I improvised a little, explaining that I was the yin to balance the yang of their agenda. I asked the audience if they believed we should kill people at work and if their repeated chants about dominating the market were really serving their customers' needs, or just those of their egos. I gently suggested to them that even if dominating the market was important to them, it was probably irrelevant to customers.

> Any intelligent fool can make things bigger, more complex, and more violent. It takes a touch of genius—and a lot of courage—to move in the opposite direction.
>
> E. F. Schumacher

So here I was, on the other side of the globe, faced with an eerie paradox: I was in Singapore, a Westerner working in the East with Easterners, who were promoting the worst aspects of Western culture—

aggression and violence—and I was now urging them to restore and embrace their natural Eastern values. A dropped pin would have been thunderous.

My speech finished, I prepared to be railroaded out of Singapore. First a few people, then the majority of the audience, told me how uncomfortable they were with the war metaphor and militaristic bombast, how they had grudgingly agreed with it, but how closely my message mirrored their true beliefs. They welcomed a message that drew from, and aligned so closely with, their cultural wisdom: the teachings of Buddha, Confucius, and the Tao. They were not critical of management, believing them to be on autopilot and using the tired metaphors of violence and war universally employed by old story leaders of global organizations.

The Dark Side of Competition

It is 1979, a basketball game in the Brandeis [University] gym. The team is doing well, and the student section begins a chant, "We're number one! We're number one!" Morrie is sitting nearby. He is puzzled by the cheer. At one point, in the midst of "We're number one!" he rises and yells, "What's wrong with being number two?"

The students look at him. They stop chanting. He sits down, smiling and triumphant.

Mitch Albom, *Tuesdays with Morrie*

The old story leader overworks the metaphors of war and sport. Without the lexicon of competition, the old story leader is lost. But the key to inspiring people to greatness comes from love, not war. A call to arms is not an effective way to engage the hearts and souls of others. Try to picture the conductor of the Boston Symphony getting up in the morning and ranting, "Let's destroy the Los Angeles Symphony!" This is the ego speaking—testosterone leadership.

Building strong relationships requires us to tame our egos. We all have egos—those little voices inside that reference our personalities to the outside world asking, "Am I beautiful?" "Am I loved?" "Will I succeed?" "Can I get more?" "Will I win?" Each of us is a unique ego, and often we compete with the egos of others. Our egos are like waves in the sea. We roll along on the surface, doing many important and meaningful things until we eventually flare out onto the beach. We don't go away—we return to the ocean—the Universal Soul, which is the sum of every soul of every living thing in the universe. Eventually a new wave arrives—another ego. But our egos always return to the ocean, the Universal

Soul—the oneness of the Divine, like the waves to the ocean. We need to see ourselves in the appropriate perspective—a small but potent wave that is an important part of a much larger picture. We don't disappear or fade away; we simply return to the Whole from which we came in the beginning. We have one body, not two, embracing our egos and our souls. We cannot separate them. We can only pretend to. We are in relationship between our egos and our souls—this is how we give meaning to each other. And the relationship between each of our souls in organizations is what gives meaning to each of us, too.

No one needs to die, and we don't need to take prisoners or scorch the Earth. There is room for us all. Innovation, creativity, synergy, collaboration, teamwork, and, above all else, love, will lead to mastery and, therefore, our success.

In July 1996, a fire roared through the Carmenet vineyards of Napa, destroying precious cabernet sauvignon, cabernet franc, and Merlot grapes. Managing director Michael Richmond, winemaker Jeffrey Baker, and three other employees hosed down the roof of the winery to prevent it from burning down. Although the winery survived, 75 percent of Carmenet's high-margin crop was destroyed. Two poor harvests in previous years combined with the blaze seemed to spell catastrophe. The day after the fire, Joel Peterson of the competing Ravenswood Winery called and pledged to replace the grapes for Carmenet a few hours later. The Sonoma Valley Vintners and Growers Alliance asked its 135 members to help, and offers poured in. "Even the smallest growers with only an acre called," said executive director Christine Finlay. "They all thought it might have been them." Local wineries sold grapes to Carmenet, even though doing so cut into their own production of premium wines. Said Ravenswood's Peterson, "It's to my advantage to have Carmenet around. They're good people, they produce good wine, and they're out in the market supporting the stuff I believe in. By selling their wine, I'm in effect selling my own."[8] That is how communities build strong relationships, thrive, and grow. It is this collaborative community-based behavior that inspires, not the scorched-earth attitude we so often see in the marketplace. As Michael Richmond told me later, "This is the very spirit of community that captured and sustained my commitment to the wine industry 30 years ago. There continues to exist within our industry a strong code of support and sharing of information. One seldom encounters any proprietary posturing or guarding of 'trade secrets.' Sharing and borrowing is commonplace, both incidentally and formally, in winemaker gatherings. This altruistic attitude, though, does seem to exist mostly among producers and administrators and is much rarer when one ventures into the culture of sales and distribution."

We are human spirits sharing the same time and space, here to serve one another, not crush one another in competition for more things. Joe Calvaruso, CEO of Mount Carmel Health System in Columbus, Ohio, puts it this way,

"We don't call other healthcare providers 'competition,' we call them 'neighbors.' When we received applications from a neighbor, I told our recruiters, 'Don't steal talent from a *neighbor*.' Even though we are not deliberately initiating the contact—we're simply running generic job advertisements—the employees of our neighbors are applying, and I don't want to harm another healthcare organization and the community's ability to improve healthcare quality by taking some of their best people."

Says Jeff Bezos, founder of Amazon.com, "Obsess about customers, not the competitors."

The New Story Leader listens to the wisdom of our elders, revisiting and reembracing their values and beliefs, based on life-affirming, not life-threatening, models. Just ask those you wish to inspire—they are the customers of your spirit and what it can offer, and what they are yearning for is a sense of community, not a war.

Building Communities of Relationships

The subatomic particles that make up the book you hold in your hands give it the appearance of a thing, but it does not exist and, therefore, cannot do anything. The relationships between me as the author and scores of other people in my life, and all the experiences that accrued from them, generated the energy that became the ideas on these pages. These ideas became keystrokes in a computer and eventually electronic code; then, after passing through the wisdom and experience of many others, they were sent by technicians to a machine that put ink on paper, which went to the bindery as a result of the skills of recycling experts and paper manufacturers and distributors, not to mention Mother Nature. Editors, publishers, lawyers, agents, publicists, reviewers, and many others created more relationships. Eventually, "a book" was produced, but a result is not a cause. Despite the fact that this book has physically passed through all these hands, it still cannot come alive until it lives in the hearts of others who like it well enough to encourage you to first buy it, then read it, and, most importantly, do something about it. Finally, you sit on an airplane or on a beach or in an easy chair and decide to build a relationship with all those people by reading this book. Even if you read every page from front to back (oh, I wish it were

> To manage a system effectively, you might focus on the interactions of the parts rather than their behavior taken separately.
>
> Russell L. Ackoff

true!), the book does not exist until you take action, which means creating a relationship with someone. Until then, it still has no meaning.

Nothing exists until it is in relationship to something else.

In the same way, organizations and teams cannot do anything because they do not exist, either. It is the relationships between people that result in actions. The Japanese do not even have a word to describe *individual* because the concept of the community and the family has such powerful societal sway in their culture. Only when we view our organizations, at home and at work, for what they are—communities of relationships—can we create reality. This reality is of two kinds: material reality, which, as we learn from quantum physics, consists of the relationships between space and tiny subatomic particles; and spiritual reality, which consists of the relationships between the souls with whom we interact in our communities, whatever configuration they might be. *Even if we have done our inner work, we need to make the outer connections.*

> In organizations, real power and energy is generated through relationships. The patterns of relationships and the capacities to form them are more important than tasks, functions, roles, and positions.
>
> Margaret Wheatley

If we continue to maintain a solely materialistic worldview, our picture of life will be made up only of discrete things, and we will tend to view people the same way. The *things-perspective* results in actions that make us feel like separate, unrelated parts. It results in actions that are good for me, but bad for you—win-lose combinations. Sometimes this shows up in careless attitudes toward the environment or toward people. The endless reorganizations, restructurings, downsizings, refocusings, and "programs" that are the quintessential knee-jerks of the old story, things-centered leaders in modern organizations have gravely damaged the quality of relationships. As a consequence, many people feel betrayed and discarded as mere things, rather than as the "most important assets" their leaders once claimed them to be.

Strong relationships are inclusionary; that is, they seek to embrace rather than repel, compete, or exclude. Organizations, of any kind, cannot be relevant if they seek to exclude by creating hierarchies, which separate people by their status or power. For example, old story leaders still cling to archaic notions such as *FTE*, *boss*, and *subordinate*. The language of separation and exclusion characterizes old story thinking,

> The greatest strength is gentleness.
>
> Iroquois saying

where it is common to hear people described as being "in scope" or "out of scope" or pigeonholed into caste systems with labels such as "hourly" or "salaried." Or they may use personality profiling to classify people, some of whom will be favored and some not. The soul seeks to belong, to create relationships, and to be part of a community. In seeking to inspire greatness in organizations and families, we need to infuse them with the power of the soul, creating communities to which we all contribute and from which we are all nourished—a holistic, symbiotic relationship built on acceptance and permission among members that leads to more than just survival—it leads to growth and evolution. Most importantly, it must lead to spiritual nourishment and regeneration, a deep and mutual caring of the souls of all members. This is the essence of relationships in a community.

Kalpan Chawla was an Indian-born, naturalized American who died tragically with an Israeli, an African American, and four other Americans when the space shuttle Columbia was lost on February 1, 2003. She learned, in the big picture of space travel, how irrelevant distinctions based on nationality or ethnic origin are. Shortly before embarking on the fateful trip, she brushed aside the media interest in the astronauts as representatives of diversity and gender, saying. "When you are in space and look at the stars and the galaxy, you feel that you are not just from any particular piece of land, but from the solar system."[9]

Thirty years ago, the Apollo astronauts who first flew to the Moon were stunned by a unique experience when they first saw our little planet from space—no political boundaries or divisions, just beauty, smallness, and frailty—Earth's vulnerability protected from the harsh void of space by an atmosphere that looked as thin and delicate as the skin of an onion. Astronauts since have given this experience a name—the Overview Effect. In *The Overview Effect* by Frank White, Rusty Schweickart, who flew on Apollo 9, described the Earth as being

> . . . so small and so fragile and such a precious little spot in that universe that you can block it out with your thumb and you realize that on that small spot, that little blue and white thing, is everything that means anything to you—all of history and music and poetry and art and death and birth and love, tears, joy, games, all of it on that little spot that you can cover with your thumb. And you realize from that perspective that you've changed, that there's something new there, that the relationship is no longer what it was.[10]

It is time for us to freshen up our perspective, from a *things* view of the world to one that sees the sacredness in relationships and communities as well as things. This is what New Story Leaders have discovered and why they are able to greatly enhance the connections among people, who, in the old story environment, resented being treated as things. They were right because they *are* more than things — they are sacred beings. We are not freestanding entities, because on our own, we do not mean or amount to anything — any more than does this book. We mean something only when we are in relationship with one another.

Mark Twain wrote that, "Principles have no real force except when one is well fed." We are all looking for more than this. What we are all yearning for is a sense of community, to belong, to experience our kinship in relationship with one another — something more than just a trough where we are well fed. We want to feel emotionally and spiritually safe, to let our guard down, to feel sacred. Elsewhere I have described these sacred communities of shared values and spirit as sanctuaries.[11] The word *sanctuary* is derived from the Latin *sanctus*, meaning sacred. As I mean it here, a *sanctuary* is not a place; it is an attitude, a state of mind, a set of shared values among people. A sanctuary is a safe environment. We may not be able to change the world around us, but we can change ourselves. In this way, though the world around us may be crazy or dangerous, in the sanctuary of our sacred relationships, we are secure. A sanctuary is like a shield, repelling the toxicity around us. Sanctuaries are often formed by groups of like-minded individuals who seldom meet, but share values, and love and trust one another and safely tell the truth among themselves. They trust and respect one another and enjoy a common code. A sanctuary is a holy relationship, an association where we give reverence to all of the people and things within it. It is a group of people connected by their souls, among whom a sacred code is practiced and members live in grace, serving and honoring one another.

Teams, departments, divisions, or corporations, as well as families, tribes, and clans are simply different-sized sanctuaries or communities. These communities can range from the very small to the very big: a city block, a hospital, a government — even a country. The rules for community building are the same as the ones we learned in the very first community to which we belonged — the family:

- Do whatever you do as well as you possibly can — Mastery.
- In a way that is good for people — Chemistry.
- In the service of others — Delivery.[12]

By becoming aware that we are communities, not organizations, we change the very nature of our relationships, making them less material and more spiritual, less mechanical and more divine, less temporary and more infinite, less cursory and more vital. Then our communities will come alive. Our natural longing to form lasting connections will cause a transformation of our affairs — and our planet. This is what the New Story Leader has learned.

From Out There to In Here

A leader who does not inspire is like a river without water.

Every follower yearns to be inspired by his or her leader. Indeed, every person yearns to be inspired by every other person. When we fail to do so, we diminish one another and sadden our souls. Thus, the role of each of us is to inspire. Inspiration is a subject that engages us in every aspect of our lives—not just in some compartments of it.

> So you think that money is the root of all evil. Have you ever asked what is the root of all money?
>
> Ayn Rand

As the drive for economic growth continues, corporations restructure and reinvent themselves, laying off millions of people to meet the pressures of globalization and competition. The social contract ("I will commit my working life to the firm if the firm guarantees to provide me with secure employment until I retire"), so long taken for granted, has been shattered, along with the dreams of many, giving rise to a new class of independent workers: independent contractors as lone eagles and employees as free agents. Corporations have never done so well, but global competition is squeezing margins and putting a lid on prices. It is like a day when the sun is out, but it is raining.

From Mechanical to Quantum Theory

The difference between old story leadership and New Story Leadership is the difference between order and chaos. Old story leaders search for order by imposing systemwide motivation; New Story Leaders accept and encourage chaos through one-soul-at-a-time inspiration. Old story leaders create processes that are designed to reinforce systemwide behavior. They prefer to control by creating order, establishing rules, and defining and achieving goals and outcomes. The New Story Leader trusts the genius of the spirit and sets it free.

> Hell, there are no rules here—we're trying to accomplish something.
>
> Thomas A. Edison

Here is another way to look at the contrast: old story leaders are Newtonian thinkers; New Story Leaders are quantum thinkers. On the one hand, the laws of dynamics govern Newtonian thinking, predicting that everything in the universe will implode into a cold and empty void—the God-as-a-clockmaker philosophy. On the other hand, quantum physics describes a universe that is constantly reinventing and adapting itself.

Newtonian thinking is by nature pessimistic and negative; quantum thinking is optimistic and hopeful. Old story leaders expect the world, and consequently their organizations, to run down, like the cosmic clock, at some point in the future. This has implications for the way that they interact with people. A pessimistic old story leader seeks control over others to limit the implosion. Some old story leaders are more optimistic—they hope that the breakdown can be held off, if only for a short time, at least until they move on. Thus, old story leaders are both short-term thinkers and pessimists in the long term. I once offered strategic advice to a CEO who rejected it on the grounds that its benefits would not be evident before his impending retirement—as if there were no life after we hand over the reins to another. Old story leaders like this believe they can influence the short-term outcomes of the organization, but in the long run the organization will die, together with all of its parts—the people within.

We often talk about organizations as if they were animated—what social scientists call *anthropomorphism*—ascribing human characteristics to what is not human. But organizations do not exist—they are merely legal constructs. It is the souls within them that exist. Newtonian old story leaders often can't see the individual, instead viewing the organization as a complete machine that can be influenced through group motivation, while quantum leaders see the quanta that are ever changing and morphing into the system—a system of individuals that influence the whole—like the unseen molecules in water.

> ❗
> So great has been the endurance, so incredible the achievement, that, as long as the sun keeps a set course in heaven, it would be foolish to despair of the human race.
>
> Ernest L. Woodward
> ❗

Organizations and communities cannot inspire, only people can, but it is possible to create an inspiring organization or community. There is just one way to do this: by inspiring people, one soul at a time. There is no other way.

The Paradox of Teams

One of the enduring paradoxes of our time is our commitment to teams and to the rights of the individual at the same time. Like so many others, I have often wrestled with how to pull these seemingly opposing notions together.

As Peter Drucker has pointed out, "No team (except for Gilbert and Sullivan) has ever accomplished anything of importance. The great musicians did not work in teams. The same is true of painters, sculptors, poets, and, to a great extent, people who built businesses." Now you may view this as the hyperbole of a lovable and brilliant nonagenarian—and perhaps a rather harsh judgment on the likes of Lennon and McCartney or Lewis and Clarke, but history is on Drucker's side. What we need is what works—and that may or may not be teams. It depends on the purpose of an organization and the context in which this is being achieved. But if we believe that teams are appropriate for given situations, we will need to adapt the affected community to fit the team culture. This includes decision-making, reward systems, learning styles, communications, leadership, structure, work styles—all of which are different in teams compared to hierarchies that celebrate the individual. Typically, we promote the concept of teamwork but reward the attainment of individual excellence—at home and at work—a classic result of the *copyfrog effect*. We do this from the beginning: In raising our children, we celebrate individual academic and sporting achievements, not the generous capacity to support team accomplishments. We are more concerned that our little Charlotte graduates with honors than that she make a contribution as a great team player who takes an extra year to graduate. By and large, we create compensation plans that reward individual performance, not that of teams. Across society, we reward individualism, while extolling the virtues of collaboration.

We live in a culture that lionizes personality, wealth, and celebrity. Frequently, it is by these criteria that we now measure our success. The contemporary measures are our levels of fame, wealth, beauty, and power—especially *over* others. We have a multiplicity of incentives for individual performance, even revering it in our Constitution and our rights and freedoms. Corporate leaders retell the stories of the great individual competitors—the heroes of our sports, corporate, and entertainment industries—and then extol the virtues of teamwork. Although they urge teamwork, payroll thinking remains doggedly resistant to rewarding cooperation, collaboration, community, love, and relationships— all essential behaviors of great teams.

Teams compete in win-lose combinations—"my team against yours"; communities flourish with win-win relationships. If we want teamwork, we need to structure for it and reward it.

In the end, we must ask ourselves, "Can I grow more through a relationship than on my own? Will an inspiring relationship with other souls help me to grow?" And we may need to remember that contrary to contemporary fads around this subject, teams may not always be the right answer—we may need to think more in terms of much wider relationships, communities, and sanctuaries.

The Voice: Source of a Great Brand

During the past 40 years, we have become experts at identifying the needs of customers. In the process, we have spawned entire fields of inquiry and practice such as marketing, selling, customer service, and quality. We have learned to perfect the science of identifying needs and motivating customer response. What potential could we unleash with followers before launching initiatives that affect them, if we used these same sophisticated marketing techniques—double-blind studies, focus groups, market testing, empirical research, and the like? What would be the happy result of investing the same level of sophistication, innovation, financial capital, and sensitivity in our followers as we routinely do with customers? Perhaps we could become as effective at inspiring others as we have become at marketing to them. We need to consider doing something too few of us do today—to look at relationships through the heart and eyes of those with whom we wish to build relationships. When we realize that employees are customers, too, and accurately identify and meet their needs, they will rise to unparalleled performance. That is the secret of success at organizations such as TD Industries, J.M. Smucker, Synovus Financial Corp., Baptist Health Care of Pensacola, Wegman's Food Markets, Timberland, Nordstrom, FedEx, Medtronic, Intuit, Microsoft, Cisco Systems, Starbucks, SAS Institute, and many others. A new science is about to be born—the *new marketing*—in which we learn that the brand of an organization is not its external reputation or advertising, but the relationships it nurtures and enjoys *inside*. These inspired relationships are the source of the energy that creates the reputation outside—its *voice*.

SAS Institute Inc. is the world leader in business-intelligence software and services, enabling customers to turn raw data into usable knowledge. It is the world's largest privately held software company. Founded in 1976 by Jim Goodnight, SAS serves more than 39,000 business, government, and university sites in 118 countries. SAS indulges its employees with a 50,000-square-foot gym, including an expansive hardwood aerobics floor, two full-size basketball courts, exercise and workout areas, a skylit yoga room, and an Olympic-size indoor pool. The company maintains soccer and softball fields, offers massages, and classes in golf, African dance, tennis, Pilates, and tai chi. A 50-person medical staff offers free medical services to employees, the cafeteria is subsidized with nourishing and healthy foods, and on Wednesdays the company provides free M&M candies (presumably adding variety to the nourishing and healthy foods!). Of SAS's 9,000 employees worldwide, more than 4,000 employees are based at its Cary, North Carolina, campus—up from 1,900 employees five years ago. While other technology companies felt the pain of a shrinking economy at the beginning of the new millennium, SAS expanded its workforce by 7 to 8 percent. In its early days, some of SAS's most highly trained female staff members left the company because they were unable to find adequate daycare. The company reacted by providing daycare in the basement for five children. Today, there are 700 children in the facility, which is the largest on-site daycare in North Carolina. Standing beside the lake on the campus grounds, I was struck by the serenity of the place—inside and out—unusual in the frenzied world of technology. Azalea and rhododendron bushes cascade down to the boardwalk that surrounds the lake. Employees are encouraged to stroll and picnic and not to work past 6 P.M., when the gates of the campus close. The clusters of low-rise buildings are nestled in the rolling campus hills, among tall ponderosa pines and shade trees. I paused to watch a snapping turtle sun itself on a bridge footing. "I've never seen anything like this in my career," said Martin Bourque, a 15-year SAS veteran.

One of the benefits of this largesse is low staff turnover. Whereas staff turnover in technology companies can typically average 20 percent a year (equal to about 1,000 employees for SAS), only about 130 leave SAS, with the result that almost 900 employees do not need to be replaced annually. Employee turnover averages about 3.7 percent and has never exceeded 5 percent. The company offers no stock option plan, and salaries are generally at the mid-level of industry norms. Yet employees are dedicated, loyal, and committed to the organization. Another benefit of treating followers like customers is performance—90 percent of the overall *Fortune 500* companies are SAS customers.[13]

SAS's "voice"—what establishes a relationship in the hearts and minds of the public—is created by, and therefore rests on, how it treats people—inside and outside the organization. People say about SAS, "That's the kind of company I want to work for," or "That's the kind of company I want to do business with." What has changed in our thinking is that the tangible assets of the organization are no longer as important as the intangible assets—Higher Ground Leaders understand that the value of an organization's brand rests more with the relationship among the people it serves, inside and outside the organization—its voice—than the expenditure of marketing dollars.

When Quint Studer became president of Baptist Hospital in Pensacola, Florida, the facility ranked in the bottom 19th percentile in customer satisfaction as measured by Press, Gainey of South Bend, Indiana. Two years later, hospitals in the Baptist Health Care system ranked numbers one, two, and three in patient satisfaction out of 600 hospitals surveyed nationwide. They now run weekly benchmarking days for a stream of hospital executives eager to learn how they achieved this stunning turnaround. Says Studer, "People around here thought I had been hired to improve patient satisfaction, but I didn't even mention patient satisfaction for the first few months." Instead, he focused directly on asking followers what their needs were and on meeting them—everything from full disclosure of financial and management information, more authority for ordering supplies, faster emergency room psychiatric assessments, night cafeteria service, coordinating security and nursing shifts (so nurses could be escorted to their cars at night), quarterly employee discussion forums, and leadership development coaching. Charts kept on employee and customer satisfaction data tell the story—as soon as employee satisfaction improved, customer satisfaction did, too—the rise in the curves is almost identical. The patient service improvement program was working, but it was working *because the employee service improvement program was working*. This is how Baptist Health Care became the best practice hospital for patient satisfaction in America—and in the process, created for itself a national brand awareness—a "voice" that spoke clearly to employees, patients, suppliers, regulators, and others.

American Airlines is a legendary airline—famous, or perhaps infamous, for its culture. In an industry that always seems to be struggling, American Airlines is often thought of as the sturdiest. Robert Crandall, American's former CEO, was often hailed as the savior of the airline industry, the inventor of frequent flier programs (the AAdvantage Awards Program in 1981), and the man who pioneered the renaissance of air travel. But inside the company, he was better known as "Fang" or "Darth Vader," a reputation that stemmed as much from his indomitable relationships with unions as for his cost-cutting techniques.[14] He once ordered one peanut removed from every in-flight package to yield savings of $100,000 a year. His successor, Don Carty, famously negotiated deep labor contract concessions from three unions to save the company from bankruptcy, after exhorting them to "shared sacrifice." But when the unions discovered that Carty had terminated the top executives' deferred compensation plans, paying them out in lump sums, and secured their retirement benefits from creditors in the event of bankruptcy, they called for a re-vote, jeopardizing the fragile truce achieved. Carty's bungling cost him his job.[15]

Southwest Airlines is a legendary airline, too, but with an entirely different voice. It is famous for its unique culture, which places employees as the number one corporate priority—*even before the customer*. Herb Kelleher, Southwest's founder, described the company's marketing strategy this way: "We market ourselves based on the personality and spirit of ourselves. That sounds like an easy claim but, in fact, it is a supremely dangerous position to stake out because if you're wrong, customers will let you know—with a vengeance. Customers are like a force of nature: You can't fool them, and you ignore them at your own peril."

Kelleher had no time for long-range planning. Instead, he preferred an integrated, customer-inspired plan that focuses on two things: What are the societal trends, and where do Southwest's leaders want the airline to be within that society? This process involves many outsiders beyond Southwest's executive circle.

Kelleher tells this story: "I was talking at the Yale Graduate School of Business some years ago. In the Q&A session, one of the students stood up and said, 'It seems to me you're talking more about a religion than a business.' And I said, 'If you feel that way about your business, I think that's good. That's a plus.' "[16]

In 1991, Colleen Barrett, Kelleher's long-time assistant and co-builder of Southwest, was appointed president. She sums it up this way: "Southwest is a cause, not a career."

The market capitalization of Southwest Airlines is greater than that of all the other major U.S. airlines together. More than anything else, we distinguish old story organizations from New Story ones by the quality of leadership observed by all who experience the results of Higher Ground Leadership. This is the value of the brand. It is not the result of the marketing dollars spent in the marketplace; it is the perception of people—not just consumers—of how they experience the soul of the organization and what values the leaders of the company stand for— the voice that becomes the brand.

The Arrival of Critical Mass

The dawning of a new millennium offered us an unusual leadership opportunity. It may be completely illogical, but we should nevertheless accept this priceless gift. The millennium energy created an awareness that had been growing during the 1990s that opened the hearts and kindled the hopes of millions of people who genuinely believed that the time was right for a radical redesign of leadership, organizations, and work. Inspiration was the growing practice and hope of this period. Great energy gathered around the possibilities, which 10 years ago would have seemed like hopelessly romantic and ambitious aspirations. Then the events of September 11, 2001, first jolted this path toward greater inspiration and then accelerated this awakening by stripping away our complacency and causing us to reevaluate our love affair with materialism. As Rushworth Kidder has written, "In a subtle way, the calibration on our internal compass has changed, and the things we always thought we wanted—material success, popular standing, personal influence—no longer lie so squarely in the line of our bearings. It's as though the promised destination . . . as familiar as the joint on your thumb . . . might not be there after all. It's as though there might be no certainty to the comforting assertion that says, This is what the journey's for."[17]

All over the world, people are beginning to ask much deeper questions about the directions of their lives. In a world where we cannot feel confident about trusting the outside world, the inner world assumes a new importance for us all. But if there is nothing in there, what then?

In his survey of Americans, sociologist Paul H. Ray found that 50 million Americans care deeply about ecology and saving the planet, about relationships, peace, social justice, self-actualization, spirituality, and self-expression. Surprisingly, they are both inner-directed and socially concerned; they're activists, volunteers, and contributors to good causes more than other Americans. He called this group "cultural creatives."[18] A critical mass within a population is generally considered to be 1 percent or higher—the number of people who are interested in nonmaterial reality far surpasses this. The New Story is well underway.

Pierre Teilhard de Chardin, a Jesuit priest and eminent paleontologist, wrote about what he called the *noosphere*. In *The Phenomenon of Man*, he wrote, "Evolution is a general condition to which all theories, all hypotheses, all systems must bow and which they must satisfy henceforward if they are to be thinkable and true. Evolution is a light illuminating all facts." He argued that matter has always obeyed "that great law of biology . . . the law of 'complexification.'"[19] He postulated that the matter-energy of the universe, since the beginning of time, has continued to evolve into greater complexity. Humanity, he believed, introduced a new level of complexity, while at the same time moving evolution to a new dimension. Teilhard described the geosphere (the nonliving world of Earth's internal cores), the many-layered biosphere covering the Earth (the outer crust and soil; the oceans, lakes and rivers; the flora and fauna; the atmosphere) from which emerged the noosphere (an envelope of thought or global consciousness surrounding the Earth). This mind layer, or human consciousness, leads, Teilhard said, to a higher consciousness, and as this evolutionary process unfolds, the material and the spiritual converge into a superconsciousness. Teilhard called this moment when life becomes self-aware the *Omega Point*—the moment in time when information is universally present in the human consciousness. It is through love that this God-Omega directs the continuation of the whole evolutionary process.

Another way of understanding this is to consider the term *critical mass*, a term very familiar to scientists (meaning the smallest mass of material that will maintain a permanent change), but which gained wider currency when James Redfield wrote about it in *The Celestine Prophecy*.[20] Critical mass occurs when awareness of a new body of knowledge becomes so widespread that it displaces the existing body of knowledge. James Redfield's name for the Omega Point was the First Insight, the creation of a critical mass that occurs when large numbers of people realize that they are experiencing a convergence of information and shared opinions.

That convergence is a renewed reliance on our inner direction, where our life compass is located—not in the rules of society or the need to please our parents or teachers, but from inside, from a deep place of knowing. In that place rest our Destiny, Cause, and Calling, and our capacity to inspire.

How Critical Mass Is Shaping Marketing

All over the world, a convergence of concern and a desire for new thinking—you can call it a *critical mass,* or an *Omega Point,* or an *abundance outlook*—are growing in human awareness. These are not just the concerned views of fringe thinkers anymore. There now exists, as never before, a powerful universal desire to set our former follies behind us and to behave responsibly to one another and to the planet, before it is too late. The millennium and September 11 are harbingers and metaphors of this critical mass—we have arrived at a new intellectual and spiritual gathering place. There is a new awareness that it is not up to "them"—and everything we do is a chance to make things better.

We now agree what the problems are: There is insufficient soul integrity among many old story leaders; we are being presented with a unique opportunity to inspire others whose need for inspiration has never been greater. A growing spiritual hunger burns in all of our breasts. Our ideas for solutions are now clear. The last piece of the jigsaw puzzle is the agreement on how we act, how we lead, and how we inspire in these times—in short, how we become Higher Ground Leaders.

One of the many indicators of the shifts in thinking being brought about by this growing critical mass is the way some forward-thinking leaders view marketing today. Business schools have for years taught models that include strategies for pricing and distribution that enable the market maker to dominate the market—an old story philosophy of scarcity and exclusion. Inevitably, high prices and limited alternatives result until similar products become available, thus transferring more power to consumers. Now think of Microsoft's Internet Explorer. Abundance thinking has propelled Microsoft's success: Their ubiquitous Internet browser was developed with the express intention of *giving it away*—a philosophy of abundance—a paradigm shift that has deeply irritated old story thinkers. The underlying theory was that if potential customers loved the product, many software developers would be drawn to writing programs for it, thus making it the industry standard. The strategy worked—Microsoft's Internet Browser became the preferred offering, despite the controversy it raised, outselling Netscape's comparable offering. Netscape succumbed to the embrace of AOL, becoming a subsidiary, and industry standards were changed and set from that time on.

Another example is the remarkable story of Linus Torvalds. When Torvalds was 10 years old, his grandfather brought home a Commodore VIC-20, on which the boy began writing computer games. In 1991, while studying at the University of Helsinki, he invented an operating system for his personal computer that he preferred to the operating system he was using (Microsoft's DOS) and to the one used by the university (Unix). He called it Linux (rhymes with cynics). Instead of aiming to be an impossibly rich techno-guru, he did something different—*he gave the software away on the Internet,* including the source code that programmers use to create software. Microsoft's Windows is the giant in the market—controlling 97.46 percent of the global desktop market, compared to just 1.43 percent for Apple Macintosh, and 0.26 percent for Linux.[21] Even so, the number of machines running on Linux exceeds 18 million and is growing at greater than 20 percent a year, thanks to millions of dedicated volunteer programmers who contribute daily improvements and add-ons to the software. Most of these programmers have never met, communicating internationally by e-mail. Linux is a virtual meritocracy—any code written for it is scrutinized closely by peers, and only the most rigorous is adopted and incorporated into the master program. Torvalds, born in 1970, moved his family from Finland to Silicone Valley to join Transmeta Corp., a microprocessor designer partly funded by Microsoft cofounder Paul Allen. Linux has gone mainstream—it was used to run special effects for the movie *Titanic,* and most of the major computer and software companies, except Microsoft, have incorporated Linux. Oracle offers Linux versions of some of its database management software. Sun Microsystems uses the program for workstations, and Datapro, a technology research firm, reports that Linux receives the highest rating for professional operating systems from users.[22] New Story Leader Torvalds views competition and scarcity as irrelevant. New Story thinking views life in terms of relationships, communities, and abundance—and the result is more for everyone.

When we turn on electric lights, nothing seems to happen for the first seven-eighths of the switch's movement. It is only during the last eighth of the movement that the light turns on. During the first seven-eighths of the movement, we could mistakenly conclude that nothing was happening. But our impatience would be a misunderstanding—lights turn on as a result of the entire eight-eighths of the movement of the switch. In terms of our awareness about inspiring and leading others, we are now in the last eighth of the process of learning and development. To some, it may appear that little is happening, but the lights are about to turn on. When they do, it will be called *enlightenment*.

The End of Fear as a Utility

This emerging critical mass has brought us to a unique place. We are experiencing a complete mind shift, and it is not just leaders who are experiencing it—the phenomenon is universal. There is an awakening among a wide range of people who have come to the realization that fear and power are not only an ineffective way of relating with people, but an uncivilized way, too. In the communities and relationships we call corporations, organizations, or families, fear is also an ineffective way to elicit high performance from others—and it is just as uncivilized there, too. More and more, we are yearning for spiritual experiences, and we are becoming increasingly aware that these can be achieved only through companionship (from the Latin words *con* and *pan*, [with and bread]—to share bread). Spiritual experiences are achieved in the company of other souls.

Many old story leaders focus most of their energy on defensive, playing-not-to-lose strategies, attempting to build permanent protection from the usual hazards and dangers inherent in all relationships, organizations, and communities. These old story leaders think of people as something to be reduced and controlled, not inspired. Consequently, they focus only on monitoring costs, lowering overheads, increasing productivity, reducing risks, protecting assets, and making decisions only after gaining the protection of a contract and the advice of legal counsel. This is not Higher Ground Leadership, but old story leadership, and it is rooted in attitudes based on fear and scarcity, instead of love and abundance. In an earlier book, I defined *management* as doing things right and leadership as doing the right thing.[23]

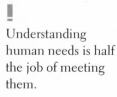

Understanding human needs is half the job of meeting them.

Adlai Stevenson

The New Story Leader is just as aware of power as the old story leader and uses managerial mastery, too, but whereas the old story leader seeks to use power to control others and to steal the power from them, the New Story Leader seeks to *give power to others*—the literal meaning of empowerment. The resulting power is far greater because it is multiplied and fueled by passion. Contrary to our current thinking, we lose nothing by giving power away. Indeed, like knowledge, it is a gift you may bestow without any loss. The

New Story Leader really doesn't give anything away, but simply enables others to become aware of the power they already have—to remember what they have forgotten. In this New Story thinking, we are not pushed toward greater and greater personal achievements. Instead, we are encouraged to ask others, "How can I be of service to you?" The results can be astounding, often reshaping the culture of families, organizations, communities, and countries.

We are now entering a new era in which power will continue to be as important as ever, but the way we use it will change. We will no longer be preoccupied with the use of power to control and dominate others to meet our own ends. Instead, we will learn to understand power as something we give to others when we serve them—this is spiritual power—what I describe in Chapter 13 as the *spiritual quotient* (SQ). Never before has there been a greater yearning by people to be served this way.

The Higher Ground Leader understands the difference between old story and New Story power—the difference between power as fear and power that comes from a loving place. We cannot inspire from fear. Higher Ground Leaders practice the generosity implied in New Story power and assume their true role as loving teachers, coaches, and spiritual guides. Their aim is not to control others, but to liberate their natural greatness.

CHAPTER

3

Step One: Defining Your Destiny—The Uniqueness within That Calls to Be Lived

Tell me not, in mournful numbers,
Life is but an empty dream!
For the soul is dead that slumbers,
and things are not what they seem.
Life is real! Life is earnest!
And the grave is not its goal;
Dust thou art; to dust returnest,
Was not spoken of the soul.
—Henry Wadsworth Longfellow

Destiny Is Authenticity

We must feel inspired before we can inspire. This singular inspiration comes from a clear knowing about our Destiny, the reason for being on this planet, the way we are connected on our journey with one another and the universe. Few of us know the reason we have been put on this planet—our Destiny—the uniqueness within us that calls to be lived. We cannot be great, nor will we earn the right to lead, until we understand our Destiny, our higher purpose. The first step toward becoming a Higher Ground Leader, therefore, is to identify your Destiny—your uniqueness within that calls to be lived.

Higher Ground Leaders have an intimate relationship with their inner purpose and the path that inspires them. Until we have clearly identified, and are then following, our own Destinies, we cannot be authentic leaders and help others to identify and follow their own true Destinies. As Max De Pree, former chairman of Herman Miller, observed, it is more important to reach our potential than to reach our goals. We cannot inspire others until we define our purpose and, therefore, our potential. A Destiny describes *why* we are here on Earth, our divine purpose.

Bill George, now professor of leadership and governance at IMD

43

and visiting professor of management at Ecole Polytechnique Fédérale Lausanne (EPFL), was formerly chairman of the board of Medtronic, the world's leading medical technology company. While at Medtronic, he told me, "I have felt since I was a teenager that I had a calling to work in the business world in a leadership position where I could influence others to work to a high code of ethics. It took a while to find a place where I could find a near-perfect match between mine and the company's values. Here at Medtronic, I feel I can really make a difference."

We all yearn to feel as secure as Bill George in our life's purpose. How did we forget who we are? And, having forgotten, how and why have we let *others* define who we are for us? Surely, we are the best suited to make these discoveries. And where will we find the answers? As we all know, but seldom acknowledge, the answers lie within.

> It is not in the stars to hold our destiny but in ourselves.
> William Shakespeare

Few of us have thought about why we have been placed on this Earth, and, if asked this question, we might become strangely tongue-tied. But how can we inspire and lead others if we can't even explain the reason for our own existence in the first place? Higher Ground Leadership is the practice of being an inspiration to others based on our own inner, authentic awareness of our Destiny. It is not something we learn; it is something we *live*. We cannot *do* inspiration. We *become* Higher Ground Leaders—it is something we express through *being*.

If we have no idea of what we are supposed to be doing while we are on this planet, we cannot know the practical purpose and sacred intent of our lives. Therefore, whatever form of relationship we have with others will have no spiritual brilliance to advance or justify it.

Without a sense of connection to a divine purpose or higher power, we tend to slip into autopilot, practicing a way of motivating and relating with others that we may have learned by reading biographies or by watching movies and TV heroes. We need a deeper sense of who we are, to be fully present as conscious beings, before we can presume to inspire other beings.

How can we tell that we are living our lives true to the noblest reasons for being alive? Surely the things we do on a day-to-day basis should lead to something meaningful, should serve others more than ourselves, and should come from the most authentic part of our being. Every action, and therefore our lives, should *amount* to something, lead to something, change something, make something better—especially one another and the world. This is the legacy we create.

What then, is our purpose on this earthly journey? What is the uniqueness within us that calls out to be lived? This is the important starting point for us all. Most of us will die with our music still inside us because, though we are given pure clarity at birth, society slowly clutters our inner awareness with its rules and pressures. And so we squeeze ourselves into the cookie-cutter molds that society deems to be best for us. With each effort to gain the approval of an external person or norm, whether these are our parents, our partners and spouses, our children, bureaucracies, institutions—"them" and "the rules"—we trade something of ourselves in exchange, until we eventually hollow ourselves out, becoming empty and, eventually, solely guided by the outer forces of life. Thus, we become inauthentic and lose our wholeness. We become not ourselves, but as others would like us to be. We live in a paradigm created by others—we become copyfrogs. As long as we are deaf to our intuition, our inner voice seeking to be heard, our true Destiny will go unrealized, and the music within us will remain unplayed.

Letting go of our constant need for approval—projecting onto others what we feel they would like us to be—is a powerful beginning on this path, because with this new freedom, we can see with new eyes, and we can make choices that come from our hearts. Caroline Myss has written, "When you do not seek or need external approval, you are at your most powerful. Nobody can disempower you emotionally or psychologically . . . You cannot live for prolonged periods of time within the polarity of being true to yourself and needing the approval of others."[1]

Like Bill George, we are each ordained to follow a specific Destiny, and for as long as we ignore or dishonor that call, we remain inauthentic. For some, because this pattern endures over a lifetime, life's lessons remain unlearned. As long as we do not heed our

> The Art of Peace begins with you. Work on yourself and your appointed task in the Art of Peace. Everyone has a spirit that can be refined, a body that can be trained in some manner, a suitable path to follow. You are here for no other purpose than to realize your inner divinity and manifest your innate enlightenment. Foster peace in your own life and then apply the Art to all that you encounter.
>
> Morihei Ueshiba

> The lesson is simple, the student is complicated.
>
> Barbara Rasp

inner voices, we remain untrue to ourselves, for we each have a uniqueness within that is calling to be heard—and lived—our Destiny.

The Awakening

Many of us blindly follow a path with no passion—we simply slip onto a moving walkway, like the ones at the airport, which stream us along with the rest of the harried and hurried crowd. We ask no questions—we are copyfrogs treading the walkway, because we see others doing so. We have no idea whether we are making a difference, creating happiness (for ourselves as well as others), or leaving a legacy. We sense a lack of connection to the universe, an absence of enchantment and bliss in our lives, and we realize that there must be more.

> !
> When one is out of touch with oneself, one cannot touch others.
> Anne Morrow Lindbergh
> !

Each of us must be awakened from our state of unconsciousness. These moments of awakening happen in different ways for different people. Some have always been aware of their uniqueness and have lived it all their lives, thus fulfilling their Destiny. Others never become enlightened this way. Many are brought face-to-face with the challenge of identifying their Destiny at some point during the unfolding of their lives.

For some, it is a rude awakening: One day, a sudden storm arrives—illness or loss of job, loved one, or relationship; a war or an act of violence; or a violation or loss—and we are shocked when our comfortable structures are torn away. In the new starkness, we become aware that we have been drifting for years. We realize that after all this time, we really have no idea of where we are, how we got there, where we are going, or the purpose of our journey. Dante described the situation: "In the middle of the journey of our life I came to see myself in a dark wood where the straight way was lost."

It's Never Too Late

In my research into the greatest leaders that have ever lived—Buddha, Christ, Mohammed, Jefferson, Martin Luther King, St. Francis, Mother Teresa—I found that many of them did not discover their Destinies until the latter parts of their lives. Christ was a carpenter for the first 30 years of His life—His greatness was compressed into His last three years on Earth. St. Francis, the son of a prosperous merchant, took part in several military operations as a mercenary soldier before he felt himself called to be a preacher and mystic at the age of 27. He founded two holy orders in the last third of his life, before his death at age 45. Buddha was a wealthy prince who did not begin his spiritual journey until he was 29, and six more years passed before he reached enlightenment.

Somewhere, something incredible is waiting to be known.

Carl Sagan

Bill Wilson was 40 before he started the organization that would change the lives of millions—Alcoholics Anonymous. Rosa Parks was 42 when she signaled the beginning of the end of segregation and ushered in a new phase of the civil rights movement in America by refusing to give up her seat to a white passenger on a bus.

Jim McCann spent 14 years as a social worker at St. John's Home for Boys in Rockaway, New York, before becoming the Higher Ground Leader who transformed a company teetering on the edge of bankruptcy into a $600 million success called 1-800-FLOWERS. Tom Bloch went the other way. As CEO of H & R Block Inc., the world's largest tax preparation company, he took a 98 percent pay cut from his $618,000 annual salary to teach math at a Kansas City Catholic school of mostly minority students.

We each find our path in different ways and for different reasons; and as these examples attest, there is no right time in our lives to discover our uniqueness that calls to be lived. The timing is unimportant. What is important is that we discover our true Destiny, and thus become authentic, before we can grow into a Higher Ground Leader. These discoveries by many great contributors late in their lives serve as a beacon for each of us as we try to define our own journeys. It is never too late.

Joe Calvaruso: Higher Ground Leader

Joe Calvaruso is the president, CEO, and *chief inspiration officer* of Mount Carmel Health System, a Catholic-based healthcare organization founded in 1886, which is part of the fourth largest Catholic healthcare system in America—Trinity Health System based in Novi, Michigan. Like many others in healthcare, the people at Mount Carmel were drawn to healthcare as a calling: to be of service to people when their need is greatest, when they are most vulnerable. Says Joe Calvaruso:

The vagaries of the marketplace and politics have created an enormous challenge for healthcare in the past decade—revenues have been declining and expenses have been rising, and we've had to figure out ways to do more and more with less and less. A few years ago, people were feeling stretched, and I was hearing that Mount Carmel was losing its soul, a soul that our people knew was still there deep inside. I didn't want to wait around. I thought we needed to reclaim our soul, reawaken spirit and values at Mount Carmel. After hearing Lance speak, I kind of just thrust myself upon him as he was going from the cocktail party to dinner, to learn more about spirit and values in the workplace. After we had dinner together, he invited me to a leadership retreat at a remote location in Canada. I was awe-struck and inspired by the retreat. There were only seven of us, and I knew at the time that this was what Mount Carmel needed, what healthcare needed, what any company in any industry needs to reclaim the spirit and soul of employees. But especially Mount Carmel, because we did have a soul, we do have a spirit, we are filled with very caring people, and I knew that they needed their souls and spirits reawakened. In fact, during the retreat I began to cry so uncontrollably that my fellow participants had to hold me up, because I realized this was what we had to do, and I was only one person.

We ran our first week-long Higher Ground Leadership Retreat with the Secretan team at the Congregational Home of the Sisters of St. Francis in Stella Niagara for our senior leadership team. Since then, over 600 executives, leaders, directors, and physicians have attended a similar retreat. I go to every one as a teacher, presenter, and faculty member. It is hard to quantify the total financial benefit of such a profound cultural change, but I am quite certain that when you have over 600 people spending eight days at a retreat, or 8,000 people who have had some kind of exposure to Higher Ground Leadership, that is good for the organization. The three years since our first Higher Ground retreat have been the best financial years in the history of the organization.

In healthcare, we have a *very* important issue that we're facing—there is a dramatic shortage of good people. In fact, I believe, it's the most important issue that we're facing in healthcare. There are shortages nationally, but Columbus is especially affected by a shortage of healthcare workers: RNs, surgical, radiology techs, pharmacists, and other specialties. Healthcare suffers from very high staff turnover, too. The national average for turnover is slightly in excess of 20 percent, which means that one out of every five workers leaves their organization every year. How can you build good customer satisfaction or deliver physician satisfaction or improve quality, if one out of every five of your workers is leaving every year—on average, every five years, you have a whole new group of employees. You can't have anything that's sustainable when you have that kind of turnover.

Our staff turnover used to be 24 percent. Since we've begun the journey to Higher Ground, two major things have happened. First, one year after we began our journey to Higher Ground Leadership, our staff turnover dropped to less than 10 percent. This kind of dramatic decrease in turnover translates not only into dollar savings; it's estimated that, for example, the replacement cost for a nurse is in excess of $50,000 according to the Healthcare Advisory Board, which is a national think tank in the healthcare industry. At 24 percent turnover of 8,000 employees, we were losing 2,000 employees every year. Cut that in half, and you are saving 1,000 times $50,000 dollars—including the cost of signing-on bonuses, education, and orientation. It takes a year or two for a nurse to get fully up to speed in a new hospital, meet physicians, see how they do things, new processes, procedures, policies. The second major movement that has occurred since beginning our journey to Higher Ground Leadership is a dramatic improvement in our employee satisfaction. We survey employees every two years using a survey from the Great Place to Work Institute. It's the same company that *Fortune* magazine uses to determine the top 100 places to work in the United States. In the two years following our first survey, our employees gave positive responses in all 55 questions asked by the independent surveyors. Every score increased! The vast majority were double-digit and high double-digit increases, including the question they use to benchmark each organization's scores against all others they survey, which goes like this: "All things considered, do you consider (Mount Carmel) to be a great place to work?" That survey answer increased 43 percent since the same question was asked two years earlier. Now coincidentally, the last time we did this survey was one month before we began our journey to Higher Ground Leadership. Our employees are now more inspired, want to come to work, and are happier at work, and are therefore happier at home; and this translates into greater productivity, less absenteeism, and reduced turnover, so we don't need to hire new people and train them again.

It also reduces our recruitment expenses. For example, a group of surgeons is building an orthopedic hospital across town, and they're doing that because some of our operating rooms have been closed in the past year or two. Because our nurse retention is now much higher than it was one year ago, we are starting to open more operating rooms, so we believe we can retain these surgeons because there will not be the urgent need to utilize another hospital for their surgical procedures. We will, therefore, retain their patient revenues at Mount Carmel, resulting in increased revenues for us. Let's take another example—providing much needed emergency services. At one of our hospitals in Columbus, we have the busiest emergency room in the entire state of Ohio, but we also have the highest diversion rates, meaning we close our emergency department more than others due to a shortage of capacity. And mostly it is capacity of workers, not the physical space. If you retain more workers, you don't have to close the emergency department and, therefore, do not need to turn away patients that we should be serving. There are all kinds of downstream effects to having staff that stay with the organization. The formula for these success stories is quite simple: We have more satisfied employees, which leads to higher retention, which leads to more satisfied physicians, which leads to their bringing more patients to our facilities, which leads to more revenues for us.

Joe Calvaruso experienced what so many Higher Ground Leaders have experienced: a defining moment, a realization of what his life could become and why he has been placed on this planet, and what he must do with his time here. This realization enabled Joe to become very clear and intentional about his life purpose—his Destiny—and to commit his life to it. The personal and organizational implications have been profound and widely acclaimed. After deliberation, coaching, and inner reflection, Joe wrote his personal Destiny statement: *To illuminate the sacredness in every Soul.* This is how Joe now leads, inspires others, and lives his life.[2]

Jerry Chamales: Higher Ground Leader

In the 1970s, Scotch and cocaine supplied Jerry Chamales' highest moments. At the tender age of 27, Chamales was, he says, "at the bottom of the food chain, bent like a pretzel." In 1977, Chamales realized this was not his true Destiny— he was not living an authentic life. He decided to dry out and straighten up his life. He founded Omni Computer Products in Carson, California, which has since grown into a $30 million producer and remanufacturer of computer supplies and recycled printer cartridges. Chamales has found his Destiny and is living it through his company—one-third of Omni's 270 employees are, like him, formerly workless or homeless, drug addicts, or alcoholics. Many are ex-convicts. Chamales recruits many of his employees at halfway houses, work-furlough centers, and recovery programs. He then assigns a mentor and puts them through a rehabilitation program sponsored by Omni. Chamales posts bail when his employees brush with the law, attends recovery programs with new hires, and maintains a close relationship with a bondsman, who puts him in touch with prospective employees. One employee worked for Omni for 18 months, but repeatedly fell off the wagon. After enrolling in a recovery program, he joined another company in the same business, being too ashamed to return. But Joe Hiller, himself a former addict and now Omni's vice-president of sales, went looking for him. "Why don't you come home?" Hiller asked the employee when he found him—and he did. Chamales is a successful businessman, but he is also a successful "therapist," rehabilitation expert, and now a conservationist, and this has helped him to become a Higher Ground Leader and to realize his Destiny.

Rhinotek is the brand under which Jerry Chamales manufactures and markets OEM-compatible toner and inkjet cartridges, ribbons, and copier and fax supplies, and saving the black rhino has become a passion for him. In 1970, the worldwide black rhino population was 60,000; 30 years later, it had dwindled to 2,700, putting the species on the endangered list. Jerry underwrote the cost of $25,000 for shipping Kusamona, a 2,500-pound black rhino from the Western Plains Zoo in Dubbo, Australia, to the Fossil Rim Wildlife Center in Glen Rose, Texas, to breed with the facility's three females there as part of the International Rhino Foundation's attempt to reverse the staggering decline of black rhinos worldwide.[3] Jerry Chamales' life is dedicated to helping rehabilitate those who are dependent on alcohol and drugs, and to saving endangered wildlife.

A *Destiny* describes *why* we have been put here on Earth. It describes our connection to a higher purpose, our link to something bigger than our immediate environments, the definition of our *sacred purpose*. Our Destiny can be stated as a clear articulation of the supreme purpose of our existence, something that, if we can edge closer to its achievement before we complete our time on Earth, will help us to know the pride and pleasure that our Creator has in us.

James Hillman has written, "The soul in each of us is given a unique daemon,[4] before we are born, and it has selected an image or pattern that we live on Earth. This soul-companion, the daemon guides us here; in the process of arrival, however, we forget all that took place and believe we come empty into this world. The daemon remembers what is in your image and belongs to your pattern, and therefore your daemon is the carrier of your Destiny."[5]

Our sense of Destiny is given to us very early in life, perhaps even before birth—and each of us has a Destiny that, in its own way, is unique. But it can lay dormant for much of our life, though it cannot remain dormant forever, because none of us is able to leave this life without first learning and understanding why we were sent here—the veil that reveals the mystery of our Destiny is lifted for everyone, even if it is in the very final minutes of our lives. And whenever in our lives that moment of revelation comes, when we discern our unique path to the fulfillment of our divine intention, we will clearly see how it is an expression of what we have known about our purpose—*our Destiny* here on Earth from the very earliest moments of our lives. We must all strive to receive this knowing so that we can live our lives fully and as an inspiration to others.

CHAPTER 4

Writing Your Own Destiny Statement

O Me! O Life!

O Me! O life! . . . of the questions of these recurring;
Of the endless trains of the faithless—of cities fill'd with the foolish;
Of myself forever reproaching myself (for who more foolish than I, and
  who more faithless?)
Of eyes that vainly crave the light—of the objects mean—of the struggle
  ever renew'd;
Of the poor results of all—of the plodding and sordid crowds I see
  around me;
Of the empty and useless years of the rest—with the rest me intertwined;
The question, O me! so sad, recurring—What good amid these, O me,
  O life?
Answer.
That you are here—that life exists, and identity;
That the powerful play goes on, and you may contribute a verse.

—Walt Whitman, 1819–1892

If you have never thought about your Destiny, you are probably wondering how to begin. Let's walk together through a process we call *reframing*.

Think of your Destiny as a solution to one or more threats to the planet and the future of humanity. We reframe the threat as a solution or a fix. We will call the threat a *Terrathreat* (*terra*, Latin for Earth) and the fix a *Terrafix*. Great manifestos, such as the Magna Carta, the Bill of Rights, the American Declaration of Independence, Vaclav Havel's Charter 77, or the Communist Manifesto were all statements of hope written in response to oppression. They described the problems deemed to be insufferable by those who drafted the manifestos at the time, and

> Eventually, all
> things merge into
> one, and a river
> runs through it.
>
> Norman MacLean

who wrote their declarations as statements of hope and antidotes for repression—cures for the issues that afflicted them. Such great manifestos provided a blueprint for the way in which an oppressive or intolerable situation could be reversed. From these sentiments of discontent were born passionate descriptions of the solutions the authors prescribed for creating a more sacred and loving planet. In much the same way, our personal Destiny statement can provide a blueprint and a higher purpose for our lives as individuals that will make the world a better place.

There are only three ways to approach anything in life:

1. We can complain about how things are.
2. We can be copyfrogs, ignoring or walking away from the Terrathreats and from the issues and relationships that we find painful or unsatisfactory.
3. We can do the nobler thing—we can roll up our sleeves and work to change things.

My own Destiny, for example, is: *To help create a more sustainable and loving planet.* By applying the reframing process, my Destiny can be seen as a positive mirror of the problems I see on the planet. It provides me with my sense of personal purpose and a blueprint for how I will contribute to the resolution of what I see to be the Terrathreats in the world. I discovered my Destiny as a response to my personal belief that there are two Terrathreats that tower above all others on Earth. I believe I am here to help resolve them, and thus bring a measure of healing to the planet:

> Tell me, what is it
> you plan to do
> With your one wild
> and precious life?
>
> Mary Oliver

1. The first Terrathreat is that there is too much violence on Earth—domestic violence, verbal abuse, hostility, anger, and the ultimate violence—war. Unless we learn to curb our aggressive behaviors and to love one another instead, we are in danger of destroying our planet and its inhabitants.
2. The second Terrathreat is that Earth, as we know it, is currently unsustainable. If we continue to consume and destroy our environment at our current pace, we will eliminate the means by which our species can survive and be sustained.

After considering these two Terrathreats, I thought about how they might be resolved by reframing them as Terrafixes—problems seen in the mirror of solution. This enables me to discern my Destiny as a commitment to reversing, in my own small way, and in my own small corner of the planet, the two major, and potentially terminal, ills of violence and environmental degradation. Through reframing, I can see that the reverse of violence is love, and the reverse of degradation is sustainability. So from this awareness, I have been able to craft the words that are the antithesis and the antidote of the Terrathreats that attract my energy and passion, which, therefore, reveal and describe my Destiny: *To help create a more sustainable and loving planet.* If I am successful in this life at all, it will be because I have helped to lessen the presence of these two Terrathreats. It is to this that I have, therefore, dedicated my life. This then becomes the articulation of my Destiny.

Here are some other examples of personal Destiny statements:

- *Joe Calvaruso, CEO of Mount Carmel Health System, a world-class healthcare system in Columbus, Ohio:* To illuminate the sacredness in every soul.
- *Susan Nind, senior faculty of The Secretan Center and a teacher of our work to corporations:* To assist the evolution of human consciousness.
- *Diane Hoover, senior faculty of The Secretan Center and a teacher of our work to corporations:* To generate spirit on Earth.
- *Michelle Lucero, corporate general counsel:* To build a spiritual, just, and inclusive community.
- *Wauleah Larson, Native American healthcare executive:* To awaken the spirit of Ho (Cherokee for "It is so") in the world.
- *Amy Feaster, technology executive:* To help those whose voices are not heard.
- *Ed Boudreau, physician:* To make the world simpler.
- *Sister Nancy Hoffman, vice president of Mission:* To help reawaken in our universe the message of God's unconditional love for all of creation.
- *Tricia Secretan, psychotherapist and life coach:* To inspire sacred passion.

As you can see, each of these statements describes a magnificent vision of a world that will be enriched by our presence here, a world that will become a better place because we have lived.

Destiny statements have a corporate application, too. Jeffrey Swartz, president and CEO of Timberland, the billion-dollar footwear and apparel company, says, "As a company, we have both a responsibility and an interest in engaging in the world around us. By doing so, we deliver value to our four constituencies: consumers, shareholders, employees, and the community. We offer the consumer a

company to believe in and get involved with; we offer our employees a set of beliefs that transcend the workplace; we offer the community an active and supportive corporate neighbor; and we offer shareholders a company that people want to
both buy from and work for." Jeffrey Swartz believes in the power of "pulling on
our boots and making a difference." Timberland employees are invited to act on
this commitment as a means to strengthen their relationships with shareholders,
customers, employees, and communities. Pulling on their boots to build a play-
ground. Pulling on their boots to clean up a park. Pulling on their boots to mentor
a child. The company is committed to "Doing Well and Doing Good," a philosophy that is guided by the values instilled by the company's founder Nathan Swartz:
Humanity, Humility, Integrity, and Excellence. One day, my call to Jeffrey's office
was answered by a recorded message saying, "Timberland's offices are closed
today. All 5,400 employees in 13 countries are working on service projects, making a difference in their local communities, and we will be back in our offices tomorrow." Timberland employees each receive 40 hours of paid time per year to
volunteer in their communities.

Don Ziraldo, founder and CEO of Inniskillin Wines, part of the fourth-
largest vintner in North America, puts it this way, "I feel that my position as a
business leader affords me a platform from which to speak about the other things
in life and make a difference in the world."

All organizations need a sense of collective Destiny—this is what makes
them great—and, to paraphrase Martin Luther King Jr., they are great because
they can serve.

A Divine Conversation

My colleagues and I have run hundreds of workshops and retreats around the
world and have coached and advised participants from many walks of life. As a
result, we have refined and polished our thinking about the concepts with which
we work and how they apply to the lives of people everywhere. Here is one approach that we have found very successful:

> Our Destiny is often revealed to us in visions or images. One way to envisage
> your Destiny is to imagine that God (or a powerful source) is speaking to you
> and inviting you to help in some great endeavor. Here is a visualization experi-
> ence to help you discern your own sense of Destiny—an imaginary dialogue
> with God.
>
> God has summoned you to an important meeting—just the two of you—
> you and God. You are about to be born on Earth, although at this moment, you
> are simply a probability. In your prehuman form, a spiritual presence, you are

deeply engaged in conversation with God in Heaven's Boardroom. This is the opportunity of a lifetime.

God opens the discussion by inviting you to participate in The Greatest Consulting Project of All. Then God gets down to business. "As a new spirit with God's Consulting Company, you will be given a very important assignment. There is a place out there called Planet Earth."

God points to a map of the universe and shows the location of the assignment He has in mind.

"It is one of our greatest successes," He continues. "The Greatest Consulting Project of All is in this dossier. It is called Planet Earth. It has been underway for a long time, and we have completed many projects over the millennia, and by and large, we are very pleased with the results. However, there are a few tasks that we agreed to undertake in our original proposal, but that, as yet, we have been unable to complete. Therefore, we have not yet been able to close this file. We need to facilitate the evolution of Planet Earth and guide it in finding better ways to create and sustain life and to improve its capacity to be a more caring, compassionate, and loving place, whose inhabitants honor the sacredness in all relationships—not only between people, but also between every other living and inanimate thing.

"I want you to go there and represent us in this very important assignment," God continues. "Planet Earth is my favorite project, and I want you to take care of our unfinished business there. Your responsibility is to dedicate your life in a way that will serve these aims and thus help make Planet Earth more like the perfect place we first envisioned. You will become a Higher Ground Leader in your community, and I will give you a century or so to complete your assignment. We will provide you with all the help you need to successfully complete the tasks. No request will be ignored or unreasonably declined. The file for this assignment is entitled 'Your Destiny.'

"I should tell you in advance that many consultants who have visited Earth before you have found that the countless distractions there caused them to lose their focus, to forget this file, and to overlook the original purpose of their assignment. These distractions are a necessary part of your learning and your journey, but they are not the purpose of life. I encourage you to remain focused on the real purpose of your life—your Destiny—while enjoying every moment of your short journey on Earth."

Through divine intervention, you are dispatched to Planet Earth, and before you know it, you find yourself busy living your life. God has given you a spiritual attaché case, which contains background data and briefing files. You review the contents for guidance. As you examine the papers, you find a helpful checklist entitled, "Defining your Destiny." Some of the suggestions included are:

- *Destiny is authenticity*: We are each called to follow a specific journey. As long as you are unaware of, or ignore or deny that call, you are compromising your authenticity. Higher Ground Leaders have an intimate relationship with their inner purpose and the path that inspires them. Your duty is to clearly identify and then follow your own Destiny, and thus become authentic. This will help you to become a Higher Ground Leader with the responsibility to help others so that they, in their turn, will be able to identify and follow their own Destiny and help others to do the same.

- *Why are you here?* This is the question that your personal Destiny statement must answer clearly. What is your purpose on this Earthly journey? What is the uniqueness within you that calls to be lived? This is the important starting point for you. Everyone has a uniqueness within that is a special purpose waiting to be lived—like a song asking to be sung, a symphony wanting to be played. Unless you can find the answer to the question of why you are here, you will be in danger of dying with your music still inside.

    To find the music that waits inside you and yearns to be played, reflect on the conditions that you see around you, that you feel are contributing to the problems being experienced on Earth. What are the most damaging and obstinate problems that are contributing to the ails of the world? How will you live your life in a way that reduces or eliminates these problems wherever you are? (Know that others have also been assigned to help you with this project—you do not have to do this all by yourself.) How will you help to change the planet for the better? I want you to be inspired to make Planet Earth more exquisite. How will you help to leave it in better health than you found it? Which are the Terrathreats that you will help to resolve, and which are the Terrafixes to which you will contribute?

- *Your higher purpose*: Your Destiny is your connection to the Divine. How does your purpose on Planet Earth connect you to the Divine? How are you integrated with the greater universe? How will your time here and the role you have assumed create enchantment and bliss in your life and in the lives of everyone with whom you are connected? How will you inspire divine results?

- *Whom does your Destiny serve?* Answering this and other questions by listening carefully as the answers are revealed to you will enable you to reach your full potential and to give birth to your whole self. This discovery and the resulting journey are the warmth that will kindle your passion, help you to fall in love with life again, and discern your Destiny. This will then lead to the life well lived, according to your true Destiny—no matter where you are on your life's journey.

- *It's never too late.* In fact, you should know that you may become sidetracked in carrying out my request and instead pursue other tasks for part of your life, but don't think for a minute that it is ever too late in your life to regroup and define your Destiny. It's never too late. Because as long as you are not following your Destiny, you risk leading an inauthentic life—Destiny is authenticity.

     You have your assignment (your Destiny) and your brilliance and passion—the Creator's divine gifts to you. How you choose to use your brilliance and passion is your gift back to your Creator. You have a lifetime in which to fulfill your Destiny. Remember, it's never too late. We *are depending on you.*

     I love you and will always be at your side.*

Understanding Your Purpose—Why Are You Here?

In the next few pages, we will work together in a process that will help you to discover the passion that burns inside you and the issues of the world that animate you, so that the higher purpose of your life will be revealed and you will be able to refine this into a clear, personal Destiny statement. Consider these questions and reflect on them for a few moments, perhaps using a journal to note the ideas and answers that come to you:

1. What Terrathreats do you feel interfere with or degrade the potential of humanity and our planet? What makes you sad when you think about the human condition? What do you think needs to be improved, changed, or resolved for these Terrathreats to recede or be reversed? What excites you and draws you to make a difference? What do you consider to be the Terrathreats that are preventing the world from becoming a place where all human and natural life can flourish and reach its true, divine potential?

2. Which of these Terrathreats are uniquely calling to you for resolution? Which ones are inviting your attention? How can you reframe these statements into Terrafixes? How will these Terrathreats be lessened by your presence on Earth? What could you do that would roll back these Terrathreats? Which of those you noted in the first group of questions are the most important to you and truly speak to your heart?

*To listen to an audio version read by Lance Secretan, or to order the CD, visit www .secretan.com/inspire.

When you have collected your thoughts on these subjects, you may find it useful to write in your notebook or journal. Don't worry about being pretty or literate — just write as fast as the thoughts come to you, gibberish and unconnected thoughts and whatever else flows. Write until it feels right, until you feel you have described and released all of your concerns, and until you feel complete.

> ❗
> Every nail driven
> should be as another
> rivet in the machine
> of the universe.
>
> Henry Thoreau
>
> ❗

Now look at your journal notes and see if you can find some common themes. What stands out? What are the main issues? How would you make a contribution to the healing of human and planetary wounds?

Write some additional, concise statements distilled from your journal writings. Don't fuss with this; just write some 5- to 10-word statements that come easily to your mind.

When you feel ready, write one statement with which you resonate. Describe how you will dedicate your life to the lessening of the Terrathreats that seem to be the most important to you. This is the first draft of your Destiny statement.

Step Two: Defining Your Cause

No vision and you perish
No ideal, and you're lost;
Your heart must ever cherish
Some faith at any cost.
Some hope, some dream to cling to,
Some rainbow in the sky,
Some melody to sing to,
Some service that is high.
— Harriet du Autermont

The Cause

The next step of the Higher Ground Leader is to identify a magnetic vision—a *Cause*. Flowing directly from the pure clarity of their Destiny, Higher Ground Leaders define and then live a Cause—a magnetic vision so powerful that it draws people and their passion to it from afar. Others feel called to contribute and add their energy, love, passion, and support to the Cause. A Cause describes how we will be in our lives or organizations—what we stand for—and it comes from within.

The greatest leaders in history all saw a beacon beckoning to them from the future—a Cause. They had a clear vision of the world they sought to create and a burning passion to bring that world into existence. For them, and for many others, their Cause defined a future world brightened by the light of their dream, and it defined how they chose to *be* in their lives and what they stood for.

People who inspire develop a vision so compelling that it becomes a magnet for passion—a Cause. They do not try to motivate—they invite inspiration with a passionately held Cause. They combine visceral energy with a clear and focused vision, founded on strong spiritual beliefs and values. This combination radiates a light so bright that people find it irresistible. New Story Leaders do not need to recruit because their Cause becomes a beacon, attracting the passion of people from far and wide. Modern corporate examples abound—Avon, The Body Shop, Centura Health, eBay, FedEx, W.L. Gore, Krispy Kreme, Medtronic, Merck, Mount Carmel Health System, Patagonia, Pella, SAS Institute, Smucker's, Southwest Airlines, Starbucks, Symantec, Timberland, Wegman's, and Whole Foods Market—just to name a few.

To determine "the profile of the global leader of the future," Accenture, a global consulting firm, interviewed leaders and aspiring leaders around the world and found that of the 14 essential characteristics, "creating a shared vision" topped the list.[1] Human resources consultant William M. Mercer surveyed employees to determine if benefits, policies, and practices influenced them when choosing an employer or improving their personal productivity. Most respondents (64 percent) said that a "clear sense of organizational purpose" would influence them more than almost all traditional employee benefits except a retirement or savings plan and a pension plan.[2] The power of a Cause to attract people to an organization and its leader matches and often exceeds any material incentive.

A grand and compelling Cause attracts the passion necessary to initiate change. In short, a compelling Cause is a covenant so powerful that it becomes a magnet that draws others to it, like a pilgrim is drawn to a sacred shrine. A Cause, whether it is a personal or a corporate Cause, stands on its own, without the need to be pitched or hawked, because it is so inherently sound and sacred. The greatest leaders in history—Christ, Buddha, Gandhi, Martin Luther King, and Thomas Jefferson among them—did not form a committee to achieve a buy-in to their mission or vision. They didn't have to sell their ideas. Their ideas were so powerful that people were simply drawn to them—their vision was a Cause. The appeal of a Cause is the profound and unique strength it holds. Think of the Kevin Costner character in the movie *A Field of Dreams*; his Cause was so powerful, he knew that he would "build it and they will come."

If one is lucky, a solitary fantasy can totally transform one million realities.

Maya Angelou

A magnetic Cause is connected to our Destiny because the Cause serves the Destiny, joining our divine purpose with our day-to-day way of being—how we show up, how we choose to *be* in the universe. A great Cause builds a beautiful bridge between the Divine and the secular, between the heavenly and the earthly, between the hoped-for future and the present, in such an elegant and thrilling way that it fires the imagination of those who hear it. Whereas Destiny describes *why* we are here on Earth—our divine purpose—a Cause describes how we will *be*, what we will *stand for*, and how we will practically meet that Destiny while we are on Earth—our earthly dreams.

The most inspiring people in history all saw a beacon beckoning to them from the future—a Cause. They had a clear vision of the world they sought to create and a burning passion that empowered them to turn their dreams into action and work toward bringing the world of which they dreamed into existence. Their Cause presented an unequivocal description of a future world brightened by the light of their dream—and so it should be for every one of us.

A great Cause always has two common features:

1. It is deeply engaging to others because it is patient, nonaggressive, and non-competitive, and it embraces the long view.
2. It is not self-serving or focused on goals; it serves and ennobles others.

A Cause is a dream that connects us from our present reality (who we are, what we do, and how we show up each day) to a richly imagined future (our dream of how things might be when the Terrathreats no longer haunt us). A compelling Cause stirs us and makes the hairs on our neck stand up. It quickens our pulse and races our imagination. It excites and arouses us into action. A Cause is the spark that fuels the ideology that blossoms into a movement. It encourages us to fall in love with the present again because it paints a clear, magical, and uplifting picture of our chosen path to the future.

I don't dream at night, I dream all day; I dream for a living.

Steven Spielberg

A magnetic Cause connects first with the Divine—a power greater than our own little worlds—and then takes us gently backwards to the reality of the present. A great Cause builds a bridge between the Divine and the temporal that captures the imagination of those who hear it. This is what draws people to a Cause.

The Higher Ground Leader responds to a clear inner voice and thus becomes the spokesperson for a richly imagined future.

When Martin Luther King Jr. delivered his famous speech in Washington, D.C., on August 28, 1963, to an audience of more than 200,000 civil rights supporters, he was deeply aware of the need for patience and holding the long view. He sought to ennoble people by proclaiming his Cause. He said, "I have a dream that one day this nation will rise up and live out the true meaning of its creed: 'We hold these truths to be self-evident, that all men are created equal.' . . . I have a dream that my four little children will one day live in a nation where they will not be judged by the color of their skin, but by the content of their character." It was a dream, not for next week, or next month, or even for next year, but forever in the future. This was, and still is, a Cause that inspires the hearts of millions of people, not just African Americans, because it appeals to the souls of all people. King was speaking to the soul. It was outrageous and irrational, given the situation at the time, but even so, millions of people found it totally enthralling. We are all yearning for a heightened level of inspiration, and we will align ourselves with a great Cause and freely undergo untold hardships to help realize a dream that ignites our passion. King achieved this by defining a Cause that was divinely inspired and far greater than himself—he spoke about an ideal, a future world that he could see in his heart, into which he was pouring his life, and which came from a higher source—and millions could identify with it and were drawn to his Cause.

> Hold fast to dreams,
> for if dreams die,
> life is a broken-
> winged bird that
> cannot fly.
>
> Langston Hughes

More than just affairs of the head, great Causes are affairs of the heart. Whereas the head may warn us that the new Cause is inconceivable and irrational, the heart tells us this doesn't matter. In fact, most compelling Causes may initially strike us as being intellectually outrageous—this is their appeal. The lasting magic created by Higher Ground Leaders such as Martin Luther King or Gandhi is the ringing passion of their Causes, which continues to this day. When Martin Luther King gave his famous speech, he was not speaking from the head, but from the heart. In an earlier period when slavery was still common practice, the Quakers, William Lloyd Garrison, and the other leading abolitionists sounded completely illogical—they spoke from their hearts with passion about a Cause that stirred the hearts and passions of millions of others who eventually changed the world. We can test the power of an idea to inspire by asking, "Does it inspire the soul?"

A Cause Is Not a Mission Statement

A compelling Cause is characterized by two vital elements:

1. It honors the sacredness of people.
2. It is the inspiration of one person.

This stands in stark contrast to the contemporary practice of writing mission statements. Old story leaders believe in two myths:

1. Organizational mission statements are developed by, and require the consensus of, a team.
2. Mission statements define quantifiable goals.

Historically, corporate and personal mission statements have tended to be litanies of goals and targets directed at others, describing how the organization or the individual intends to become larger, stronger, more powerful, dominant, or successful—statements flowing from old story thinking. After a while, these earthly, egocentric visions all start to look alike. This is not surprising—the same texts are used so widely to develop mission statements that everything eventually starts to look the same. I often joke with clients that if we were to place all the corporate mission statements in a pile in the middle of the room and shuffle them before randomly returning them, most people would not know if they had received their own or someone else's.

We can no longer afford small, self-serving missions. Small missions are already too commonplace, lackluster, and dispiriting. Goethe urged us to "Dream no small dreams, for they have no power to move the hearts of men."

In Bill George's words:

> People must be motivated by a deeper Cause. Our Cause is not maximizing shareholder value. One of the things that I like to do is talk to shareholders about our Cause. Recently, we were having a breakfast meeting with the board of directors of one of our largest shareholders. They had made a huge profit in the value of their shareholdings. They asked about Medtronic. I said that Medtronic is not in the business of maximizing shareholder value; we are maximizing the value to patients, serving them well. Through serving patients, we are ultimately serving the shareholders well. One of the keys to our success is continuing to reinforce that. Medtronic is a Cause-inspired company. We talk about our Cause every day. Every decision is made with the purpose of "restoring people to full life and health." Our Cause is central and core to everything that the company does. It inspires our people. I believe that people don't come to work to earn money for themselves and the company. They come to work because the product does something worthwhile, and this is what gets people inspired.

Medtronic's Cause was crafted by the company's visionary founder Earl Bakken (inventor of the external pacemaker) in 1949. Not one word has been altered since. When new employees joined the company, Bill George gave each of them a card and a book describing the company. They watched a video about the founder, and Bill George told anecdotal stories about how being at Medtronic affected his life. "At the end of this, each employee came up, and I gave them a medallion that is three inches across and has a picture of a person rising because he or she has become well. On the back is part of our Cause. I would say to each of them, 'I ask in accepting this that you accept the Cause of Medtronic and look at it and display it to remind you that the purpose of your being here is to restore people to full life and health. If you get frustrated, note that there is a higher Cause.'"

It is important to make this distinction between traditional mission statements and a Cause, as we are using these terms. A mission usually tends to be defined in terms of *our* needs, whereas a Cause is always defined in terms of the needs of *others*—it defines how we intend to serve. Whereas a mission might say, "To be the best health system in America," a Cause would state, "To create the healthiest community in America." Jeff Bezos, the founder of Amazon.com, might have created a mission such as "To be the dominant e-trader on the Internet." Instead, Amazon.com's Cause is other-centered and demonstrates servant-leadership: "To be the world's most customer-centered company." His other-centered passion has paid off—Amazon's score on the American Customer Satisfaction Index is the highest ever recorded, not just online or even in retailing, but in *any* service industry.

A mission often draws its energy from the ego, describing the rewards we hope for when our mission is realized. A Cause draws its energy from the soul, describing the way we plan to honor the souls of others, how we will recognize their sacredness, improve their lives, and serve them. A mission is self-centered; a Cause is other-centered. A Cause creates passion because it describes passion. Although a mission may refer to the same future, a Cause inspires because it puts others—their personalities *and* their souls—first.

Hunter (Patch) Adams, the doctor whose fame grew when Robin Williams portrayed him in a movie very loosely based on his life, has a magnetic Cause. Adams plans to build the Gesundheit! Institute, a unique healthcare facility on 310 rural acres in Pocahontas County, West Virginia. The Institute will be a theme-park-like, 40-bed facility that offers free healthcare to patients from anywhere in the world. A planned eye clinic will be shaped like an eyeball, and a sewer treatment center shaped like a backside. Without any advertising or recruitment, Adams' vision of compassionate, humor-filled, patient-centered wellness programs has created a magnetic Cause so powerful that it has inspired more than 1,000 physicians to apply to work gratis at the Gesundheit! Institute.

The Myths of Buy-In and Shared Vision

Unlike the old story model of leadership that calls for the orchestration of a buy-in from the rest of the organization, Higher Ground Leaders create Causes so compelling that organizing a buy-in is unnecessary. If the Cause is so magnetic that it attracts followers who are eager to support its aims, what need is there to orchestrate a buy-in? Coercing others to believe in a Cause amounts to tacitly transferring the responsibility to others for crafting and articulating the right Cause in the first place. If the Cause is inherently brilliant, it attracts hosts of dedicated followers; if it is a weak Cause, it needs to be sold to followers, even those on our own teams or families. This is the difference between a brilliant Cause conceived by a visionary Higher Ground Leader and one designed by a committee.

One day when Mahatma Gandhi was on a train pulling out of the station, a European reporter running alongside his compartment asked him, "Do you have a message I can take back to my people?" It was a day of silence for Gandhi, part of his regular practice, so he didn't reply. Instead he scribbled a few words on a piece of paper and passed it to the journalist: "My life is my message."

Higher Ground Leaders have dreams, passions, Causes. They want to change or improve the world and help people to realize their dreams because they know that the best way to predict the future is to create it. Their Cause is a divine undertaking drawn from deep within their hearts. Sometimes, when first articulated, their Cause may appear to be frail because, although the conceiver may see the magic clearly, they may find it more difficult to find the words that give voice to their imagined future. A unique and great Cause describes a world that does not yet exist, and it is difficult to describe tomorrow in today's language. Often, for this reason, the natural human reaction is to resist the change offered by the Cause—it describes a new paradigm.

Lack of literary elegance need not necessarily diminish a great Cause because great Causes have their own energy. What a great Cause may lack in precision and polish will be made up by its passion, beauty, and magnetism. Although it is best to have all of these, passion is the most important ingredient of a great Cause, and it is the passion that attracts others to the Cause—passion generates passion.

> When the legends die, the dreams end; there is no more greatness.
>
> Tecumseh of the Shawnees

> Is not life a hundred times too short for us to bore ourselves?
>
> Nietzsche

The Singular Vision

Another contemporary myth about vision-crafting is that it should be a shared idea, thus reducing the risk of others failing to buy into it. As a consequence, missions and visions that were once extraordinary ideas are adapted, modified, and pummeled until their fire and passion have been squeezed out of them. These "consensus" missions and visions reach for the lowest common denominator where an accord can be built—egalitarian and democratic no doubt, but soulless and lacking in magic. In other words, they suffer from a fatal flaw—compromise— and this leads to mediocrity.

If Thomas Jefferson had not bent to the pressures of his peers, he would have written the American Declaration of Independence (a Cause if ever there was one) differently, and it would, therefore, have been necessary for Martin Luther King to search for different words for his famous speech. Jefferson originally penned the phrase, "We hold these truths to be sacred and undeniable."[3]

We hold these truths to be sacred, not "self-evident." This change, when compared to the original, has the feeling of a great visionary work diluted by a committee. Benjamin Franklin convinced Jefferson to alter the words. How would history have been affected had the original intent of sacredness been retained? What might have happened if the Declaration of Independence had required that "life, liberty and the pursuit of happiness" be considered sacred? How would it have affected our thinking, philosophy, and approaches to the world? If life were considered sacred today, would violence have become as prevalent as it has? How would sacredness have shaped our attitudes toward guns, war, prisons, poverty, and crime? If liberty were considered sacred, would our levels of incarceration and recidivism still be among the highest in the world?[4] What would Martin Luther King have said instead? Would King have needed to make the speech at all?

The power of a compelling Cause rests in the soul of its creator, because a Cause springs from the soul. It is a spiritual statement from one soul and cannot be the result of many. It comes from a deep place of knowing—some conviction that a richly imagined future could, in some way, dramatically and positively change the world. Others can offer their input, help, advice, and even help to fine-tune, strengthen, and wordsmith it. But in the end, a magnetic Cause is a one-of-a-kind thing that cannot be cobbled together by a committee or a team.

Let me tell you how the Cause of my own organization, The Secretan Center Inc., came about. We are a worldwide consulting organization, working with corporations, healthcare, education, law enforcement, and not-for-profit and governmental organizations and individuals. We have a worldwide faculty who teach our work internationally. Our faculty members teach and consult in partnership and independently with us, using our proprietary concepts and their own rich and diversified gifts. In addition, we have a growing worldwide family called The Higher Ground Community, numbering several thousand, which is linked together in a global network, committed to changing the world by bringing greater spirituality and higher values to the workplace. We hold international conferences and retreats, run workshops and seminars, and maintain a web site (http://www.secretan.com), where you will find an Internet discussion forum and many worldwide initiatives.

Higher Ground Leaders know that the global network of organizations, especially commercial corporations, has become one of the most powerful forces on Earth. Half of the world's largest economies today are corporations, not nations. Other institutions, like the great religions or the world's political systems, cannot match their reach, intellect, power, talent, and money, and, therefore, the opportunity to influence the world. This influence can be positive or negative—the choice is ours. So New Story Leaders see organizations as one of the greatest instruments of positive social change known to humanity and have thus reframed their role as leaders accordingly. Our future success will not be measured by market share, profit, and increased shareholder wealth alone, but by our effectiveness as custodians of the human spirit.

Higher Ground Leaders know that to make this world of ours work a little better, we must use the most powerful institutions that exist on the planet to effect the changes we seek. We also know that people want to be inspired, which can only be achieved one person at a time. We know, too, that when a group of inspired people commit to reawakening spirit and values at work, they become an inspired team; and when a number of inspired teams connect, they become inspired communities, and many inspired communities will lead to a more inspired world.

But change does not happen to organizations. It happens to people—one soul at a time—not executives, physicians, fire-fighters, or teachers—but *whole* people—which means their whole lives as parents, lovers, spouses, children, friends, and citizens. Transformational change in organizations is achieved through transformational change in people—one soul at a time. So the Cause of The Secretan Center became:

To Change the World by Reawakening Spirit and Values in the Workplace.

Every day, people call, write, and e-mail us inquiring about our work because they have been drawn to our Cause. This is one of the ways we try to practice what we teach—and, like everyone else, we have our good and bad days.

Our sincere intent is to inspire those with whom we come into contact. This Cause is the focus of all our work and all our energy. It is why we come to work every day, and it is how we touch the lives of others.

The Cause That Inspires

The first objective of a grand Cause is that it speaks—or more accurately, sings, croons, cheers, and shouts—to the soul. It engages the heart and the mind. When others learn about a Cause, it makes such a complete connection with their minds, hearts, and souls that they yearn to share the same vision, to experience the same passion and exhilaration, and to invest their energy in the Cause that they now share. It is a visceral experience. A Cause speaks to our inner knowing, to our spirit, to something that is intuitive. A great Cause is not so much about the material as it is about the metaphysical. It is more about magic and dreams than economics and efficiency. A Cause engages us at a level that is mystical, rising far above mundane goals or targets.

One of the great benefits of Higher Ground Leadership is that it works. Joe Calvaruso of Mount Carmel tells the story of how he created the Cause for his organization:

> During a Higher Ground Leadership Retreat, my colleagues said to me, "Joe, we don't have a Cause. We want one. We need one. We would benefit from knowing the purpose of the organization. But please understand, we know it can't be a committee thing—we don't want a *Jefferson-compromise* effect here. We need *you* to develop it." They said, "Joe, you must write it." So, for the next two weeks, I was very focused on creating our Cause. I knew, right away, what would be at its essence—it would be about people. In the first rough draft, I included the word *honor* and the word *service* or *serving* because of the servant-leadership connection, and I included the word *love*. I wanted the "L" word in there, because I knew this would differentiate us from most other companies. It also had to be inclusive—I didn't want it to be just about patients, or just about patients and physicians, or just about patients and families. I didn't want it to be focused on an abstract idea like wellness or wholeness. I also wanted it to be a standard against which we could make decisions. I wanted it to be something that could be easily recited and memorable, and I wanted it to be consistent with what I knew Mount Carmel stood for and could be once again. It couldn't be something that just sounded good—it had to be *authentic* and ring true to who we are. I knew what I wanted to accomplish, and I spent a week or two wordsmithing before developing our Cause: *Honoring every soul with loving*

service. I didn't want it to be a committee decision, but I did ask a few people for their feedback, and they reviewed it with a few of their staff. I got about 30 e-mail comments, of which roughly half said, "Great. This inspires me." The other half said, "I love it, with the exception of 'love.' It shouldn't be in there. The word love doesn't belong in the workplace. Why don't you substitute a word like compassion or caring?" I thought about it for a while, and I thought, "Blah, blah, blah, blah, blah . . ." How many organizations have mission statements with "compassionate" or "caring" in them? It doesn't differentiate us. It doesn't make us stand out. It isn't inspiring. It wouldn't be a magnet for passion that would attract people or inspire people to stay at Mount Carmel. So, I said, "Thank you very much, but . . . we need to be courageous. Love belongs in the workplace." We kept the word *love* in, and I'm so glad we did. An example of why I feel this way: An emergency department physician from Florida came up to one of my colleagues at the end of his presentation and said, "I want to come and work for you. This is the way it should be done." In another situation, one of our nurse executives was attending a national conference. In an auditorium filled with 1,000 nurses, the presenter stopped using her own examples of mission statements to illustrate her presentation (which she had thought were the best she had ever seen) and instead focused on our Cause, stating that it was more inspiring than any other example she could give. In yet another case, I heard from a new employee, "We heard about your Cause. I've just joined Mount Carmel from another organization. They don't believe in your kind of thinking, and that's why I'm here." Another woman said, "You know, I'm going to bring five nurses with me." That's the power of a great Cause—it is a magnet for passion that is so powerful that it inspires people to bring their talents to align them with our Cause.

As Pierre Teilhard de Chardin wrote, "Someday, after mastering the winds, the tides, and gravity, we shall harness for God the energies of love, and then, for a second time in the history of the world, man will have discovered fire."

Because a Cause rises above the mundane, it enables us to see magic where others see problems. A Cause combines ideas so that new realities are created. Above all, a Cause inspires because it is always rooted in love. A Cause is magnetic because it draws people to it and inspires them to rethink their options in creative ways that will manifest reality.

The late Konosuke Matsushita built a globe-straddling business from scratch to $90 billion, employing more than a quarter of a million people. Today, Matsushita is the world's largest consumer electronics company, embracing names such as Panasonic, Quasar, National, Technics, and Victor, and through thousands of innovations and patents, Matsushita built an organization that has improved the lives of millions. Matsushita's beginnings were modest, but they were inspired. Early in his career, he was invited by a client to the head temple of the Tenrikyo religious sect, and this visit had a profound effect on his life. He wrote later, "There was something to be learned from the way [the temple] was apparently thriving, from the mountains of donated logs, from the energetic and dedicated way the members of the sect threw themselves into the construction work." Matsushita reasoned that if a corporation were as meaningful as a spiritual practice, it would greatly benefit people. Two months later, on May 5, 1932, he unveiled his Cause to 168 office workers at the Osaka Central Electric Club. He began by reminding them of their impressive achievements: The company was only 15 years old, but already employed 1,100 people, generated annual revenues of 3 million yen, owned 280 registered patents, and operated 10 factories. Then he made a proclamation that defined his Cause: "The [Cause] of a manufacturer should be to overcome poverty, to relieve society as a whole from misery, and bring it wealth." Using tap water as a metaphor because it is freely available to almost anyone, he continued, "This is what the entrepreneur and the manufacturer should aim at: to make all products as inexhaustible and as cheap as tap water. When this is realized, poverty will vanish from the Earth." Since that defining moment, the Cause of the company became aligned with important human values.[5]

Planning at Matsushita is established over a 250-year time span. Matsushita built a remarkable business without centralized structure, excessive bureaucracy, internal focus, high costs, or slow response time, while embracing optimistic and ethical purposes, communicating these widely, and helping others to excel.

Causes come in all sizes, big and small, and we can all craft a Cause that is so magnetic it draws people to our richly imagined future.

The Courage to Speak Your Truth

I have proposed that a Cause contain spiritual as well as intellectual and material components, and we cannot create a magnet for passion without embracing the language of the spirit. If we say that others are not ready to hear or use the language of the spirit, of Higher Ground Leadership, and that words like *love* and *soul* will not sit well with our colleagues or family, we may be describing the way *we* feel, rather than the way others feel. This is what I have described earlier as *projecting*.

Joseph Swedish is president and CEO of Centura Health, the largest healthcare system in Colorado and the fourth-largest employer in the state. Centura was formed in 1996, when two organizations came together, each of whom had been operating independently for well over 100 years. For three years, until

Joseph Swedish came on board as CEO, Centura attempted to make sense of this alignment, but as a business proposition it failed miserably, so much so that the company was borrowing money to make payroll—for 12,000 employees. The atmosphere was characterized by anxiety, fear, suspicion, dejection, and a sense of failure and skepticism about the ability of the company to survive. People thought that it would eventually just break apart and the original organizations would return to their original status: stand-alone enterprises in an unforgiving marketplace. Joseph formed a "workout team" and turned a $50 million loss into a $50 million profit in two years. He says:

> Having completed the workout phase, our team moved into the turnaround phase: rebuilding the infrastructure to create more lasting change and stability. In the final phase, which we called "strategic deployment," we began to build on the recognition that the organization had (1) a very, very strong role in providing services to the community and (2) significant standing because of its long history in healthcare. We now needed to change the fundamentals, continue to build on the revitalized core assets, and find a way for both of the founding organizations to talk to each other on a common platform. This is when we made our commitment to Higher Ground Leadership. It contained a message that resonated with everyone—the opportunity to go to Higher Ground irrespective of our history or background. It truly gave us a common language. When we speak about fiscal responsibility—effectiveness—we now do it in a truthful manner employing all of the Higher Ground Leadership principles to guide how we relate to one another, how we make decisions, and how we act on those decisions. I am totally comfortable with all my associates performing in a way that is a systematic, soulful way of behavior. Opportunities for conflict are vastly minimized because we now have a common language.
>
> It takes courage to overcome fear. I think the biggest fear we have as human beings is public speaking. But I would submit that *private speaking* is just as difficult as public speaking—it's the same coin, just different sides. It takes a lot of courage to privately speak with other individuals in a way that advances us all toward a Cause. After two people talk, misunderstandings can often still exist. When those two people leave the room, they may each go and communicate with somebody else and the message can become distorted again, and again, and again. But if I have the ability to talk in a common language, a common tongue, I can be courageous and speak the truth. With courage, I know I can challenge someone and do it in a loving manner, a respectful manner, and they will know I am coming from that place. The journey to Higher Ground Leadership has given us the ability to speak courageously. Because we are able to speak courageously in private, we are better able to speak courageously in public because we have a strong new foundation from which to speak.

In 2003, Joseph Swedish won an Ernst & Young Entrepreneur of the Year Award for the state of Colorado, an extraordinary achievement, considering most entrepreneurial awards are typically associated with business start-ups. Centura is no "started-in-a-garage" small business — it is a complex company with $1.3 billion in revenues, more than 750 managers and supervisors, 12,000 associates at 12 different hospitals, eight senior living residences, plus home care and hospice services. An important component considered by the judges was Centura's culture and its sustainability, which Higher Ground principles are helping to transform.

A Cause contains the power to mobilize extraordinary performance, as Higher Ground Leaders like Joseph Swedish demonstrate for us all.[6]

CHAPTER

6

Writing Your Own Cause Statement

What Is Your Cause?

In this chapter, I will guide you through the process of creating your own Cause statement.

What is a Cause? It is the earthly bridge between your Calling, or vocation, and your Destiny—how you intend to *be* and what you will stand for. A Cause is a litmus test for the decisions in our lives—"Am I taking this action or making this decision in such a way that it is consistent with my Cause and helps to achieve it?" It is something that we stand for and believe in with so much passion that we are prepared to dedicate our lives to it. (By the way, it is not something we are prepared to die for—it is something we are prepared to *live* for.)

As we discussed earlier, our Destiny describes **why** we are on this Planet— our divine purpose. A Cause describes how we intend to **be** in order to achieve our Destiny.

To use my own example again, my Destiny is: "To help (I can't do it all on my own!) create a more sustainable and loving planet." My Cause describes how I will *be* every day in my life to make that aspiration a reality. In my case, I plan to achieve my Destiny by *inspiring others to see the sacredness in all relationships* because, I reason, if everyone saw the sacredness in others, it would lead to a more sustainable and loving planet. Do you see how this works? *My Cause leads to my Destiny* (see Figure 6.1).

Whereas our Destiny reveals *why* we are here, why we have been put on this planet, our Cause answers the question: *How will you be in your life to achieve this Destiny?* For me, the answer is that if I succeed in any measure in inspiring others to see the sacredness in all relationships (in my case, I am saying *all*, not just some), we might find that teachers and students begin to see the sacredness in each other, lawyers begin to see the sacredness in the argument of the opposing lawyer, wardens and prisoners recognize the sacredness in each other, Israelis

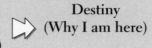

> **Cause**   **Destiny**
> (How I will be—   (Why I am here)
> what I will stand for)

Figure 6.1 Cause to Destiny.

and Palestinians see an emerging sacredness in each other, management and unions see the sacredness in each other, husbands and wives hold each other as sacred, and so do children and their elders, physicians and patients, liberals and conservatives, and CEOs and employees and shareholders. Technicians might see the sacredness in their technology and equipment, and lumberjacks the sacredness in trees. If this became the prevailing ethos of the world, it would lead to a more sustainable and loving planet. Do you see the connecting logic? Can you feel the passion that powers my Cause, which, in turn, fuels my Destiny? The connections are important here.

Let's look at an excellent example of a Cause statement.

Tricia Secretan is a therapist, teacher, and also vice president of The Secretan Center. Tricia's Cause is:

To lift the spirits of others with love, light, and intimacy.

If you knew Tricia, you would understand how supporting, encouraging, inspiring, and loving others is at the very core of who she is and how she lives her life. Notice how the successful implementation of Tricia's Cause will lead to the realization of her Destiny, which is:

To inspire sacred passion.

Tricia believes that the Terrathreat that causes her the most concern is the lack of passion on Earth, the lack of fiery will to mend and heal people and the planet. So, she reasons, if she lifts the spirits of others with love, light, and intimacy, it will inspire the sacred passion required to transform and heal the world.

Notice, also, how the successful practice of Tricia's Calling (we discuss how to develop our personal Calling statement in Chapter 8) will lead her to the achievement of her Cause. Tricia's Calling is:

To be a muse and empath.

An *empath* is a person who senses the feelings, emotions, thoughts, and energy of another. The character Gem in *Star Trek* was a famous empath. By being a muse and empath to others, Tricia is able to lift their spirits, and if she does this well, she may inspire their sacred passion, thus empowering them to change the world.

Destiny, Cause, and Calling statements are powerful stuff—powerful enough for every one of us, no matter what our status or role, to make a difference in how this world works and how it will evolve. Let's look at another example.

Elaine Callas is the senior vice president of information technology at Centura Health, Colorado. Her Destiny is:

To guide people, teams, and communities to their full potential.

She has answered the question "Why are you here?" She believes that if people, teams, and communities (countries, ethnic groups, companies, etc.) are encouraged to reach their full potential, the world will be a better place. So her Cause describes what she will do to help make this happen, how she will *be*, and what she will stand for:

To nourish inspiring partnerships that help others to grow.

Elaine sees her role as an agent of personal growth for *others*, through the development of partnerships and relationships—joining her expertise with the gifts of the person or team she is inspiring.

Elaine's Calling, the *what-she-will-do* part of her life, is:

To serve others through listening, advocating, coaching, teaching, and writing.

If she does this well, it will lead to the nourishment of inspiring partnerships with others (which is her Cause), and if she does this well, it will lead to the world's reaching its greater potential (which is her Destiny). Taken together, this is a humble, elegant, and beautiful statement of servant-leadership and all the pieces fit together in a graceful and congruent way. Although Elaine is a technology expert and her work is focused on providing information technology leadership to a 12,000-person-strong organization, she has not made the one mistake people tend to make more than any other—assuming that our lives can be defined only by our work. Notice that technology is not even mentioned in Elaine's

Destiny, Cause, or Calling. It is *one of the means* by which she aims to achieve her Destiny, Cause, and Calling.

How Will You Serve?

1. Considering the Terrathreats that you identified in Chapter 4 and that you believe are currently limiting the potential of humanity and our planet, ask yourself:
   - What special circumstances, assets, and opportunities exist that could be used to deal with these Terrathreats and thereby improve the world?
   - What is the *practical* interpretation of your Cause while you are here on Earth that will enable you to gather the necessary resources, find the right channels, take the right actions, and be a special, positive influence on the future of people and the planet?
   - How will you serve?
   - In what way will your day-to-day activities—corporate and personal— contribute toward a richly imagined future?
   - How will your Cause positively influence what you believe is in need of improvement, change, or resolution on Earth?
   - What actions would overcome the Terrathreats you have defined?
     Take a moment to put your thoughts on paper.
2. In what way will your life be dedicated to the resolution of these Terrathreats?
   - What is your vision—your Cause—that, when realized, will make the world a better place?
   - What must happen (described in your Cause) for your Destiny to be fulfilled?
   - How can your life (and/or your organization) be an instrument for this aspiration?
     The difference between the Destiny and the Cause is that a Destiny is connected to a higher purpose, whereas the Cause is very much concerned with the here-and-now—our earthly activities and aspirations. Remember that the Cause should serve your Destiny, and try to describe your Cause in a way that will lead to the successful realization of your Destiny.
     Take a moment again to put some of these thoughts on paper.
3. Think about the values in your professional and personal life that are the most important to you. What concepts or principles do you hold most dear

to your heart that speak to you personally and directly and that call to you to be lived? Choose two or three that resonate for you—that are absolutely essential to the sacred practice of your life.

4. Now look at the words and phrases you have chosen:
   - Will they inspire others to support you in your work?
   - When you think of actions that you wish to take to create a magnetic vision that will invite the passion of others—your Cause—which words fit comfortably?
   - Connect these words. How well do they link or connect?
   - What ideas and concepts are evoked?
   - What phrase is beginning to come to mind?
   - Does a complete thought emerge?
   - How could you fashion those words into a statement of your Cause—a statement that will be a magnet for passion (yours and others), which, in turn, will lead to the achievement of your Destiny?

5. Do these words and phrases describe:
   - How you will *be*?
   - What you will stand for?
   - How you will serve?
   - The way you will *live* your life?
   - The impact and influence you will have on others and the environment to support the *reason* you are here: to contribute in your own way to the healing and growth of humanity and the Earth—your Destiny?
   - How you will contribute to the resolution of these human and earthly shortcomings—the Terrathreats?
   - How you will inspire others to action, to share this vision, so that they are moved to resolve these issues, too?

Don't worry if the words haven't jumped out at you yet. Just use the words that work for you. What we are doing here is not trying to "get it right"—there is no magic formula and no need to be perfect. Remember the words of actor *Michael J. Fox:* "I am careful not to confuse excellence with perfection. Excellence I can reach for; perfection is God's business." The purpose is to get your creative juices flowing and to invite your Soul to describe what you yearn to do with your life. Be intuitive.

6. Imagine that what you now think of as the end of your life's story is actually the middle. How would you complete the rest of the story?

7. Try to describe how you will *be*, how you will become a Higher Ground Leader, and, through your example, what you will teach and how this will lead and serve others. Describe the positive effect that you will have on people, how you will touch them, inspire them, and make their lives and the world better.

> !
>
> Ah, but a man's reach should exceed his grasp, or what's a heaven for?
>
> Robert Browning
>
> !

8. Last, do not expect finality here. This process of redefining the meaning of your life will probably last much longer than the time it takes to read this book or complete these exercises. You may be fortunate and find that everything falls into place. It is more likely that everything will need to marinate in the juices of your consciousness over the next few months. Describing the meaning and purpose of our lives is new to us—it is not, therefore, likely to be completed overnight.

CHAPTER

7

Step Three: Defining Your Calling

The Path with a Heart

Anything is one of a million paths. Therefore, you must always keep in mind that a path is only a path; if you feel you should not follow it, you must not stay with it under any conditions. To have such clarity you must lead a disciplined life. Only then will you know that any path is only a path, and there is no affront, to oneself or to others, in dropping it if that is what your heart tells you to do. But your decision to keep on the path or to leave it must be free of fear or ambition. I warn you. Look at every path closely and deliberately. Try it as many times as you think necessary. This question is one that only a very old man asks. My benefactor told me about it once when I was young, and my blood was too vigorous for me to understand it. Now I do understand it. I will tell you what it is: Does this path have a heart? All paths are the same: they lead nowhere. They are paths going through the bush, or into the bush. In my own life I could say I have traversed long, long paths, but I am not anywhere. My benefactor's question has meaning now. Does this path have a heart? If it does, the path is good; if it doesn't, it is of no use. Both paths lead nowhere; but one has a heart, the other doesn't. One makes for a joyful journey; as long as you follow it, you are one with it. The other will make you curse your life. One makes you strong; the other weakens you . . . the path without a heart will turn against men and destroy them. It does not take much to die, and to seek death is to seek nothing. For me there is only the traveling on paths that have heart, on any path that may have heart. There I travel, and the only worthwhile challenge is to traverse its full length. And there I travel looking, looking, breathlessly.

—Don Juan[1]

After achieving pure clarity about their Destiny, then defining and championing the Cause, Higher Ground Leaders first reaffirm their commitment to their own Calling and then coach others to find and master theirs. A Calling is a sense of authenticity and knowingness about our capacities and genius. It is the intersection of our passion and our talents and gifts, and an awareness of their relevance and applicability to a Cause. It is the awareness of how the alchemy of this passion and talent can be used to serve the world.

Mark Twain said: "Work is a necessary evil to be avoided." Perhaps he meant that if we don't love what we do, we may come to think of it as merely *work*, but if we are passionate about what we do, we may think of it more as a Calling. H. Jackson Brown Jr. put it this way, "Find a job you like, and you add five days to every week."

All the greatest leaders in history found their Calling, and all who are inspired have found theirs, too.

I have worked with and studied thousands of leaders around the world and come to realize how few have really thought clearly about their Calling, much less followed it. I suspect that more than half of these leaders would exchange their current work for a Calling if they were presented with an opportunity to do so. We cannot inspire others to find their true Calling if we have not done so ourselves.

How We Become Lost

Many of us are incapable of living our dreams at work and are frustrated in our attempts to achieve clarity around our vocation. We have erroneously come to believe that we can't live a full life while making a living. We fantasize and, therefore, blur the boundaries between fact and fiction, thus becoming immobilized between the two. As a result, we fail to put energy into our search for our real Calling. In *The Secret Life of Walter Mitty*, a classic 1947 movie loosely based on a James Thurber story, Danny Kaye plays the role of a magazine proofreader who merges the pulp fiction fantasies he reads for a living into his real life. Concocting elaborate delusions, he variously passes himself off as a world-famous surgeon, a swashbuckling sea captain, a criminal attorney, and a World War II fighter pilot. Eventually, no one is sure which is the mask and which is the real Walter Mitty—least of all Walter Mitty. More recently, the film *Catch Me If You Can*, based on the true story of Frank W. Abignale, describes how, as a runaway teenager without even so much as a high school diploma, he passed himself off as a college professor, doctor, lawyer, and airline pilot and, in the process, successfully cashed millions of dollars of fraudulent checks before being caught. He then switched sides and became an FBI specialist catching imposters just like himself. Some of us slide into a Mitty-esque entrainment in our lives, becoming so inauthentic that we eventually cannot tell the difference between the real and the surreal, between what we would like to do and what others believe we should do, and between our ego and our soul.

Few of us ever discover the work we love, our Calling. Instead, we acquire skills based on an I-must-earn-some-money logic and then become prisoners of this path. We remain asleep in the illusion of ego. We answer the question, "What career do I want to pursue?" instead of "How will I use my passion, gifts, and talents to serve the universe?" This causes us to be trapped in work that is not our Calling, that we do not love, and that does not inspire our heart. The questions are not, "What am I good at?" but "What do I love?"—not "What do I want?" but "How do I want to feel?"

> After one has discovered what he is made for, he should surrender all of the power in his being to the achievement of this. He should seek to do it so well that nobody could do it better.
>
> Martin Luther King

We become trapped by the fantasy that the needs of the soul can be deferred while we feed our egos and that the soul can operate independently of the ego. We fool ourselves with the myth that if we can get just one more promotion, one more mortgage payment, and one more child through college—we will turn our attention to our spiritual aspirations. But "just one more" always leads to "just one more." Like the horizon, it never comes closer, even though we advance toward it. As a result, our soul retreats from our work, and we feel empty. Doing work we love, which summons and engages the soul, cannot be achieved by pursuing our skills alone. Our hearts and souls will be fully engaged only when we discover our natural gifts and then put them to great service in our lives. Our Calling is the work we love, the activities that we undertake that make our hearts soar and provide deep and lasting moments of bliss.

> Inside every old person is a young person wondering what happened.
>
> Terry Pratchett

Some of us don't have an inner voice shouting clear directions, so we respond to the urgings of parents or other well-meaning individuals who guide us into business, law, dentistry, medicine, a craft, trade, or profession, believing it to be "the best thing" for us. We respond to the external voices and urgings that are speaking to our egos and fail to hear or listen to the inner voice that speaks the truth directly from our soul. We cruise along the highway of life in this way until, at last, one day, we realize there is more. The subtle urging from our soul has been pleading all along, yearning to be heard. We suddenly realize that we have been longing to follow our dreams, to paint in Technicolor instead of monochrome. We have been longing for meaning and fulfillment so that we can honor our souls. We dream about flying at last.

I always wanted to be somebody. I see now that I should have been more specific.

Lily Tomlin

Some hear the call, but are distracted by the mundane and the commitments of their current lives. In other cases, the messages are heard clearly, but must be tested. During my early career, I quickly became an executive with a very successful organization while still only in my mid-20s. The years passed, and, by many measures, I was thriving, but by others, I was somehow incomplete and restless. Some years earlier, I had read *My Life in Court* by Louis Nizer, the famous American trial lawyer, and it had reignited my long-dormant desire to become a criminal lawyer. My wife, who was raising our family, and my oldest daughter, who was finishing high school, urged me to quit and study law. They presented me with a plan—they would both go to work so that I could quit my lucrative executive position and go to law school. Presented with the opportunity and the loving support of my family, I had the chance to realize my dreams—to bring greater justice to the world. But when it came time to act on my dreams, I did not pursue a career in law, because I was not being called from within, from my soul, by a voice that cheered. It was a prize that someone else had described as being right for me, not a Calling I had discovered for myself from a place deep within.

Most people are other people. Their thoughts are someone else's opinions, their lives a mimicry, their passions a quotation.

Oscar Wilde

The important thing is to always listen and to discriminate—there is just one Calling for each of us at any given time in our lives, just one perfect intersection of passion and talent.

Often, we confuse a Calling with a career or job. It is neither. *Our Calling is the spiritual union of our passion with our essential, inherent talents, which results in a perfect alignment of spirit with function.* A job or a career limits us and encourages our smallness; the grandness of a Calling invites us to grow. A Calling is not a product of the ego or the personality; it is an extension of our soul. A Calling is just that—something we are being "called" to, by our muse, by an inner voice, by a higher presence, by something greater than us. A Calling draws us from our inner world to the outer world and integrates the two. A job may sometimes lack integrity and authenticity; a Calling demands and invokes both. A Calling moves us from our dreams to actions. We honor our soul by responding positively to our Calling.

Reflect for a moment:

- What are the gifts with which I have been blessed, but which have been hidden from me or set aside because of my fear of failure?
- Am I engaged in work I value or work that merely pays the bills?
- Is my work spiritually and materially rewarding?
- Is my work my Calling?
- Do I love my work?
- What do I love to do?
- What activities engage my passion?
- What are my authentic, natural gifts?
- When am I most happy in my life?
- What am I doing when that happens?
- How can I turn those activities into my life work?
- How can I make my work my spiritual practice?
- What is holding me back?
- How can I overcome those obstacles?

Millions of people today are asking profound questions about their work. Dramatic shifts in the balance and style of our lives can pivot on the answers to questions like these—and our reaction to them. We cannot become inspired, and, therefore, cannot inspire others, until our gifts and our vocation are aligned, until we are using our gifts and talents to serve, until we are practicing our Calling. All the greatest leaders I researched knew this: We have to live our Calling before we can inspire others to find theirs.

> You can tell whether a man is clever by his answers. You can tell whether a man is wise by his questions.
>
> Naguib Mahfouz

Finding joy in our work depends on the relationship between our soul and our work and on the degree to which our work engages and nourishes our soul. Before embarking on a search for the work you love, test the relationship between your current work and your soul. Your answers will provide insight into the level of soulfulness in your work—whether you have found your Calling.

Is Your Calling Aligned with Your Soul? A Check-Up

Few people fail at something that engages their hearts; they fail at things that are driven by negative energy or pursued to feed the ego. The negative energy of fear—especially of poverty, inadequacy, loss of status, change, and other frailties of the ego—often drive our career choices and, paradoxically, this inevitably leads

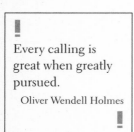

Every calling is great when greatly pursued.

Oliver Wendell Holmes

us to failure—the thing we fear most. And most of this thinking is our own projection anyway. What makes great artists, poets, athletes, writers, or leaders unique is that they are among the few who have discovered their gifts and turned them into work that they love. For them, it is a Calling—a vocation—and this, more than anything else, explains their brilliance in their fields. For them, none of their greatness springs from fear; on the contrary, it springs from love.

The questionnaire in Table 7.1 uses two words that are familiar to us everywhere in our lives, but often not at work: love and soul. Many old story leaders recoil when they hear these words, fearing that crystals and incense will follow—but if we keep an open mind here, we can avoid the trap of projection discussed in Chapter 1.

The dictionary defines *love* as a deep and tender feeling of affection. Most people yearn for the opportunity to have deep and tender feelings of affection for their work and their colleagues. They want to do work they love, with people they care about. These are natural human aspirations that are strangely absent in the modern workplace. And then there is the "S" word—the soul. The very notion of the soul, let alone the thought of having soulful experiences at work, mystifies many people. We all experience soulful moments in our lives—when we are at the symphony, when we watch a sunset, when we gaze into the eyes of a loved one, when we hold a baby, when we play with a puppy, when we are deeply appreciated, when we are practicing our highest mastery, or when we are connected to the Divine. We all want to feel the same way at work and throughout our lives. There is no reason this should not be so.

TABLE 7.1
The Soulscreen

Please place a tick beside each question to which you are able to answer YES

1. I look forward to going to work on Monday mornings. ____

2. At my organization we believe in and practice noble values. ____

3. At work we tell the truth to employees, customers, and suppliers. ____

4. At work my colleagues keep the promises we make to employees, customers, and suppliers. ____

5. We have happy relationships with all employees, customers, and suppliers. ____

6. The leaders where I work do not use fear as a motivator. ____

7. I love the people with whom I work. ____

8. I have fun at work. ____

9. I love the work I do. ____

10. My work has meaning and richly rewards my soul. ____

11. My physical working environment is inspiring. ____

12. My organization doesn't try to win by beating our competition. ____

13. The products and services we sell are friendly to people and the planet. ____

14. I have all the information I need and I am empowered to do my job. ____

15. I trust everyone with whom I work. ____

16. My organization is not bureaucratic. ____

17. I am encouraged to use all my creative potential at work. ____

18. I am truly inspired by my work and my colleagues. ____

19. My work is valuable to my community. ____

20. Every dollar earned by our organization makes my soul proud. ____

   TOTAL YES SCORE ____

How to Score

Total the number of Yes ticks and check your score against the numbers below to determine the interpretation that is appropriate for you.

17-20: In your organization, work is a spiritual practice – cherish it! Your are in that sacred space where work, Calling, and spirit are aligned.

13-16: Congratulations! Your workplace is becoming a sanctuary—a community of kindred souls in which your soul can flourish and soar.

9-12: Your organization makes a valuable contribution to your soul. There is much to do, but you are on your way. The prospects for a fusion between your soul and your work, between Calling and Cause, are excellent.

5-8: Your work is beginning to stir your soul—nourish this. By doing so, you will regenerate yourself.

0-4: Your soul is endangered by your current work, which is harmful to your spiritual well-being.

Adapted from *Reclaiming Higher Ground: Creating Organizations That Inspire the Soul* by Lance Secretan.

Being in the Moment: Clarity,
Choice, and Commitment

The Kingdom of Heaven

> We do not have to die to enter the Kingdom of Heaven. In fact, we have to be
> fully alive. When we breathe in and out and hug a beautiful tree, we are in
> Heaven. When we take one conscious breath, aware of our eyes, our heart, our
> liver, and our nontoothache, we are transported to Paradise right away. Peace is
> available. We only have to touch it. When we are truly alive, we can see that
> the tree is part Heaven, and we are also part of Heaven. The whole universe is
> conspiring to reveal this to us, but we are so out of touch that we invest our re-
> sources in cutting down the trees. If we want to enter Heaven on Earth, we
> need only one conscious step and one conscious breath. When we touch
> peace, everything becomes real. We become ourselves, fully alive in the pres-
> ent moment, and the tree, our child, and everything else reveal themselves to
> us in their full splendor. The miracle is not to walk on thin air or water, but to
> walk on Earth.
>
> Thich Nhat Hahn, Touching Peace[2]

We often hear that life is a journey, but perhaps it is not so much a journey
as a collection of moments. We are not destined to achieve a certain standard
of living or a particular set of career goals—such ambitions are typically modern, narcissistic notions that have become the hall-
mark of the last half of the twentieth century. Real
living is not about tolerating the moments of work
along the journey to retirement in order to build a
fat retirement fund. The point of life is not to slave
away to the age of 65 and then say, "Phew! Glad
that's over!" We are destined to live each moment
joyfully, passionately, and in the service of others.
This is a definition of bliss, and bliss is an essential
requirement of the soul—whether at work or at play.

> Use what talent you
> possess: the woods
> would be very silent
> if no birds sang
> except those that
> sang best.
>
> Henry Van Dyke

Finding the work that you love is not complicated or difficult. We need to curb our addiction to
personality (or ego) gratification and open our hearts
to options that nourish the soul. Think about your health. There are no mysteries to becoming fitter, nor is it complicated or difficult. To lose weight, for example, you need clarity, choice, and commitment:

1. *Clarity*: knowing that you must change, and establishing a goal, such as, for example, how much weight you want to lose.
2. *Choice*: changing diet or exercising, restoring greater balance in your life.
3. *Commitment*: following the regimen.

> I've found that every time I've made a radical change, it's helped me feel buoyant as an artist.
>
> David Bowie

If we are not prepared to make these choices and commitments, we are unlikely to progress toward our aspirations, even if they are clear, and when we cling to the status quo, we are saying to ourselves, "I do not have the courage to change."

It is the same with our work. Identifying work that would inspire our soul is not a difficult process. The difficult part is having the courage to make the appropriate choices and committing to them. If you are enjoying all the creature comforts that material success can buy, but hating every moment of your work, the choice is simple: Change your experience of work, or quit and find the work you love. The question is, "Do you have the courage to give up the security, toys, and perceived esteem that being materially successful, but spiritually empty, provides?" Millions of people, nearly half the working population, according to our research at the Secretan Center, cannot bring themselves to make the sacrifices needed. They stay in a rut and complain for the rest of their lives that they never found the work they loved. This is the old story: no pain, no gain. The

> They say that time changes things, but actually, you have to change them yourself.
>
> Andy Warhol

real pain comes from being imprisoned in work that does not inspire the soul. On the other hand, finding work that is our spiritual practice is achieved when we make the personal commitment to reduce dependency on the things that feed the personality and instead find and develop pursuits that nourish the soul.

Following Your Intuition

Many, though, set in their ways for so long, think it is too late. They seem incapable of thinking outside the box, let alone burning the box, because it seems so outrageous at this stage of their lives. There is an old story about a middle-age woman who yearned to play the piano. After deciding to follow her lifelong dream, she announced to a friend that she had changed her mind and was abandoning her plans. When her friend asked why, she explained that it would take 10 years to learn how to master the piano, and that because she was 50, she would be 60 before she achieved her goal. Her friend thought for a moment before observing, "But darling, what difference will it make—you will be 60 anyway!" Too often, we invent roadblocks and convince ourselves that our dreams are beyond our reach. We rationalize our resistance to change. We become copyfrogs.

Scott Adams toiled in cubicles for seven years at Crocker National Bank (he was twice robbed at gunpoint) and then for nine years at Pacific Bell "in a number of jobs that defy description, but all involve technology and finances. . . . My business card said 'engineer,' but I'm not an engineer by training." He was "downsized" by the firm in 1995.[3] This personal inconvenience proved to be just the catalyst he had been waiting for to release his pals Dilbert, Catbert, Dogbert, Ratbert, and the Boss from his imagination into an unsuspecting but eager world. Today, Scott Adams is one of the world's most successful cartoonists, having found his Calling by speaking to the hearts of millions of cubicle dwellers around the globe.

In 1994, Jeff Bezos gave up his cushy job as a vice president on Wall Street and headed for the West Coast with the idea of selling books over the Internet. Five days later, he had set up his new company in his basement. Today, Amazon.com is the most successful company on the Web and the largest bookseller in the world. Bezos had found his Calling: redefining merchandising in an electronic marketplace. His motto: "Work hard, have fun, make history."

For some, their Calling becomes very clear early in their lives. Steven Spielberg won his first film award for a 40-minute fully scripted action movie when he was 13. Fred Smith, founder and chairman of Federal Express, conceived the idea for an overnight delivery service while an undergraduate at Yale University. Leo Burnett borrowed against his life insurance policy and mortgaged his home to come up with the money to establish one of the greatest advertising agencies in the world. In 1922, 21-year-old George Gallup took a job at the *St. Louis Post-Dispatch* surveying city readers to determine their interests, and the eponymous Gallup Poll entered into our lexicon. In 1951, Lillian Vernon was a young expectant housewife who used her wedding gift money to place a $495 advertisement for a personalized purse and belt in *Seventeen* magazine. She received $32,000 in orders, and her business was launched. Starting from her kitchen table, she eventually formed the Lillian Vernon Corporation, which now processes more than five million orders annually. Virgin Group Inc. chairman and CEO Richard Branson ran his first advertisement for Virgin Records in the final issue of his magazine, *Student*, when he was—a student. Michael Dell ran classified advertisements for computer upgrades and souped-up PCs that he sold from his dorm at the University of Texas, undercutting local retailers by 15 percent. When he reached sales of $25,000 a month, he decided to abandon his premed studies to establish Dell Computers. When David Geffen was fired by CBS TV, he told the receptionist on his way out how much he loved show business and yearned to remain a part of it. "What can you do?" she inquired sympathetically. "Nothing," he replied. She thought a moment before replying, "You could be an agent!" The joke was lost on Geffen, who went to work in the mail room at the Morris Agency, rising over the years to sign acts such as The Eagles and Laura Nyro and create Asylum Records and Geffen Records, which he later sold for $700 million to become a founding partner of DreamWorks with Steven Spielberg and Jeffrey Katzenberg. Paul Orfalea is dyslexic, can't spell, and doesn't like to read, but he started selling notebooks on the campus of the University of California at Santa Barbara in 1970 and grew this modest enterprise into Kinko's (the nickname given to him by his college buddies because of his curly, reddish hair). Today, Kinko's has 1,100 branches that provide "Document Solutions—Done Right, Anytime, Anywhere" in the United States, Canada, the Netherlands, Japan, South Korea, Australia, the United Arab Emirates, China, and Great Britain.

> One must not always think so much about what one should do, but rather what one should be. Our works do not ennoble us; but we must ennoble our works.
>
> Meister Eckhart

"Don't I have the best job in the world?" my friend Moe Dixon says to me. Moe spends the summer and fall living on top of a mountain in the Columbia Gorge embraced by a 360-degree view, where he plays his unique brand of music at concerts and folk festivals, records a CD, and kayaks, wind-surfs, and mountain bikes until the snow flies. Then he moves to Copper Mountain, Colorado, where he's the number one après-ski entertainer in America, playing his rendition of country-and-western, classical pop, traditional folk, and blues during the winter and spring ski season to hundreds of enthralled patrons who raise the roof nightly. During the year, we work together combining our talents to inspire audiences to *change the world by reawakening spirit and values in the workplace.* He is a world-class summer and winter sports athlete and entertainer. Does this sound like the best job in the world? Talk to Moe Dixon and he will tell you that this is what he has chosen—he didn't just stumble on to it. He has spent 20 years shaping his life so that he is able to live the life he loves, by finding his true Calling.

Bernie Krause began studying classical music at the age of 3 in his native Detroit. He graduated to composition at age 4 and then to guitar as an adolescent. After college, he worked in radio and concert promotion and as a studio musician for the Soupy Sales Show. After a year as a member of the Weavers folksinging group, he became a producer and studio musician for Motown Records before moving to Los Angeles. With his then business partner Paul Beaver, Krause invested in one of the first Moog synthesizers, eventually contributing to more than 250 albums, including productions by The Byrds, The Doors, Mick Jagger, and George Harrison.

Krause worked on a project called "Wild Sanctuary," the first album to use sounds collected from the natural environment. Though Krause had not yet found his true Calling, he relied heavily on the most important asset of those searching for their Calling: intentionality. The experience of tape recording the sounds of the California surf and blending them into lush orchestral instrumentation led to an epiphany for Krause. "From then on," he says, "every spare moment, I was outside with a microphone."

Being alert to our inner voice during the search is critical to discovering the right livelihood. Krause pushed the envelope, searching for ever more exotic sounds. When scientists would not let him accompany them because they felt he was unqualified for scientific expeditions, he countered their skepticism by studying successfully for his Ph.D. in bioacoustics. This enabled him to travel to the Alaskan tundra, to famed primate expert Jane Goodall's camp in Tanzania, to Borneo, Indonesia, Sumatra, rainforests, mountains, oceans, deserts, and the Amazon. He recorded ants, frogs, insect larva, sperm whales, earthworms, gibbons, and snails. He recorded the sounds of a water-parched cottonwood tree drinking noisily after an intense rainfall. He gained national recognition as the "Pied Piper" whose audio wizardry lured Humphrey the Wayward Humpback Whale from the Sacramento River Delta back to the Pacific Ocean. He has amassed 3,500 hours of habitat sounds during his 30-year career, recording the voices of 15,000 creatures. During that time, 20 percent of their habitats have been lost or destroyed, and Krause sees his work as a Cause—he donates a percentage of his profits to organizations such as the Nature Conservancy. His CDs have sold more than 1.5 million copies, and he has contributed to more than 130 feature films, including *Apocalypse Now* and *Rosemary's Baby*. He has been assaulted by a cobra, hurled by a gorilla, and put upon by a polar bear, but he found his Calling, and every day of that Calling is an earthly day in heaven for Bernie Krause.[4]

If there is any point at all to life, surely it is to live out our dreams, to serve, to follow our bliss, to release the music within us, play it with joy, and to share it with others. Surely we have a responsibility to finally listen to and honor the siren calls of our souls that have been silenced by our egos throughout our lives. How else can we connect with our essence, the source of our Calling?

There Is No Calling without Caring and Service

Researchers have shown that caring, or serving others, is a necessary condition of happiness, both in work and in life generally.[5] A Calling without a significant component of service is not a Calling. When we serve others, we transform work into a Calling.

Albert Schweitzer said, "I don't know what your destiny will be, but one thing I know: the only ones among you who will be really happy are those who will have sought and found how to serve." Our talents and gifts are opportunities to serve, and they mean little if they cannot be used to serve others.

Wynton Marsalis, the world-renowned jazz trumpet player, spends much of his life touring, recording, and winning Grammy awards. But he also uses his talents to serve—teaching underprivileged children—in more than 1,000 schools during the past decade alone. Marsalis knows he is a great musician, but he also knows that one of his greatest gifts is to listen to the soul of a musician. He says, "When they play and I hear their sound, I can tell what kind of grades they make in school and what kind of habits they have. I can just hear it in their sound. I know what they're saying. Sometimes what they're saying is 'Help.'"[6] The opportunity to serve by sharing our gifts is the highest Calling, and we are enriched with the highest rewards in return: Our hearts are inspired by moments of pure bliss.

> I slept and dreamt that life was Joy, and then I awoke and realized that life was Duty;
>
> And then I went to work—and, lo and behold, I discovered that Duty can be Joy.
>
> Rabindranath Tagore

Our Calling is enriched when we are able to serve, because service to others is how we make a difference in the world and, therefore, soothe our souls. Sting (aka Gordon Sumner) has attained global success as a singer, composer, musician, and actor, but he has also spent much of his life serving—campaigning and fund-raising for environmental causes, taking part in Band Aid, Live Aid, participating in Amnesty International's Human Rights Now! tour, and working with the Rainforest Foundation. He has probably raised more awareness for the plight of

> I once asked my history teacher how we were expected to learn anything useful from his subject, when it seemed to me to be nothing but a monotonous and sordid succession of robber baron scumbags devoid of any admirable human qualities. I failed history.
>
> Sting (Gordon Sumner)

the indigenous people of the Brazilian rainforest than any other person alive. In 2001, Sting received the Kahlil Gibran Spirit of Humanity Award for his "efforts to promote cross-cultural understanding" from the Arab-American Institute Foundation. Bono (aka Paul David Hewson), lead singer for the rock band U2, is another gifted entertainer who has looked beyond the material and commercial success reaped from his talents to follow a second Calling by being heavily involved with NetAid and Warchild (to whom he donated the profits from the single "Miss Sarajevo"). Bono is actively involved in campaigning for the poor and has perhaps done more than anyone alive to publicize the tragedy of African countries stemming from debt and AIDS. He visited Ghana, South Africa, Uganda, and Ethiopia with former U.S. Treasury Secretary Paul O'Neill, has petitioned the Pope, considers U.N. Secretary General Kofi Annan, Canadian Prime Minister Paul Martin, and Bill Clinton as friends, and has continued to work with DATA (Debt, AIDS and Trade in Africa) with the support of several world leaders and financial backing from the Bill and Melinda Gates Foundation.

Seventy-one percent of U.S. adults can name a member of the band U2, but only 15 percent can name the Chief Justice of the United States![7]

Writing Your Own Calling Statement

Our Calling is a siren that sings to our heart throughout our lives. Sometimes it sings softly, sometimes our egos suppress it, sometimes it sings like Callas or Pavarotti. Whatever the intensity, whatever the style, our Calling strains to be heard, sending signals to us throughout our lives in an endless stream of creative efforts to become noticed. Our purpose is to listen attentively, to use every means we can to turn up the volume of the siren within, so that we can clearly hear the song of our Calling. The striking thing about a Calling is that it never goes away.

So what is the point of your role in life? What are your unique gifts and talents that, if polished and practiced with mastery, could help you to become matchless? Why are you following the path you have chosen? What is your path? What is the way in which you can best serve? Beyond all your instinctive responses, beyond the material, the metrics, and the mundane—what is the *real* point of the task you undertake every day? What is meaningful, noble, or divine in your daily practice that lifts the hearts and souls of others and stirs their passions? Is there something greater, something more inspiring than just going to work each day, making your widgets and your budgets? Do you not deserve to be inspired by what you do in your work through the sure knowledge that what you do and how you contribute will make the world a better place?

> The toughest thing about success is that you've got to keep on being a success. Talent is only a starting point in this business. You've got to keep on working that talent. Someday I'll reach for it and it won't be there.
>
> Irving Berlin

Maximizing the metrics of our work and our lives is important, but not the *most* important, or the only, thing. As I wrote in *The Way of the Tiger*, "Profit is like oxygen; essential for our survival, but not the reason for our existence."[1] We don't wake up in the morning, throw open the windows, and proclaim, "Ah! I'm going to have a great day breathing today!" any more than most of us would say, "Ah! I'm going to have a great day making profits today!"—even though we know that both are essential to our well-being.

We can best guide others to discover their Calling by modeling the sure and brilliant practice of our own. The legacy of inspiring people is often defined by how much they have helped others to learn, grow, flourish, and discover their true selves during their lives.

To inspire others, we must first be inspired ourselves. Keeping a stiff upper lip and setting aside our needs so that we can dedicate ourselves to the greater good of the organization is absurd. *This confuses service with sacrifice.* In our striving to serve others, we must maintain personal boundaries that protect us from *overserving* to the point where we are *sacrificing* and depleting the reserves needed by us to inspire others. Like every successful psychotherapist, my wife learned long ago that she needed to take care of herself first, so that she could protect her own resources necessary to nourish those of others—so that she could be more effective in serving them. We all need to have this awareness. It is not selfish; the most effective way to serve others is from a place of abundance rather than depletion, from love rather than fear. Sacrifice and overwork are the shadows of the Calling.

Each of us can recall days of disappointment or despondency, and in moments of honest reflection, we might all admit that on these occasions, we were less than our inspiring best to others. As we mature, we question our journeys. The accidents of biography, the serendipitous moments of our lives that somehow get connected together and that have brought us to our current professions, often begin with an involuntary journey that takes us to places we would never have consciously chosen.

Then again, some of us simply lose the passion for our Calling. In my experience of working with leaders in many fields, I have observed that many leaders have become so dejected with the minutiae, the administrivia, and the frustrations of their work, including budget cuts and the desperate shortage of great leadership, people, resources, facilities, and money, that they have lost sight of the noble Calling that summoned them to their vocation in the first place—to contribute, to make a difference, to excel, to achieve meaning and fulfillment, and to make the world a better place. They live as victims rather than the instruments of change they could be.

Listening for the Calling

Reflect for a moment and ask yourself: Am I doing the work I love? Is it time to re-invent myself? Have I been so seduced by the trivial, the mundane, and the processes that I have overlooked the noble essence of my work and the many ways my spirit and that of others can be moved by what I do? Am I open to receiving the messages of the universe?

Gregg Levoy begins his book, *Callings: Finding and Following an Authentic Life* (Three Rivers Press, New York, 1997), with this story:

Some years ago, along a country road outside of Fresno, California, on a windy spring day, a part of the invisible world was made, for a brief moment, visible to me.

I saw, in the light lancing through a row of trees, great streams of yellow pollen, sweeping by on the wind, every speck filled with information—blueprints for making perfect blue flowers, the dark musculature of the tress, meadow grasses.

I saw in that moment that the whole sky is filled with furtive transmissions—pollens and seeds, radio waves and subatomic particles, the songs of birds, satellite broadcasts of the six o'clock news and the Home Shopping Network. And I saw that what is necessary to make substance or meaning out of any of it is a receiver, somebody to receive.

Years later, struggling to make sense of a stunning aggregate of symptoms and synchronicities in my own life that appeared to cluster around the question of whether or not I should leave a job, I realized that my own life was similarly flooded with signals of which I was only dimly aware but that seemed to indicate the necessary steps I should take to make my life literally "come true." Until then, unfortunately, the receiver had usually been turned off, so these incoming calls fell lemming-like into silence.[2]

To live a full and authentic life, we must *listen*; we need to be tuned in to the signals we receive every day. Thomas Moore, in his book *Care of the Soul*,[3] cites "repression of the life-force" as the most common reason his clients sought his advice in therapy. Many people are trapped in activities that force them to live a lie—they are not happy. Tomorrow morning when you put on your make-up or shave, look deeply into your eyes and ask yourself: Have I found my true Calling—am I being authentic? Am I doing the work I love? Am I living a life that I love? Am I in "flow" with my Calling? Am I following my passion—my Calling—not my career or my training? Whether your answer to these questions is positive or negative, heed the advice of Dennis Waitley: "Follow your passion, not your pension."

How to Connect with Your Calling

Here is an example of an excellent Calling statement infused with passion:

> Helen Morley is a senior faculty member with The Secretan Center Inc., a teacher, facilitator, consultant, and writer. Helen's Destiny is: *To advance human unity*. Helen believes that the world is suffering from disunity. Her Destiny is a play on words. She feels that she can bring greater unity to the world through her Cause, which is: *To return souls to their wholeness*. But it is in Helen's Calling that she describes the actual tasks she will perform every day that will lead her to her Cause and her Destiny. Her Calling is: *Through facilitation, teaching, and writing, illuminate the inherent wisdom of every soul*. Helen is a wonderful facilitator and teacher, and she uses these gifts to illuminate the wisdom that lies within others.

Notice how Helen's Calling is very focused—the mark of a Calling with passion—and it describes exactly what she does: She facilitates, teaches, and writes. This is a good example of creative, yet elegant and succinct, phrasing, which is, at the same time, very clear in its meaning. My Calling, as mentioned earlier, is: *To lead and serve through my writing, teaching, and speaking*. Again, no frills, just the facts.

> Only one who bursts with enthusiasm do I instruct; only one who bubbles with excitement do I enlighten. If I hold up one corner and you do not come back to me with the other three, I do not continue the lesson.
>
> Confucius

Erin Denholm is the vice president of a major home care organization. She is passionately committed to her work, which is her living ministry—her spiritual practice. The nature of the work that has called to her is clearly evident in her Destiny, Cause, and Calling statements. Her Destiny is: *To alleviate human suffering*. Erin does this through the organization she leads, but also through her family, including her two beautiful daughters. Her work is a very important focus, and Erin sees the team she leads as her means for leveraging her Destiny. Her Cause is: *To inspire individual empowerment and team kaizen.* So Erin's Calling—the *doing* part—what she *does* every day with mastery and passion that will lead to the

---

* *Kaizen* is a Japanese word that means continuing improvement in personal life, home life, and working life, involving everyone.

achievement of her Cause and, therefore, her Destiny is: *To lead, speak, coach, and teach courageously and truthfully,* because these are her talents and natural gifts. This is her training, what she loves to do, and how she has chosen to serve.

Sister Nancy Hoffman, SC, is a Roman Catholic nun. Her Destiny is: *To help reawaken in our universe the message of God's unconditional love for all of creation.* Sister Nancy is a deeply committed woman of faith, and her Cause is: *To strive to act justly and to love tenderly in all situations.* Knowing Sister Nancy as I do, I have learned how much she strives to live up to these high standards. She once told me that Saint Thomas Aquinas had said, "Love is to will the good of the other." This inspired her, so she has made her life vocation, her daily commitment, her Calling: *To mentor, partner, and walk with others on their journey to wholeness.* This is the mastery that Sister Nancy practices every day, because she believes that by doing so, she will "act justly and love tenderly in all situations," and if she does this every day, she will be able to "help reawaken in our universe the message of God's unconditional love for all of creation." Can you see how the Destiny, Cause, and Calling all fit so beautifully into one another, like a set of *matrioshka* dolls?

Here is another example of someone who has made her life's work her spiritual practice. Karen Hoskins runs a nursing home for elderly patients and has dedicated her life to this work. Her Destiny is: *To inspire others to see the wisdom of the ages.* Karen works with seniors every day and has come to not only value the wisdom of the elders, but honor it in her Destiny. Karen's Cause is: *To restore dignity and respect to all seniors,* and her Calling is: *To lead others by following the values of respect, integrity, teamwork, and promise-keeping.* Notice how beautifully Karen's work is woven into her Destiny, Cause, and Calling.

> It's amazing how many cares disappear when you decide not to be something, but to be someone.
>
> Coco Chanel

Higher Ground Leaders first reaffirm their commitment to their own Calling and then coach others to find and master theirs. Chuck Yeager, the legendary test pilot, said, "If you are going to fly, do it right. What I really admire in a flyer is professionalism and consistency. I'm really impressed by a guy or gal who goes out there day after day and does it right—not fancy or flamboyant, but just constantly good performance. Lots of pilots talk a good game, and sometimes their stories get better with each telling. Don't measure yourself by the stories of others. Seek to improve yourself—that's the mark of a true pro." A Calling is a sense of authenticity, true mastery, and knowingness about your gifts and talents and an awareness of its applicability to a Cause. This vocational mastery and bliss must be experienced before it can be taught. *A Calling is a compact, succinct definition of our personal mastery—the intersection of our passion and our most effective talents, tasks, and skills that we will use to achieve our Cause and live our Destiny.* Our Calling is the work we love, how we are when we are *in flow*, whether it is being compensated for in the conventional sense or not—think of parents and volunteers.

Considering the Terrathreats that you earlier defined as currently limiting the potential of humanity and our planet, what is your personal mastery, your unique gifts and skills that you wish to contribute and that could lead to their resolution?

- In what fields do you excel?
- Where are your natural gifts?
- What activities, skills, and practices call to you that, given the chance, you would pursue?
- In which new fields could you excel with appropriate training or coaching?
- What special talents and expertise do you possess that could be used to deal with these Terrathreats and, therefore, improve the world?
- What gifts do you bring—such as special knowledge; personal, intellectual, or physical characteristics; intuition, natural abilities, or material circumstances—that might enable you to be a special influence?
- In what way could your special talents, your personal mastery—both those already realized and those yet to be revealed and tested—be used to serve others and to improve, change, or resolve the Terrathreats of the world?

Reflect on your personal mastery (personal mastery describes the special talents and skills that are unique to you, which you love to practice and which you do very well)—the exact skill you practice when you are doing whatever it is that you do best, or would like to do best, to the highest standards of which you are capable. Choose two or three competencies that best describe the skills, trained proficiency, or natural gifts that, when you practice them well, truly inspire you—where your deepest passion lies (e.g., teaching, speaking, consulting, coaching, nursing, caring, selling, parenting, painting, or a task definition such as long-distance transport driving, neurosurgery, computer code writing, performing music). Be specific and succinct. You may wish to answer these questions by writing in a journal or elsewhere:

- Which two active verbs describe the specific activities or skills you are practicing when you are at your very best at work or how you would like to be at work—your highest levels of personal mastery?

- When you are relating with others and you are inspired and inspiring them, what tasks are you performing?
- What would you like to see happen in these situations?
- What outcomes are you seeking?
- What would you like to be different as a result of the application or sharing of your skills, gifts, and talents with others? For example, my passion comes from being able to lead and serve—servant-leadership—in every way I can. So it shows up in my Calling: *To lead and serve through my writing, teaching, and speaking.*
- What are the two or three words that describe what you are doing when you are in flow? Perhaps your passion might be ignited by teaching, serving, inspiring, leading, honoring, and so on.
- Which active verbs best describe this passion and exhilaration for you?

Reflect for a moment on these questions.

What is your Calling? Put it all together to describe your Calling.

Don't worry about making this pretty—eloquence or literacy is not a priority at this stage; just capture the essence, so that it describes the longing deep inside you. Now you are ready to meditate on your calling.

Meditation

To access something as vital and personal as our Destiny, Cause, and Calling, we need to go deep within ourselves. Meditation offers a powerful way to access energies, information, hidden awareness, and understanding. Before guiding you through this approach to accessing your own inner wisdom, I will review the concepts behind meditation.

It has been said that the dramatic rise of technology has been responsible for the equally dramatic rise in contemplative practices, such as Eastern meditation and the centuries-old Christian practice of contemplative prayer. Our psyches have required a balance to the heightened electronic stimulation of daily life. Few people have the constitution to cope with today's turbocharged pace of life without a compensating mechanism—the capacity to go within, to go deep to recharge and renew the mind, body, and soul.

We need to listen, to follow our inner voice, and pay heed to the spiritual call, what Carl Jung called the "unavoidable vocation toward individuation." In this way, we may live our passion, deliver our best work, and make our best contribution. The meditation I will share with you in this chapter invites you to open your inner ear so that you can hear the siren within singing to your heart, inviting you to recognize your Calling.[4]

Meditation is the uninterrupted flow of energy toward the subject on which we are meditating. One of the elements of meditation is stillness, which is a part of all great religions and wisdom teachings. One of the purposes of meditation is a paradox: to find things by letting go of them. What we need to know is inside us all.

Meditation is one of the most powerful ways of calming our minds, reducing the mental chatter in our heads, and opening our subconscious to information that we do not normally see, hear, or sense in any other way. Without meditation, we tend to be blocked, to miss the obvious, and to be closed to information and energy that is striving to connect us to our Destiny, Cause, and Calling. Meditation is a powerful way to open the heart and the soul, as well as the mind, to the boundless possibilities that might be ours if we pay attention. After all, we are nothing more than potential; we are spiritual and human beings seeking a relationship with our appropriate future.

> The world is what we think it is. If we can change our thoughts, we can change the world.
>
> H. M. Tomlinson

Daily meditation has roots in all the major spiritual practices of the world and has been used for centuries to invite the spirit to move beyond the anxieties, distractions, and confines of the body. When practiced regularly, meditation can help to lower stress and blood pressure and enhance our state of awareness. Studies have also shown that meditation may decrease the risk of heart disease, possibly because we are able to release stress and fatigue, rest the body, and thus allow it to heal naturally by reducing the toxic chemistries of stress. At the Kings County North Rehabilitation Facility, a correctional institute near Seattle, only 56 percent of inmates who meditated for 10 days, 11 hours each day, returned to jail within two years, compared to a 75 percent recidivism rate among those who did not meditate.[5] The enormous and growing daily assault we experience from sensory inputs causes our minds to hyperactivate in the process of thinking. We watch and listen to the news; read books, magazines, and papers; experience advertising; study and write reports; compute and surf the Internet; engage in conversation; and solve hundreds of problems every day. Processing these normal activities requires a constant mental commentary, and most people are unaware of the overload this causes. Watch people talking to themselves in rush-hour traffic and you will know what I mean.

Peak-performing athletes know that after concentrating their efforts superbly for short periods of time, they must then regenerate and replenish their resources. If we wish to work at peak performance, we must do the same.

There are many different forms of meditation, each with discrete techniques appropriate for different temperaments and personal needs. The best-known practice in the West is transcendental meditation, which is based on ancient Hindu teachings. Transcendental meditation typically uses a mantra, a phrase with no obvious meaning that keeps the mind, at least temporarily, from being embroiled in the pressing matters of your day—freedom from what Buddhists call the "monkey mind." Some meditation practices involve concentrating on an object, such as your breath, a mandala, a flower, or a candle. The Vietnamese Buddhist monk, Thich Nhat Hanh, has popularized the practice of mindful meditation and walking meditation in the West. Christian meditation has a long tradition, too. "Be still and know that I am God" from Psalms 46:10 refers to the meditative practices of thousands of years ago.

Meditation creates a refuge for the mind, so that it can settle down from contemporary hyperactivity and move into a more peaceful, calm, and focused mode. The result is personal rejuvenation and greater effectiveness. Over time, the number of random thoughts that interrupt the tranquility of the mind diminishes. Even more rewarding is that your attachment to, and identification with, these thoughts declines. It is useful to try several forms of meditation practice until you find the approach that best meets your particular needs. Try starting with 5 to 10 minutes of meditation each day and increase the time as you grow in practice. The best attitude in meditation practice is to not have any expectations, because to do so can create unnecessary strain in the practice. The rewards will soon become apparent with daily practice. Even a few moments of meditation, whether at the airport while waiting to take off or land, before making a speech or beginning a meeting, or while commuting on the train, are helpful. With practice, any venue can become a sacred space for meditation where relief from daily stress can be gained.

Here are some tips for meditating:

- Try to find a tranquil location—one free from distractions. If this is difficult, learn to tune out distractions.
- In your office or home, decide whether you'd like to have soothing music in the background.
- Avoid stimulants (coffee or smoking), depressants (liquor), or eating (which stimulates the metabolic system) immediately before meditation. All of these interfere with and reduce the physiological benefits and effectiveness of meditation.
- Select a comfortable chair or place to sit—the floor will do, too—and assume a sitting position with your spine relatively straight. You may find it helpful to lean against a wall to provide greater support for your spine.

- Close your eyes. Remove eyeglasses if you wear them (you won't be needing them when your eyes are closed!).
- Breathe in deeply, allowing your chest and stomach to expand as you inhale.
- Exhale fully and slowly.
- Concentrate your awareness on your breathing and the feelings of deeper relaxation.
- Allow thoughts and feelings to enter your mind. Don't worry about being distracted by these thoughts—this is natural. Acknowledge them, allow them to pass through, and then return your focus to your breathing.
- When you have completed enough time, and when you are ready, open your eyes and enjoy the feeling of being more relaxed and centered. Don't rush— allow yourself time to return to your daily routine. The world will continue to turn, without your help, for a few moments more.

Many companies have recognized the benefits of meditation by building non-denominational meditation rooms for employees. Many organizations incorporate meditation into their board and management meetings. CEOs such as Bill George of Medtronic and Joe Calvaruso of Mount Carmel Heath System have practiced daily meditation for many years. Meditation is being practiced in organizations such as AstraZeneca, Palle Computer, Yahoo!, Google, McKinsey, Texas Instruments, Raytheon, Hughes Aircraft, and Deutsche Bank.[6] Marc Benioff, the founder of Salesforce.com Inc., is an advanced practitioner of yoga and a regular meditator. How does Benioff stay so calm while building a booming technology company? Robert Thurman, the first Western Tibetan monk, a friend of the Dalai Lama and a professor at Columbia University, says, "He meditates. He doesn't put stress on himself."[7]

Meditation is one more way for us to become whole humans. One of the benefits of meditation is that delicious *still-point* when the world is suspended; wisdom and creativity flow and emotions that get in our way simply dissolve. Yogi Amrit Desai put it this way: "Prayer is you talking to God; meditation is you listening to God." This is one of the secrets of greatness.

The meditation that follows will help to crystallize your Calling, but first, I will explore four concepts that will prepare you for the meditation experience and help you to identify a Destiny, Cause, and Calling that is truly yours—not small, but large:

1. The Preprobability Plane.
2. Intentionality.

3. Synchronicity.
4. Letting go.

The Preprobability Plane

For each of us, there is one true Calling. It is our potential, waiting to manifest. It is not something we strive for—it is something we are called to. We do not bend ourselves to fit something, but we embrace that which invites us. Contrary to what many of us were taught to believe and contrary to the theories of many psychologists, we are not the result of our social conditioning or our genetic heritage. James Hillman points out, "By accepting the idea that I am the effect of a subtle buffeting between hereditary and societal forces, I reduce myself to a result. The more my life is accounted for by what already occurred in my chromosomes, by what my parents did or didn't do, and by my early years now long past, the more my biography is the story of a victim."[8] We are capable of identifying our Calling through the use of insightful tools and releasing our intentionality into the Preprobability Plane, where there reside the conditions, opportunities, networks, skills, training, knowledge, and wisdom necessary for us to follow our Calling.

The underlying source of all life is the Preprobability Plane, the reality from which all life emerges. At the subatomic level, the universe consists of raw energy, and in this Preprobability Plane, this raw energy isn't anything—it just is. The Preprobability Plane is not empty; it is full of everything that ultimately manifests itself on the surface of life—what our senses detect. The Preprobability Plane represents potential and probability, with the capability of manifesting into consciousness. It is from here that we are able to change probabilities into realities, dreams, and thoughts into action. When we do this, we are converting the invisible into the visible. These probabilities reside within the Preprobability Plane.

> Once you can accept the universe as matter expanding into nothing that is something, wearing stripes with plaid comes easy.
>
> Albert Einstein

Intentionality

Whether these probabilities are manifested into the conscious energy field—the universal awareness of all living things—depends on our intentions—our *intentionality*. Intentionality is energy from the conscious energy field calling on the

Preprobability Plane for the information necessary to activate and convert probabilities. A plant must call on the unrealized energy of the sun to sustain itself and grow. It must also monitor the entire celestial domain to ensure that it is perfectly receptive to nutrients and light, and rest when necessary to conserve energy, grow, and replicate. It also draws data and energy from the Preprobability Plane to build cells, create roots, and establish systems of osmosis, nutrition, and photosynthesis. An acorn without intentionality is just a little oval nub that will remain an acorn. An acorn with intentionality will reach into the Preprobability Plane and draw the information necessary from the universe to become a mighty oak tree.

Examples of intentionality bringing about the desired outcome are evident every day in our lives. A placebo is intentionality disguised as a pill. Prayer is intentionality in the form of an invocation. Miracles are the results of collective intentionality. Complementary medical practices such as acupuncture and homeopathy are techniques of intentionality designed to activate the knowledge desired from the Preprobability Plane—the healing knowledge that is already within us, but that we have forgotten. Intentionality eventually removes the hard covering that we have layered over our inner knowing.

The science of intentionality has been validated by many leading researchers. One of them, Dr. Fabrizio Benedetti, a neuroscientist at the University of Turin, has conducted experiments with patients suffering from Parkinson's disease, an ailment caused by degeneration of nerve cells located in the substantia nigra (the middle area of the brain), which results in tremors and muscle spasms. Parkinson's can be alleviated by electrical stimulation of the brain. In Dr. Benedetti's experiments, when the patient was unaware that stimulation was being applied, the symptoms continued unabated, but as soon as the patient was told that the stimulation had begun, the symptoms were reduced.[9] Intentionality is causal power.

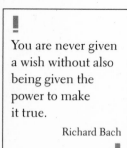

You are never given a wish without also being given the power to make it true.

Richard Bach

I live and work in the countryside. Animals of all kinds visit us from nature, and many plants choose to live around us, beyond the ones that we have planted. A few years ago, I had the driveway to our offices paved so that it could better withstand the growing traffic. But the intentionality of the lilies of the valley, now paved over, remained as strong as ever and my ego (the asphalt) was subdued by the intentionality of the lilies of the valley, which thrust through the blacktop. The lilies had registered their intentionality and called for the information necessary from the

Preprobability Plane and, consequently, manifested the reality they desired. Relatively speaking, the asphalt is a very large obstacle, which, scaled up to the human level, would probably thwart most of us. What determines outcomes is the relative power of the intention.

How do we build this level of power? Paradoxically, we do it in the opposite way to what we might assume: We let go.

Intentionality is thought, and thought is energy. Energy operates at various frequencies; consequently, humans (who are a manifestation of energy) function at different frequencies. The most commonly experienced frequency is our body—our physiological energy frequency. Indeed, for many people this is the only frequency of which they are aware. Our personal growth and spiritual evolution access different, higher frequencies—spiritual energy frequencies. When we meditate, we are functioning at yet another, higher frequency. When our meditation reaches the level of trance, where our physiological activity slows or stops but our experience continues, we have reached yet another, higher level of frequency. When we experience a sense of being one with the universe, we are operating at another, higher level of frequency; and when we sense the experience of being one with God, we operate at the highest frequency. At this level, we are close to the Preprobability Plane, and it is here that we are closest to the field of unrealized probabilities, the state of raw energy and potential. This is the subquantum level, the quantum void, before the conscious energy field is activated by intentionality. This is where we access our soul.

The issue here is not just whether we can mold future events through the power of our intentionality. It is also whether we sometimes inadvertently use intentionality to *limit* our potential. Claude Steele, professor of psychology at Stanford University in Palo Alto, California, has described clear empirical psychological evidence indicating that when African American students believe they are being judged as members of a stereotyped group rather than as individuals, they do less well on tests. He calls this mechanism the "stereotype threat."[10] Whereas popular prejudice suggests that women do not do as well in mathematical or science exams, Steele has found that differences in performance are largely to do with confidence more than competence. Sexual stereotyping seems to work in the same way. Professor Steele:

> . . . discovered this by administering a math exam to a set of equally qualified men and women, all of whom were studying the subject at Stanford. As the test was being distributed, one group was informed that it had proved to be sex-neutral: men and women performed equally well in it. To the other group, which acted as a control, no such comment was made.

As popular prejudice predicted, men outperformed women in the control group. In the experimental group, however, not only did the women do better than their sisters in the control group, but the men did worse than their brothers there. The result was an equal performance by both sexes.[11]

Here is the question for each of us to consider: Do we find it easier to say, "I can't" or "I will"? "I can't" means "I don't believe I am capable enough or have the power to shape the future so that it conforms to any criteria I choose." "I will" means "I have the power to shape and bend future outcomes in any way I choose, if I *really* want to." The first gives away our power to external forces—the second claims our power and recognizes its potential. The choice is ours. *A Course in Miracles* says, "There is no order of difficulty in miracles." We often think that miracles happen only in mythology, to contemporary saints, gurus, and bodhisattva. But mere mortals like you and I can open ourselves to the possibility of miracles every day. We must become comfortable trusting the universe and learning to appreciate the extraordinary as ordinary. Perhaps the only limits to what can be manifested from the Preprobability Plane are those imposed by our minds.

> !
>
> You are searching for the magic key that will unlock the door to the source of power; and yet you have the key in your own hands.
>
> Napoleon Hill
>
> !

Thus, our Destiny, Cause, and Calling will be limited only by our limited thinking.

Synchronicity: The Result of Intentionality

Traditionally, we are encouraged to survey the marketplace to identify the strengths and range of opportunities, occupations, and the careers that offer the greatest potential rewards and meet our future needs. After gathering this information, we embark on paths designed to secure our ideal career—dentistry, law, medicine, teaching, business, crafts, or the arts, for example. Some of us have no plan, accidentally falling into a life lived as a "victim" or as a "result." In these circumstances, we are the product of our heredity, our genes, and the external environment—and the absence of intentionality.

What all this presents is a picture of humanity as prisoners of limited possibility thinking. It is a unidimensional view that does not go beyond our own ego and personality or the personalities of others; it fails to consider the spiritual potential within each of us and within the Preprobability Plane.

By listening to the siren within, however, and by following paths fueled by our passion and inner knowing, our values and the energy of our intentionality, and then using this to access the energy resting in the form of potential in the Preprobability Plane, we can manifest any Calling that our heart and soul desires. It is only our lack of faith in the Divine, our sense of frailty, unworthiness, and insecurity that causes us to invent words like *synchronicity*.

> The greatest discovery of my generation is that a human being can alter his life by altering his attitude of mind.
>
> William James

Synchronicity is the arrival of a timely reality manifested through intentionality from the Preprobability Plane. Synchronicity is proof that we can manifest realities that on the face of it seem absurdly ambitious—even miraculous.

Synchronicity is normal behavior. Look at the formations of nature; the flight paths of birds and insects; the directions, shapes, and sizes in which grass grows; the shapes, strengths, direction, height, content, and impact of clouds; the physical, emotional, and energetic diversity of humans. Synchronicity is the rule of nature, not the exception. Synchronicity is where the factors of intentionality converge. Though synchronicity may seem random to the untrained eye, to the mystic, to the Higher Ground Leader, it is nothing less than the manifestation of intended outcomes.

Letting Go

Now let's prepare for a meditation to help you learn the practice of letting go. Please read the following sentences slowly, pausing after each one, inviting their meaning to trickle gently into your consciousness. After each sentence, reflect and then breathe deeply and pause before proceeding to the next one:

- Acknowledge your desire to be an instrument of the universe. *I am an instrument of the universe.*
- Give thanks for life as it is. *I give thanks for life as it is.*
- Let go of your anger, sadness, and fears. *I release all emotions of the ego now.*
- Move your heart and mind out of your current space/time awareness. *My heart and mind are released into the universe.*
- Adopt an attitude of surrender; go with the flow. *I surrender. I go with the flow.*

- Think like a mystic, in Thomas Merton's definition of this term: Adopt a complete, unqualified sense of wonder about life. *I hold each moment of life in wonder.*
- Be ready to receive what you need to know from the Preprobability Plane. *I am willing to receive that which I need to know.*

Close your eyes and practice these thoughts; repeat them in the same sequence for a few more moments . . . then read the following sentences slowly, pausing after you read each one to let them infuse your consciousness.

It is from this mystical perspective that we are enabled to manifest what we need from the Preprobability Plane. Here is where the information lies that will help us define our own Destiny, Cause, and Calling. It is from this framework that we ready ourselves to call in the information from the Preprobability Plane, which we do in the following way:

- Gather your intent and release it into the universe.
- Keep your ego out of the equation. No matter how difficult this may seem at times, it is an essential prerequisite. If you find yourself asking questions about the effect on you or the payoffs of a thought or action, stand aside, observe yourself and the thought, and let the thought pass.
- Close your eyes and practice these thoughts; then repeat them in the same sequence for a moment or two.
- Practice the concept of detachment from the outcome.

The Calling Meditation

(Note: Find a friend to be your guide for this meditation. This should be someone close to you whom you trust and who will support you in every way in this quest for your Calling. Ask your friend to read the following meditation very slowly, modulating his or her voice, articulating and enunciating deliberately and slowly. Invite this friend to take his or her time, pausing regularly, and help you remember to concentrate on your breathing. Please do not begin the meditation unless you have the necessary uninterrupted time available. Once you have begun, try not to rush any of the phases of the meditation and ask your guide to be aware of your transcendental state and safety at all times. If you know a meditation teacher or master, invite his or her support in guiding you through this meditation. **Do not complete any part of this meditation if it could trigger any personal physical, emotional, or mental issues you might have or if it**

could pose any medical risk to you. Based on our experiences with thousands of retreat participants who have undertaken this Calling Meditation in our workshops and retreats, when you have completed the meditation, you should rest, write in your journal, and reflect on the life-altering experience that you will feel washing over and through you. Or perhaps you will simply experience a delicious sense of calm—let whatever this experience brings be what it is.)[12]

First, find a comfortable place in which to sit. If you meditate regularly, you will probably find a cross-legged position comfortable. If not, sit on a chair with your feet flat on the ground, your back upright and pressed firmly against a solid support, thus permitting energy to freely flow directly up and down your spine. Place your hands on your knees with your palms upright, thus inviting the universal energy to flow through you.

If you wish to play music that soothes the soul, do so very softly. Make sure that the music provides a background support rather than a distraction, so that it will not be necessary to interrupt your meditation to adjust it.

If you wish, and you can safely do so, light a candle. Make sure that there are no distractions around you and that you will not be disturbed.

Get into a comfortable position. Now allow your eyes to close and begin by focusing your awareness on your breath. Breathing in and breathing out. Breathe in easily and effortlessly. Breathe out easily and effortlessly. Each breath allows you to become more relaxed and comfortable. Let any outside sounds only serve to allow you to go deeper inside. Let them be a reminder of how good it is to leave the noise and stress of the outside world and journey into the quiet and peace of your own inner world.

As you sink deeper down into quiet and ease, imagine a golden cord dropping down from the back of your spine. Imagine it going down deep into the center of the Earth. Imagine there is something to which you can anchor the cord to so that no matter where you travel on your inner journey, you will feel solidly connected to the Earth.

As you allow yourself to sink deeper into a state of relaxation, reflect back to a time when you stood beside a pond or a lake where you experienced the peace and gentleness of the quiet. Drop a pebble into the water and notice the waves rippling outwards. One wave after another, flowing outward, farther and farther. The waves slow down and become farther apart until the water settles and is calm and peaceful once again. Imagine that your body is like that body of water. Drop a breath, like the stone, into the pool that is your body. And, as you drop a breath into the center of your body, experience the waves of relaxation rippling outwards. Waves of relaxation flow through your body, up through your torso into your chest, shoulders, and back. They flow up through the vertebrae and spread out into each and every muscle of your back and neck. The waves flow through your shoulders and arms, up through your neck, your jaw, your face, your scalp. Enjoy those waves as they relax your body, as your muscles let go and become soft and loose. Now, feel the ripples of relaxation flowing toward the lower part of your torso, flowing through your abdomen and your pelvis, down through your thighs, calves, ankles, feet, and toes. With every breath that you drop into the center of your body, you become more relaxed. And as you become more relaxed, you find yourself becoming more quiet and peaceful.

(Pause . . . focus on your steady breathing)

This is a meditation of intentionality, so let's begin with the intention of healing your body, the temple for your soul.

(Continue to concentrate on your breathing)

Think for a moment about those things that you are currently angry about.

(Pause . . . focus on your steady breathing)

Now let them go. Gently release them from your mind. Continue to concentrate on your breathing.

Slowly repeat to yourself the phrase, "I invite the Divine presence of the Creator." (The Creator is the Higher Presence, as you understand it.) Repeat this several times—"I invite the Divine presence of the Creator."

Continue to repeat the phrase for four or five minutes.

(Pause . . . focus on your steady breathing)

Think for a moment about those things that you are currently afraid about.

(Pause . . . focus on your steady breathing)

Now let them go. Gently release them from your mind. Continue to concentrate on your breathing.

Slowly repeat to yourself the phrase, "I invite the Divine presence of the Creator." Repeat this again several times—"I invite the Divine presence of the Creator."

Very slowly, scan your body with your third eye. As you do so, silence your mental chatter. Focus your energy within your physical body. After a few moments, slowly scan from the top of your head to the tip of your toes. Pause as you observe in your mind, every part of your body. Along the way, continue to gently relax every area of tension. Don't forget areas like your throat, your cheeks, your eyebrows, your jaws and tongue, your chest and tummy, elbows, arms and hands, knees, calves, feet, and toes—including each knuckle and joint.

Continue to concentrate on your deep breathing and repeating, "I invite the Divine presence of the Creator."

Bring your awareness to your heart and become conscious of its beat as it sends the life force throughout your body. As you concentrate on your heart, gently slow your heartbeat down.

(Pause . . . focus on your steady breathing as it slows down with your heartbeat)

Bring your awareness to the blood flow within your body, and become aware of the friendly role your heart is playing in this process. Notice any areas in your body that are painful and concentrate on them for a moment, bringing heat to them. Become aware of the tingling and warmth in these sensitive areas as the blood flow and temperature increase.

Continue to breathe slowly and deeply in an even rhythm.

Continue to let go of any remaining anger.

While you are breathing deeply, your body is healing, and your mind is clearing itself of all other things.

(Pause . . . focus on your steady breathing)

Bring your awareness to your passion—to what gives you the greatest joy in your life. Now define all of the mastery you could imagine you possess when you see this passion flourishing. Imagine your passion as a Calling and yourself practicing this Calling to the highest levels humanly attainable. Image your Calling being practiced by you to perfection.

Capture this picture in a ball of white light and hold it in your heart. Keep breathing steadily and deeply and repeating the phrase, "I invite the Divine intervention of the Creator."

While holding this image within the ball of white light in your heart, travel now to the Preprobability Plane, where all the information you need for your Calling rests as pure potential. Bring your attention to the spot between your eyes, your third eye. Imagine a bright, white light there. Imagine the intense whiteness of this light between your eyes. Now, imagine this bright, white light becoming a beam that extends out into space. Follow that beam as it leaves the building you are in, as it travels above your town. It continues outward, and now you can see the entire countryside; and now the entire country. Keep traveling farther and farther into space and notice the curvature of the Earth. As you keep traveling in space, farther and farther, you find yourself enveloped by the softness and the quiet of space. Notice below you the big blue-green ball and the white clouds that are caressing it. Allow yourself to enjoy this perspective for a moment. Keep traveling, traveling, until there is nothing more to notice, just the void. This is the quantum void. You are now in the Preprobability Plane—that place of knowing wherein resides all the information you need to achieve pure mastery in your Calling.

(Pause . . . focus on your steady breathing)

Prepare yourself to receive all of the guidance you need to find your Calling by saying softly and silently to yourself, "I am ready to receive." Repeat this phrase for four or five minutes. Keep your awareness on your breathing, which should be rhythmic, steady, and deep.

Stay calmly in this place for a few moments.

(Pause . . . focus on your steady breathing)

Now, gently return from the Preprobability Plane by riding an arc of light back to the ball of white light in your heart, thus connecting the future to the present.

(Pause . . . focus on your steady breathing)

It is now time to let go of your intentionality because you have now put it out into the universe, into the Preprobability Plane. Your desires will manifest themselves in space/time reality—of this there is no doubt. It is only the timing that is uncertain. This is in the hands of the Universe. Repeat silently "I trust the Universe."

(Pause . . . focus on your steady breathing)

Prepare yourself to slowly return to an awakened state. Keep your eyes closed.

(Concentrate on your breathing)

When you are ready, slowly return to the present moment. Take your time. Without opening your eyes, rub your hands briskly together to warm them and then cup them over your eyes, but without touching them. Feel the warmth and energy from your hands. When the moment is right, with your hands still cupped over your eyes but not touching them, gently open your eyes, looking into the warmth and darkness of your cupped hands, then slowly let your hands fall away.

Now rest. Journal if this feels appropriate. Allow the experience of the Calling Meditation to do its work, by being present in this moment, without interruption or distraction. Let the experience you have just completed do its good work by creating magic and healing and new awareness for you.*

---

* If you would like to be inspired by the Destiny, Cause, and Calling statements of other readers, clients, and workshop, seminar and retreat participants, or if you would like to post your own, please go to the Secretan Center website at http://www.secretan.com /inspire.

Step Four: Aligning Destiny, Cause, and Calling

Creating a Seamless Fit

So far, we have been discussing Destiny, Cause, and Calling—our "Why-Be-Do"—as three freestanding ideas—but in reality, they are one. When they become seamlessly integrated within us, we can experience a liberating sense of joy—a life lived on purpose.

Inspired people want to know five things about their work:

After achieving pure clarity about their Destiny, defining and living the Cause, reaffirming their commitment to their own Calling, and coaching others to find and master theirs, Higher Ground Leaders align Destiny, Cause, and Calling by enabling followers to invest the energy of their Calling in service of the Cause. When followers hear about, and are drawn to, the Cause, the Higher Ground Leader then asks them, "What is your Calling?" and proceeds to help them identify their true Calling and develop their mastery within it. Thus, followers make a passionate and seamless connection between their Calling and the Cause, achieving full alignment with the two, and then direct both toward living out their Destiny.

1. How does my work help to achieve the Cause?
2. Does my work enable me to use my deepest creative gifts?
3. Will my work make a difference to the world, will it have meaning, and will it make the world a better place?
4. How does my work meet my spiritual needs?
5. Is this how I want to be in the universe?

These are some of the issues that Higher Ground Leaders think about frequently, ensuring that satisfactory answers are found for each of them.

Higher Ground Leaders know that lifting the hearts of others is achieved through providing positive answers to questions like these more than through targets and goals. This is not to say that the latter are not important, just that they lead us to the path of *motivation*, and we are more concerned here with finding the path of *inspiration*. Higher Ground Leaders work hard to help followers align their work to the Cause, searching for a perfect, seamless fit between the work and each individual's Calling and the Cause. We cannot live out our Destiny unless we can live this alignment. This enables us to become authentic.

According to *USA Today*, the international arm of Philip Morris submitted a report to the Czech government claiming that the country saved as much as $30 million in 1999, thanks in part to the "indirect positive effect" of smoking. The report argued that people who die prematurely from smoking-induced diseases save governments money they might otherwise spend on healthcare, pensions, and housing payments. In 2001, as news of the report was picked up by the Czech media, it quickly spread around the world, and the public outrage caused CEO John R. Nelson to tell employees that the company's critics were right in suggesting the report "exhibited a callous and cynical disregard of basic human values." Alignment and authenticity gets put into question here: Philip Morris has spent $150 million a year on a public relations campaign to prove that it is a responsible and caring organization, that it should influence proposals in Congress on new federal tobacco regulations, and that the public should trust its judgment on the health risks posed by new tobacco products it may market.[1] Philip Morris has since renamed itself Altria Group.

We all yearn for greater alignment than this, to be internally congruent. We yearn to align our values, beliefs, and dreams, which is how we achieve our Destiny, Cause, and Calling. A great Cause positions the connection we have with our work and the world on higher ground. It shifts our consciousness so profoundly that we completely reframe our view of our work, so that it is no longer a boring functional statement, but a brilliant spiritual one that defines our connection with the Divine and the way we serve others. It moves work from the mundane to the inspiring. Here is how Bill Pollard, Chairman Emeritus of ServiceMaster, puts it:

> We have found that people want to work for a Cause, not just a living, and when there is an alignment between the Cause of the firm and the Calling of its people, a creative power is unleashed that results in quality service to the customer and the growth and development of the people serving. People find meaning in their work. The Cause becomes an organizing principle of effectiveness. Why is Shirley, a housekeeper in a 250-bed community hospital, still excited about her

work after 15 years? She certainly has seen some changes. She has moved from 2 West to 3 East and cleans more rooms today than she did five years ago. The chemicals, the mop, and the housekeeping cart have all been improved. Nevertheless, the bathrooms and the toilets are still the same. The dirt has not changed nor have the unexpected spills of the patients or the arrogance of some of the physicians. So what inspires Shirley? Does she have a mission in her work? Is her job just cleaning floors, or is she part of a team of people that helps sick people get well? Is she recognized not only for what she does, but also for what she is becoming? Does she know that she is needed and is providing an important contribution? Shirley sees her job as extending to the welfare of the patient in the bed and as an integral part of a team supporting the work of the doctors and nurses—she has a Cause—a Cause that involves the health and welfare of others. When Shirley first came to us over 15 years ago, no doubt she was merely looking for just a job. But she brought to her work an unlocked potential and a desire to accomplish something significant. As I talked with Shirley about her job, she shared with me her Cause when she said: "If we don't clean with a quality effort, we can't keep the doctors and nurses in business. We can't serve the patients. This place would be closed if we didn't have housekeeping." Shirley was confirming the reality of our Cause.

If you ask John Dornan what the mission or vision of SAS Institute is, he will tell you that there isn't one now, there never has been one, and there probably won't ever be one. He simply observes that SAS has always tried to do the right thing for employees, because when you do, it translates into effective services and solutions for customers. As Jim Goodnight, the company's cofounder, is fond of saying, "If you treat employees as if they make a difference to the company, they will make a difference to the company." This sounds like a better plan than the usual corporate mantras. Jim Goodnight believes that if you treat people well and help them to find their Calling and grow, they will then take care of customers because they are inspired. This is a philosophy shared by Southwest Airlines, Timberland, and Baptist Health Care of Pensacola, among others.

The greatest leaders in history worked closely with others to ensure that they had found their true Calling. Once this was confirmed, they helped them to increase their mastery, to stretch and tackle extraordinary opportunities, often before they were fully ready. They were transformative leaders—leaders who changed people and helped them to grow.

I worked for a Higher Ground Leader at Manpower Limited. Jim Scheinfeld trusted me to run an entire business when I was just a 27-year-old rookie. He spent the next 14 years teaching, encouraging, supporting, and, when necessary, defending—and always inspiring—me. The gift he gave me was the feeling that

I have never worked a day in my life because I have always known and followed my Calling, I have loved the people I have worked with, and I have always aligned my Calling with a Cause that enables me to live out my Destiny. After 14 years, Jim left and a new chairman took over, who had different values and no clear and magnetic Cause. For the first time in years, I felt that my Calling was no longer aligned with a Cause I believed in, and, therefore, I was no longer inspired. Sadly, this could not be resolved, and I resigned. But Jim's gifts to me as a Higher Ground Leader were not lost because I had experienced the bliss that comes from aligning my Calling with a Cause, and to this day I have never settled for anything less. If we wish to live authentic lives, we cannot live out of alignment with our Destiny, Cause, and Calling.

Aligning with a Noble Cause

Monsanto Corp., whose corporate motto is "Food—Health—Hope," is one of the world's leading biotechnology companies and a pioneer in the development and production of genetically engineered seeds. They manufacture pest- and herbicide-resistant seeds for a variety of crops from corn to canola. For tens of thousands of years, farmers the world over have planted seeds, harvested their crops, saving some for seed to replant in the fall. More than 1.5 billion people, primarily poor farmers, rely on farm-saved seeds as their primary seed source for the following crop year. To ensure a revenue stream for Monsanto's expensive research, the company asked farmers not to save their seeds, even requiring them to sign agreements to this effect, arguing that Monsanto needed the revenues from new seed purchases to make such research financially viable. But farmers were not easily persuaded to follow these urgings, especially in developing countries. So Monsanto developed a plan to ensure that farmers did things their way. The company designed a new strain of chemically reengineered seeds that produce a healthy crop, but after they mature, their seeds become sterile and unable to reproduce. Critics of these tactics have built a movement, fuelled by the Internet, naming these genes *Terminator*, and making dark predictions about seed monopolies, bankrupt subsistence farmers, and toxic clouds of pollen drifting from these "super seeds" that might result in irreversible sterilization of great tracts of natural vegetation.[2]

In the face of intense worldwide opposition, Monsanto dropped its Terminator Seed technology in 1999. Hope Shand, research director of Rural Advancement Foundation International, a nonprofit international civil society organization headquartered in Winnipeg, Canada, said: "The company finally realized that *Terminator* will never win public acceptance. Monsanto would never have abandoned the profit-generating potential of sterile seeds just because it was an immoral technology. *Terminator* had become synonymous with corporate greed, and it was met with intense opposition all over the world."[3]

Regardless of the arguments in this case, it raises questions of alignment, congruence, and leadership such as, "What is the Cause at Monsanto?" Is it about "Food—Health—Hope," as claimed, helping to feed the world, improving the lives of farmers, and liberating the poor, or only about increasing shareholder value, raising the share price, overwhelming the competition, and dominating market share? If I work for an organization or leader who espouses these kinds of behaviors, attitudes, and strategies, how will they help me to live out my Destiny? Followers are rarely inspired by greed or selfish aims for very long. To inspire people over the long term, we need to ensure that the Cause is rooted in something higher than self-interest, something beyond personal or corporate gain, something that recognizes and invokes a higher purpose. Inspiration is created when followers understand how their Calling fits and serves this *higher purpose* and how this alignment will resonate for them. Inspiration is generated from a perfect fit among Destiny, Cause, and Calling—but the Cause must be meaningful or noble. Monsanto missed an opportunity by frightening people instead of framing their ambitions as a noble Cause and thus inspiring them.

Identifying and Aligning Passion

In the early pioneering days of Manpower Limited, part of what has today become the largest employer in the world, I was the CEO of a team committed to building one of the most people-centered, inspirational, and soulful businesses in the world. One of the reasons we became so successful was our total commitment to people and to honoring the Calling of each one of them. Instead of hiring "skills"—branch manager, controller, technical director, and so on—we simply committed to building the best team in the world. I had learned that finding skilled and talented people was relatively easy; what seemed to be far more difficult was to find people with *passion*. We knew that if we found talented but, more important, inspired and passionate people with a strong commitment to spirit and values, we would be able to build successful businesses around them. It was the passion and the spirit and the values we were building a company on, not a series of tasks or an agglomeration of functions.

One day an ex-helicopter pilot contacted us. He had heard about our Cause and wanted to be part of our dreams. As we got to know him, we knew that he would be a terrific human being to add to our team. He had the kind of passion we needed, and we agreed that we would all love to work together—but we weren't quite sure how. So we asked him what his Calling was. He told us he loved to fly and that he was a gifted pilot. We liked him very much, and, fortunately, he felt the same way about us. We invited him to become a member of our organization, although we had no idea what he would be doing. So we began to brainstorm ideas to align his Calling with our Cause. He described how he had been flying personnel between the mainland of Scotland and the North Sea oilrigs during the booming development phase of the North Sea oil industry. He explained that there were now many companies in this business, but that they were uninsured, dangerous, and in need of organizing and leadership. With his expert advice, we put a plan together that resulted in the formation of a new company to maintain the helicopter fleets servicing the oilrigs. He became the president of the new operation, and through his efforts, we became the industry leader in that field. We were always on the lookout for passionate people—"helicopter pilots," we called them—to inspire our business.

We repeated this approach many times during my 14 years with the organization. We found many wonderful people—not functions—who were drawn to our Cause, and we helped these "helicopter pilots" to align their Calling with our Cause, so they could create magical careers for themselves, while, at the same time, investing their passion in our Cause. We became the largest truck-driving organization in the country, we helped to design some of the most important arterial highways in the nation, we were the first company in our industry to sign an agreement with a labor union, and we pioneered information technology testing and training. The company became an international case study and an exemplar for people-centered growth and Values-centered Leadership®. The organization was hugely profitable and admired. We had a team assigned to receive visitors who toured the company daily to learn our leadership "secrets." And our "helicopter pilots" inspired and built our success by aligning their Destiny, Cause, and Calling.

Addressing an audience of 1,100 engineers at Pratt & Whitney, makers of the jet engines that power over half the commercial airlines in the world, I asked if they put their heart and soul into their engines. Because I ride on their jet engines three or four times a week, I had more than a passing interest in this matter. I told them that it would greatly comfort me to know that each engine is invested with the spirit and passion of each follower—rather like Japanese house-builders who carve their initials with pride into the beams of buildings, even though their personal hallmark will be forever hidden from the buyer somewhere deep in the structure. I would feel differently about those engines if I knew they were not just the result of Pratt & Whitney's famed engineering genius, but also the result of each employee's loving care. What I learned from the Pratt & Whitney people is that they consider every passenger riding on their jet engines a precious, sacred being and are, therefore, inspired to build the best jet engines in the world. This is Higher Ground Leadership at work and, in this case particularly, an inspiring confirmation for a frequent flyer like me.

Releasing the Music within You

Today, I run a worldwide consulting organization. The first question we ask prospective consultants who wish to become teachers of our work is, "What is your Calling?" Some people offer the trite responses we all learned from career counselors: "I love working with people," "I want to help people," or "I want to make a difference." But these have the feeling of mere bromides. Some people are afraid to own up to their heart's inner yearning and, therefore, die with their music still within them, intimidated, afraid, or unaware, and missing the opportunity to live the uniqueness within. But we press them for their truth. One very successful management consultant privately longed to be a classical pianist, but was afraid to reveal this in a "business setting." He felt that there would be no application for his talent in a bottom-line world. I told the consultant of my experience years ago, when I attended a workshop in which a pianist trained at the Julliard School of Music sat down in front of a grand piano and gave a virtuoso performance of Franz Liszt's Liebsträume No. 3 in A flat minor. Then he rose and addressed the audience of business executives. The audience applauded wildly to show their appreciation for his talented performance. But his purpose was just as much about business as it was music.

"Liszt was an entrepreneur," he began. "He wrote music that was impossible to play on anything that had been invented at that time. His music was simply too fast for keyboard instruments of the day. So the contemporary music industry created one for him. It became known as the pianoforte, what we now call the piano—an instrument designed to play at the speed that Liszt imagined in his mind—*bLisztering* speeds, you might say! In the middle of the nineteenth century, Liszt's genius and inventiveness energized an entire industry—just as entrepreneurial genius does today. It is the same now: Software developers write programs for which no hardware has been developed—hardware and microprocessor manufacturers respond to these entrepreneurial challenges with new machines and chips. Entrepreneurship and creativity always determine market directions, not the other way around. Liszt was not fazed by the limitations of available technology; he was an original thinker."

By using the analogy of a musical genius, the speaker was able to make his point vividly and in an entertaining way that the audience would never forget. He showed that Liszt was a breakthrough thinker, unconstrained by the limitations of available technology. He linked his gifts and knowledge of classical musicianship with a metaphor about modern technology to make his strategic business and leadership points. If being a pianist was this particular consultant's dream, I asked him, why couldn't he think outside the box, too—using his musical skills to teach leadership principles? If he was moved to follow his Calling with us, we could benefit from his musical skills to help us in our work—teaching values and spirituality in the workplace? His gifts could help us teach and inspire others to transform their cultures, if he was moved to align his Calling in service of our Cause.

I heard recently about a pastor in Colorado who has a passion for movies. Every week, he selects appropriate movies around which he can build a theme for his Sunday sermons. His Calling (apart from his ministry) is about movies, his Cause is to bring the Christian message to his congregation and beyond, and he has successfully aligned the two. His congregation is enthralled and growing, while other churches in the neighborhood struggle to reverse their declining attendance. This is what happens in the face of passion—the alignment of your Calling with a noble Cause in pursuit of a Destiny results in energy, enthusiasm, and vigor that inspires those who experience it.

You see, we need to connect the dots. If I want to be a pianist, and I truly believe that this is my Calling, the thing I was born to do, I need to ask the question, "How will my piano playing change the world? What difference will it make to others? How will it serve them and make the world a better place?" If I am a pastor and I love movies, I need to ask, "How can I use my passion, my Calling, to be a movie maven, to further the Cause to which I am connected?" This is how we validate our Calling. Then we connect the Calling to the Cause by asking, "How does my Calling serve the Cause?" In my case, my Calling is to "Lead and serve through my writing, speaking, and teaching." So the question I must ask is, "How will this invigorate my Cause?"

> All men should strive to learn before they die—what they are running from, and to, and why.
>
> James Thurber

A client, one of the largest pharmaceutical companies in the world, learned that one of their employees wanted to pursue her Calling as a scuba diver instead of a chemical engineer. An old story leader would have failed to connect the dots or even listen to this deep yearning for authenticity from an employee. But this employee was fortunate to have a Higher Ground Leader as her mentor, who pointed out that one of the company's divisions manufactured chemicals designed to remove barnacles from the hulls of ships. He then asked her if she would like to travel to Puerto Rico and do some underwater research on behalf of that division!

During one of Mount Carmel's 20 Higher Ground Leadership Retreats, the director of finance responsible for accounts receivable discovered that her Calling included music because she was a passionate pianist. So her leader, the CFO, bought a reconditioned piano, fixed it up, and placed it in the lobby of their building. Since then, during lunch hours, the director of finance entertains employees and visitors with her recitals on her new piano, releasing her rekindled passion for their enjoyment—as well as her own. In this way, she practices and develops her Calling, while contributing to the Cause of Mount Carmel: *Honoring every soul with loving service.*

There are no limits to the imagination when it comes to aligning Calling and Cause—we simply need to learn how to say yes instead of no. This is how we inspire people.

Understanding Your Gifts

In my book *Reclaiming Higher Ground: Creating Organizations that Inspire the Soul,* I argue that mastery is one of the *primary values* of outstanding leaders.[4] I define *mastery* as "Undertaking whatever you do, to the highest standards of which you are capable." A bonus for practitioners of mastery is that if they do it better than anyone else, they and others will reap handsome rewards. It is a wonderful law of life. If you cycle better than anyone else, like Lance Armstrong, or play hockey like Wayne Gretzky, or golf like Tiger Woods, or dance like Nureyev or Karen Kain, or sing like Pavarotti—or if you lead like Jeffrey Swartz of Timberland, James Blanchard of Synovus Financial Corp., Andrea Jung of Avon, John Thompson of Symantec, Colleen Barrett of Southwest Airlines, the late Bill Gore of W. L. Gore & Associates, Inc., Donald Ziraldo of Inniskillin Wines, Yvon Chouinard of Patagonia, Dave Duffield of PeopleSoft, John Mackey of Whole Foods Market, Joseph Swedish of Centura Health, Joe Calvaruso of Mount Carmel Health System, or Jack Lowe of TD Industries—not only will you accumulate spiritual and material wealth, but the energy of your Destiny, Cause, and Calling will create opportunities and jobs for others and revenues will blossom—as the track records of each of these examples attest.

Tiger Woods won the Masters championship when he was 20 years old, breezing past the best golfers in the world by a record 12 strokes. He was being hailed as the next Jack Nicklaus, considered by many to be the greatest golfer of all time. Where most players, even those twice his age, would have been content to practice more of what was working so well, Tiger Woods chose to pursue mastery and kaizen. He told his coach he wanted to overhaul the way he struck the ball.

"I knew I wasn't in the greatest position in my swing at the Masters," said Woods, "but my timing was great, so I got away with it. And I made almost every putt. You can have a wonderful week like that even when your swing isn't sound. But can you still contend in tournaments with that swing when your timing isn't as good? Will it hold up over a long period of time? The answer to those questions, with the swing I had, was no. I wanted to change that."[5] Tiger Woods knew his gifts and his potential, and he knew that, through greater mastery, he could raise the bar even higher than those who admired and coached him thought. In Chapter 7, we reviewed the importance of clarity, choice, and commitment. Tiger Woods chose the path of clarity—knowing what he wanted to do, choice—choosing to do it, and commitment—he and his coach Butch Harmon pounded hundreds of practice balls, reviewed tapes of the swing again and again, and did more of the same until he had reinvented his style—and thus achieved a new, higher level of mastery.

Leveraging Your Talents

We sometimes forget what our real gifts are and become distracted or unfocused, and this causes us to become confused about how we apply the magic of our Calling in the service of others. Sometimes the processes of our work, what we make, or the functions we provide—the means—become confused with the ends: *why* we do what we do. The ends, our Destiny and Cause, are far more important than the means with which we achieve them.

Some years ago, one of Manpower Limited's quarterly board meetings was being held close to Christmas. As the president of the company, I made a proposal that would engage us very directly in our community. The centerpiece of my suggestion was that we personally visit less fortunate families in the major urban areas in which we operated to deliver Christmas dinners to them.

The reaction to my proposal surprised me. The senior executive responsible for day-to-day operations raised his eyebrows and peered at me intently. "Are you crazy?" he asked.

What do you say to someone who asks if you are crazy after you have just suggested an act of generosity? I mumbled something in an effort to buy time while I collected my thoughts.

He looked me squarely in the eyes as he advised me: "We have built a business from scratch that today employs 72,000 people—10 years ago, those jobs didn't even exist. In all probability, each of those 72,000 people has at least one dependant and one friend. Therefore, the jobs we have created are directly or indirectly benefiting the lives of over 200,000 people. Creating over 70,000 new jobs is the finest work we could do for our community. Why would we divert our talent from this good work to something for which we are untrained and unprepared?"

He had a point.

Most of us want to support charities and it is good that we do so. But it is not the only way to give. If leadership is your Calling and your greatest mastery, it may be a better gift than cash because it can be leveraged into so much more. The most precious gift of all is your time and talent and, in sharing it, we share our best with others. As Lao-tzu said in the sixth century BC, "Give a man a fish, and you feed him for a day. Teach a man to fish, and you feed him for a lifetime."

Ever since my colleague taught me this lesson, I have politely declined most (but not all) requests for cash donations to charities. In my particular case (and I am not saying this is the same for everyone), giving money is like giving the fish. Whatever small talent I possess lies in leading organizations, inspiring others, and teaching others how to do the same, and I am more than prepared to share these gifts and my time for a worthwhile endeavor—to align my gifts with the Cause.

A great concert pianist might be asked to donate a day's income to charity, but the charity would gain more if they received the gift of her time and talent for a day. With this gift, they could organize a charity concert and collect all of the gate and box office receipts. The contribution by the great concert pianist remains the same but, through leveraging, the benefit to the charity is far greater. We are always greater when we align Destiny, Cause, and Calling.

The pursuit of mastery in the service of humanity is one of the greatest contributions we can make on this planet. The lesson is to be aware of our gifts and to share them in the best interests of others, to leverage them as strongly as possible. In this way, our Calling becomes our joy because it becomes joyful for others and aligned with a Cause.

Aligning Your Own Destiny, Cause, and Calling Statements

Some Clarifying Questions

Now that you have arrived at a measure of clarity about both the divine and the pragmatic purpose of your life, it is important to test the alignment of the components, because nothing is as reassuring as the certain knowing that you are living your life *on purpose*. The sense of wholeness and freedom that comes from this alignment can be completely uplifting.

Until we clearly identify and follow our own Destiny, making it real by defining and then following a Cause and doing this by using our gifts to serve—our Calling—we cannot be authentic leaders and help others to identify and follow their true paths. Higher Ground Leaders have a very clear understanding of their Destiny, Cause, and Calling. They have an intimate relationship with their personal purpose and the path that inspires them.

Another way to test the integrity of these statements is to reverse the order and test their flow (see Figure 10.1).

1. If I have found my true Calling, that unique intersection between talent and passion, and if I practice it with exquisite mastery, will it help me to achieve my Cause?

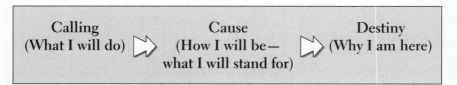

Calling	Cause	Destiny
(What I will do)	(How I will be— what I will stand for)	(Why I am here)

Figure 10.1   Calling to Cause to Destiny.

2. . . . and if I am successful in achieving my Cause, will it make a difference in the world; will it lead to my Destiny?

So aligning our Destiny, Cause, and Calling is an important step toward the validation of our lives, confirming that the new sense of clarity we are experiencing is not an illusion, that discovering and being thrilled to know our Destiny, Cause, and Calling is not just "an exercise," but a *real* arrival at a new stage in our personal growth and development.

A rigorous way of aligning your Destiny, Cause, and Calling, is to ask yourself some clarifying questions about how and whom you are serving and how the world could become a better place through the practice of your Calling.

Thus, you might ask:

1. Why is my Calling as I have described it?
2. How will my Calling serve my Cause and therefore lead to a better world?
3. How will my Cause contribute to a noble legacy?
4. If my Cause is successfully achieved, will it lead to the realization of my Destiny?

Answer these questions quietly to yourself.
Pause.
Reflect.
Then ask them all over again. Do this slowly, reflectively, and with sacred questioning, listening, and understanding. As we absorb the meaning and learning that comes from reflecting this way, we ease closer and closer to the essence of why we have been placed here on this Earth—our Destiny. We ease closer and closer to a true alignment between the tasks we do every day—our Calling; and how we will harness these skills and tasks in the interests of others—servant-leadership; the way we will make our time count while we are on Earth—our Cause; and the divine reason for doing these tasks, the reason we are here on this planet—our Destiny.[1]

The point is to ensure that the sacred practice of our Calling, using high levels of personal mastery and service, will inexorably contribute to the realization of our Cause, and that this will, in turn, lead us to our Destiny.

The Three "Whys?"

An old technique for testing the logic of an assumption is to ask "why" three times. Here is how it works: Beginning with your Destiny statement, ask three

"Whys" in consecutive order. Begin by asking and then answering the first question "Why?" fully, before asking and then answering the next question "Why?" and so on.

The idea is to test the logic of your Destiny, Cause, and Calling statements. For example, suppose you have written a Destiny statement like Diane Hoover's that I described in Chapter 4, *To generate spirit on Earth*, then you would ask the question like this: "Why?" meaning, "Why do I think it is a good idea to generate spirit on Earth?" "What would happen on Earth if more spirit were to be generated?" "What would generating more spirit on Earth lead to?" Perhaps your answer might be something like this: "People would love each other more, and the world would be more peaceful, and we would have greater reverence for each other and nature," and so you would offer this answer (or write it in your journal). It can be very helpful to ask a friend to be your learning partner and to be the one who asks you this question, and for them to take literal notes of your answers, without editorial comment.

> Forgive, O Lord, my little jokes on Thee
> And I'll forgive Thy great big one on me.
>
> Robert Frost

After repeating this sequence once, repeat the process by asking "Why?" again. Why is it important, and what would be the beneficial results if, to use the earlier example again, you had answered, "People would love each other more, and the world would be more peaceful, and we would have greater reverence for each other and nature"? Reflect on your answer, perhaps asking a friend or learning partner to pose the question to you and to fully record your responses in your journal.

Now let's repeat this process one last time by asking "Why?" yet again. Look at your response to the second "Why?" question. Using this statement, ask why this is so important, and what would be the beneficial results if the positive outcomes you have described to the second "Why?" question were to be realized. What improvements would result for the universe? Reflect on your answer, and again, ask a friend or learning partner to pose the question to you and to fully record your responses in your journal.

What this exercise will do for you is help you to polish the logic, intent, desired outcome, and language of your Destiny, Cause, and Calling. It will help you to align all three, so that they serve each other and lead to the achievement of each. Many people find it easier to start the other way around, by beginning with their Calling, and asking "Why?" "Why would I practice this mastery?" "What larger purpose will it lead to?" "How will the vision that I hold, the Cause that I live for, be advanced through the practice of my Calling?" Then one can ask

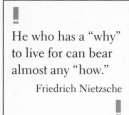

He who has a "why"
to live for can bear
almost any "how."

Friedrich Nietzsche

"Why?" again—"How will my Cause, if realized, lead to the achievement of my Destiny?" "How will my Cause contribute to the resolution of the Terrathreats?" Be sure that there is a solid, logical, and spiritual connection that flows from your Calling to your Cause and to your Destiny: "If I practice my Calling really well, it will lead to the achievement of my Cause, and if my Cause is realized, it will enable me to live out my Destiny."

Sleep on It

Defining your Destiny, Cause, and Calling is no small accomplishment. Something this important in your life is unlikely to be accomplished quickly or without reflection. Teri Watson, vice president of marketing at Mount Carmel, describes her journey:

> When I was at the Higher Ground Leadership retreat with the Secretan faculty, and we began to work on defining our Destiny, Cause, and Calling, I was terrified. I thought "Oh no, here's where we get into all that philosophical stuff about the meaning of life." One of the first exercises we did was to read over a list of words and select those that "spoke" to us. Well, I sat there and analyzed every word, assessing whether it was something I would like to be known for, whether it was a good word, and so on. This was very frustrating. Eventually, I decided to just go with the flow. So, I began again and read each word without analysis or judgment. Soon, I had a list of words that spoke to me, although I wasn't sure why. By the end of the evening, although I did not have a final Destiny, Cause, and Calling, I felt a growing sense of comfort that I was getting closer, and I gained an important insight during the process. The insight was that, even though I do not work in direct patient care, the fact that I was drawn to healthcare means something. It is a way that I can use my skills in planning and marketing to help people. I could have gone into marketing toothpaste, laundry detergent, or underwear. But I didn't. I was called into healthcare because it was a way that I could help others (even though I didn't know it at the time) by planning new services and programs to meet community needs and educating people about treatments, hospital services, and how to stay healthy. And that made me feel good—as marketing often gets a bad rap for taking advantage of people or manipulating attitudes. After the retreat, I didn't think much about my Destiny, Cause, and Calling for several months. Then, one day, I got my notes out and looked through them. I played around with words for a while and

thought about what I really enjoyed doing: (1) communicating information in a way that even difficult messages are easily understood; (2) creating things—whether it's sewing, painting, or completing a PowerPoint presentation; and (3) helping others figure out what they need to do. I played around with these thoughts and before long, I had what I think is pretty close to being a final version: Destiny: *To bring clarity and courage into the world*; Cause: *To help others make wise decisions and navigate through uncertain waters*, and Calling: *To serve others through creative thinking, communication, and action.* I have always enjoyed my work, but the exercise of exploring my Destiny, Cause, and Calling gave me a deeper awareness and understanding of how my work is important and how I am using my talents to make a difference in the world. I encourage everyone to explore their Destiny, Cause, and Calling. It could prove to be a very valuable experience!

When you have completed this portion of this book, find a special piece of paper—parchment, or a card that has special meaning for you, or perhaps your journal. Write the three statements of your Destiny, Cause, and Calling, such as they are at this stage, on this special writing material and place the writing under your pillow, and sleep on all this for the night. You have done an awesome thing—something very few people ever do in their entire lives—you have clarified your life's purpose and vastly improved the likelihood that you will live a meaningful and fulfilling life that enhances the lives of others and our planet—a life lived *on purpose*.

Tomorrow morning, look over your Destiny, Cause, and Calling with the eyes of a fresh day. Do they resonate with you? Are you excited? Moved? Challenged? Do you feel whole and clear? If you feel complete, then, for now, this part of the task of changing your life is done. (I say "for now" because, practically speaking, self-discovery is never "done.") You have greatly increased your capacity to inspire others and serve the world.

Read on!

CHAPTER 11

Step Five: Serving Followers

Service to others is the rent you pay for living on this planet.
Marian Wright Edelman, U.S. social reformer, lawyer, and author[1]

We encourage violence when we practice violence. The dysfunctional actions we observe in others are sometimes the response of their unconscious self to our conscious behavior. Old story leaders focus the majority of their attention on the attainment of the goals that meet the needs of their personality. The selfish pursuit of budgets, targets, quotas, performance criteria, goals, strategies, plans, and so on will elicit selfish behavior in response. Violence and love are at opposite ends of a continuum, with selfishness at one end and loving service at the other. What we give is what we get. This is one of the foundations of Higher Ground Leadership.

After achieving pure clarity about their Destiny, defining and living the Cause, reaffirming their commitment to their own Calling, and coaching others to find and master theirs and then aligning that Calling with the Cause, the Higher Ground Leader sincerely asks others, "How may I serve you?" More than anything else, we yearn for leaders who genuinely seek to serve us, for this is a signal of love—and love inspires.

The all-too-frequent tendency to focus so much of their time on their own needs—achieving their own goals, objectives, and strategies—can cause old story leaders to become blind to the needs of others. Self-focused people tend to invest all their available energy into motivating or manipulating others, dreaming up incentives that will cause others to meet their goals. They will tell you that this is demonstrating their ability to focus on the goal. In truth, they do this because they need to—selfish behavior does not have inspiration as its primary objective. On the contrary, it

If you wish to be a leader, you will be frustrated, for very few people wish to be led. If you aim to be a servant, you will never be frustrated.

Frank F. Warren

causes people to feel used, alienated, and ignored. When we are self-focused, we send repeated signals to others that their needs are secondary to ours. In this environment, resentment is caused because we sense that the relationship is merely functional, that we are viewed, and being motivated, merely as a means to an end.

Servant-Leadership

The first priority of the Higher Ground Leader is to serve. The servant-leader knows that others yearn to be heard, to be engaged—not in debate, but in genuine dialogue—not mind to mind, but heart to heart—a dialogue that springs from a loving intent and thus inspires.

Service is the raison d'être of the Higher Ground Leader. It is in serving others that we best serve ourselves. Once we have defined our Destiny, Cause, and Calling, and have aligned them tightly, then we can ask, "How may I serve you?"

Here is how Robert Greenleaf, who first coined the term, described servant-leadership:

> The servant-leader is servant first . . . It begins with the natural feeling that one wants to serve, to serve first. Then conscious choice brings one to aspire to lead. He or she is sharply different from the person who is leader first, perhaps because of the need to assuage an unusual power drive or to acquire material possessions. For such it will be a later choice to serve—after leadership is established. The leader-first and the servant-first are two extreme types. Between them, there are shadings and blends that are part of the infinite variety of human nature.
>
> The difference manifests itself in the care taken by the servant-first to make sure that other people's highest priority needs are being served. The best test, and difficult to administer, is: do those served, grow as persons; do they, while being served, become healthier, wiser, freer, more autonomous, and more likely themselves to become servants? And, what is the effect on the least privileged in society; will they benefit, or, at least, will they not be further deprived?[2]

Once, working with a client who was the senior partner of a very large dental practice, I gave this advice: "Tomorrow morning, please open your management meeting by asking everyone the following question: 'How may I serve you?'

You may feel a little odd, even awkward, but please just try it and see what happens." The next day, he called me to report on the outcome. He said, "You should have seen the looks on their faces . . . their jaws all dropped, and they just stared at me. They had never heard me say anything like this. I always wanted something *from* them. Here I was offering to *serve* them. They were stunned. Afterwards, they told me that it had the effect of completely changing the dynamics and the chemistry of the team. It was amazing."

After working with the American Heart Association, Tina Zarifes, the regional director in Los Angeles, asked me how to invite Larry King to become the honorary chair of the annual Griffith Park Heart Walk in Los Angeles. I suggested to her that she avoid the usual approach of building a watertight case, with a snappy proposal, to "sell" him on why he should become the honorary chair of the walk. Instead, I suggested that she ask him some questions, such as, "How can I serve *you*?" "What are *you* looking for when you become involved with charities or sponsorships?" "What are *you* trying to achieve in

> There is no higher religion than human service. To work for the common good is the greatest creed.
>
> Woodrow Wilson

your life?" "How can the American Heart Association help you to achieve some of your life's goals?" "How can I serve *you* through the AHA?" She called me a few days later to let me know she had used this approach, and Larry King had agreed to become the chairperson of the Los Angeles AHA Griffith Park Heart Walk.

Joseph Swedish of Centura says, "I find myself consistently asking the question of people, 'How can I serve you?'—it's just that simple—and the reaction is shock! When posed at the end of a conversation, it's a question that is taken as a very constructive inquiry, particularly because it probes their needs. It doesn't focus on *my* needs. It opens up a dialogue that previously would not have been there. My life as an executive, in the main, is focused on problem solving, and so, shifting emphasis from me to you when you are dealing with a problem with someone, by asking, 'How can I serve you?' is very disarming. Often, a person with a problem is dealing from a state of frustration. There's friction. There is fear. So, when you turn the conversation by saying, 'How can I serve you?' it removes all of that baggage, and it gets to the root cause of the issue, and it puts the other person's needs ahead of yours. There have been a lot of success stories at Centura of Higher Ground Leaders who have risen to the occasion and are now doing more because of this approach. Our commitment to serve others has inspired them to go beyond the normal boundaries."

The Ideal Parent: The Ultimate
Servant-Leader

The parent is one of the most enduring role models in our society. For some, the experience of the parent/child relationship is one characterized by power and control, permissions and requests, giving and taking. For these people, the result is that they become emotional orphans—their parents don't know who they are. The corporation, the employer, the government, the law enforcement officer, the priest, the educator, and the physician all occupy a similar "parent" role in which we expect them to provide control, exert their power, and supply answers, while never really knowing us. Perhaps we have been drawing the wrong conclusions and learning the wrong lessons from the role model of our parents.

Somewhere deep in our hearts, we never lose the need to be cared for. If I think about some of the moments of pure joy in my life, many are associated with being nurtured—as when someone defends me, spoils me, bakes me a cake, rubs my back, gives me a hug, tells me a story, cares about me when I am unwell, or straightens my clothing. Do we ever "mature" to the point where we become indifferent to the magic ministrations of a caring soul? Is there not an important lesson for us here? Should we not all learn a little of the magic of kind and caring mothers and fathers?

At their best, parents offer unconditional love, consistent communications, support, loyalty, and commitment to followers, even as they invite discipline and order. They create community and bonding among "family." They promote growth and development, health and safety, ethics and morality, beauty and comfort, nourishment and balance, spirit and values. They inspire and teach, always in a loving way. They are boosters who cheer and encourage. They hug and serve. They make peace. They provide wisdom, vision, and hope. Aren't these the finer qualities of any inspiring person? This suggests that the model of the ideal parent may be the first and best example of servant-leadership that each of us can experience. What greater characteristics could we be looking for in a coach, mentor, leader, or friend?

People Whisperers

For many of us, the parent in us shows up strongly in our relationship with animals—we are drawn to nurturing, protecting, serving, and loving them. Real animal lovers have never relied exclusively on the theories of Ivan Petrovich Pavlov (1849–1936), the Russian physiologist and Nobel laureate, best known for his studies of conditioned reflex behavior. He became famous for his linear theory of motivation: Punish failure until it stops, and reward success in order to encourage its repetition. Over the years, Pavlovian philosophy has evolved into a kind of meta-theory, and the behaviorist school of psychology developed by John Watson grew from Pavlovian thinking and has influenced our theories of leadership ever since. Most animal training is based on this principle, as are most reward and compensation systems. Most leadership and motivational theories also follow this philosophy.

Those who enjoy a loving bond with their pets have always sensed that these harsh techniques might indulge the teacher, but they don't do much for the student. Smacking a dog when it piddles on the rug is not a loving action. To the nose of a dog, one hundred times more sensitive than that of a human, a swat on the snout with a folded newspaper is the human equivalent of a whack on the side of the head with a steel girder. Few sensitive beings, whether they have two legs or four, relish having a folded newspaper scrunched in their ears every time they displease another.

Similarly, violent techniques are frequently used to train horses. We "break" horses. Horrifying though it may be to some, horses are "broken" by blindfolding them, hitting and whipping them, lassoing their feet, and tying them to stakes — all in an attempt to break their spirit. Cowboys are called bronco-*busters*.

This paradigm of motivation isn't what happens in a loving relationship. Let's look at the parental model of servant-leadership for a moment. When a baby is learning to walk, we don't punish it. If a baby falls over, we don't say, "Boy, you're dumb. I don't think you're ever going to get it. I'm not sure you have the potential to be a good walker. I'm going to give you one more chance, and then you're toast! Now, get with it!" When your toddler first tries to raise herself from the floor and collapses after two paces, you pick her up, dust her off, tell her how beautiful and wonderful she is, and how much you love her, and then start all over again. Parents repeat this process in a loving, supportive way until they, and their children, are rewarded with those magical "baby's first steps." We praise them and love them, speak to their souls and hug them into learning. We call this inspiration, a successful system that is based on love, not on the fear-drenched, carrot-and-stick formulae of Pavlov. Children who grow up in such a nurturing and supportive culture become whole adults. My wife and I are excellent examples of this theory. Her adoring parents praised and inspired her to success, whereas I was alternately rewarded and kicked around by mine, depending on how well I met their ever-increasing demands. Both my wife and I love our parents, but from my perspective, my struggles to shed the baggage I accumulated in my early life have seemed, to me at least, harder than hers. When my wife came home with straight As and one B, her parents praised her and encouraged her. When I did the same, my parents scolded me for the errant B. It has taken me decades to realize that I do not have to be perfect by someone else's yardstick in order to be a complete and spiritual human. My parents loved me and did the best they could with what they knew at the time when it was common to transfer Pavlovian theory to child-raising—but this is still true for many parents today.

> ❚
> Lead and inspire people. Don't try to manage and manipulate people. Inventories can be managed, but people must be led.
> Ross Perot
> ❚

Leadership theory has not advanced much from this basic model—at home or at work—we still practice the carrot-and-stick method of leadership. We reward behavior we wish to encourage with incentives, bonuses, raises, benefits, promotions, and so forth; and we discourage the behavior we want to see less of with salary and job freezes, budget cuts, poor performance reviews, and even termination or dismissal. Many practice a similar style at home, too. Our leadership practice has not evolved much in the century since Pavlov first introduced this thinking.

As long as we remain slaves to the Pavlovian concept of motivational leadership, we will fail to inspire. There is a better model for our age. The work of horse whisperers offers a perfect metaphor. Horse whispering is the age-old technique that favors silent communication and physical cues to teach and communicate with horses. Horse whisperers modify the behavior of a horse with hand gestures and body movements, instead of yanking on the reins, or using spurs and whips. They use touch and gesture to create a spiritual connection with a horse, sending a clear message of love. This enables a horse whisperer to take a wild stallion into a barn and emerge two hours later with a rideable mount.

> ❚
> My life's goal is to leave the world a better place than I found it, for horses and people, too.
> Monty Roberts
> ❚

Horse whispering has gained much publicity in recent years, following the publication of Monty Roberts' book, *The Man Who Listens to Horses*, and the release of the movie starring Robert Redford, *The Horse Whisperer*. As a result, the old story of horse training is slowly changing. We need the same thing to happen with people.

We need *people whisperers*.

The old story of motivation, leadership, and training, and the old way of getting a horse to accept a saddle and rider was to break its spirit—old story leadership. A horse whisperer is a Higher Ground Leader who, instead of motivating, inspires, who avoids bribing a horse or cheating it by withholding food, and instead copies and perfects the actions of the matriarchal mare who causes the other horses to yield when moving through their midst—a lesson from parenting.

Kent Williamson, a horse whisperer from Millarville, Alberta, says, "If a person leads a horse by pulling or forcing, the horse learns from day one to resist pressure and go against it. From then on, you always have to make the horse do things, as opposed to asking and maybe receiving through willingness." Monty Roberts, from Solvang, California, argues that no one has the right to motivate by saying, "You must or I will hurt you" to any other creature.

This includes humans. We need to inspire the behavior we seek through love. This requires us to communicate in a way that empathizes with others, by communicating spiritually with them and giving spiritual power to them—the Higher Ground Leader in action. The result is an act of conspiracy—from *con*, which means with, and *spirare*, which means to breathe—to breathe together. Conspiring together is to serve each other, as horse whisperers do when truly serving the needs of the horse by conspiring with them. We truly breathe together so that we both grow toward our full potential.

Williamson demonstrates this philosophy as he moves his body toward one of the pressure points of a horse, its hip, to cause the animal to step away. When he turns to walk, the animal follows. It is about engaging the spirit, not breaking it. As Monty Roberts puts it, "The object of the teacher is to create an environment in which the student can learn."

This new logic of gentleness over violence, inspiration over motivation, has led the U.S. Bureau of Land Management to set up a program in several states called Wild Horse Inmate Programs (WHIPs). When prison inmates learn and experience the techniques of horse whispering, coaching wild stallions with love and sensitivity instead of aggression and violence, they often hold this attitude for the rest of their lives. If hardened criminals can be transformed this way, replacing terror with trust and shedding their violent habits in favor of relationships built on compassion and caring, then so can our leaders, in the corporate setting, in organizations, or at home.

Michael served his third prison term at the Susanville, California, correctional center, this time with a 20-month sentence for possession of methamphetamines and assaulting a police officer. "You've got to take your time [with a horse]," he says. "I was kind of nervous when I first got out here. But you can't win a fight with a wild horse. They'll kill you first." The spiritual connection he has made with horses has deeply affected him.

"This is about as good as it gets for me," he said then. "I've learned a lot here, and I like getting off the prison yard. Every horse I've trained I'd like to take home with me." A plumber by training, Michael decided to work with horses following his release, hoping to own and train horses.

We may respect a leader, but the ones we love are servant-leaders. They are the ones who teach with love and who learn and grow with us, listen and empathize, and honor us from deep within their souls—thus making a spiritual connection together—they are people whisperers.

Like Higher Ground Leadership, horse whispering is taught through experience, by apprenticing with masters, as I did with Jim Scheinfeld, who was one of my servant-leaders. It is a gift that is passed on, like the wisdom of elders. One of the dozen horse whisperers in North America is Buck Brannaman of Sheridan, Wyoming, who learned from another horse whisperer named Ray Hunt, who teaches "thinking harmony with horses" at his horse clinic in Ribera, New Mexico. In turn, Hunt's own mentor was a legendary master teacher named Tom Dorrance, who still teaches a technique he calls "true unity," the willing communication between horse and human. Notice how all these techniques and metaphors transfer easily to people. Instead of saying "the willing communication between horse and human," we could just as easily say "the willing communication between human and human."

It may be more than mere coincidence that many horse whisperers were raised in abusive environments—Brannaman, Hunt, and Dorrance all had abusive backgrounds ranging from alcoholism to beating, violence, and abandonment. The personal experience of these three legendary horse whisperers has perhaps informed their philosophy of life and leadership—they learned the hard way that there is a better way. Monty Roberts' father, Marvin, a Salinas, California, horse trainer, hit him with stable chains and dominated horses with similarly rough treatment. "I believed there was a better way," said Roberts, and he decided to find it.

Growing up in Whitehall, Montana, Brannaman says, "I was always kind of scared of my dad. He was pretty mean to us boys. I remember we'd come home from school for lunch, and my mom would drop me off at school again on the way to work. She was a waitress in a town about 50 miles away, and my dad had a shoe repair and saddle shop in town. I remember from about eight or nine years old, I would beg her not to go to work every day, 'cause I was terrified of being at home alone with my dad for the four or five hours after school, before she'd get home."

A domestic heritage of violence, aggression, punishment, control, and abuse of power can result in different lessons. Some of us will carry forward the cellular memory of our familial experiences and, through projection, convert them into negative models for parenting or running organizations. These experiences are stored as anger, which is released as violence and aggression—which hides in the shadow. This results in organizations and families that are as dysfunctional as their families were because their leadership philosophies are modeled on the leadership experiences they grew up with. Many people recognize the pathologies of their families in their organizations, having seen and experienced them in their earlier lives.

Other leaders take the same experiences and convert them into different lessons. One of the leaders who loomed large in my early career was as paranoid as anyone I have known. He once hired a private detective to report on the off-work activities of my sales team. But we learn from every experience, and I learned what *not to do* from this teacher.

Some horse trainers have imported their macho experiences into their work—these are the bronco-busters. Horse whisperers have learned a different lesson from the same experiences. They have learned that horses should be "started," not "broken," because an intelligent horse has as much to teach us as we have to teach it. This is the heritage of horse whispering handed down from Tom Dorrance to Ray Hunt and Buck Brannaman. As Ray Hunt puts it, "You're not working on the horse, you're working on yourself." Years ago, Ray Hunt asked Tom Dorrance where he'd learned his skills. Dorrance replied, "Ray, I learned it from the horse." This is universal wisdom. We learn it from the follower.

The metaphor of the horse whisperer transfers easily to the servant-leader. Higher Ground Leaders transfer power to the follower, as a horse whisperer does to a horse. The result is a union, which is a magical thing to observe. This expression of honoring that horse whisperers and people whisperers make to each other by serving is vital. We each need to know that others regard us as sacred. Then we become inspired.

"How Can I Be Kind, Instead of Right?"

Often, being a servant-leader can be made easier by asking ourselves the question, "Who am I serving right now, my ego or the soul of another being?" When our relationships or our communications become tangled or toxic, it is often because we are serving ourselves and our ego's need to be right. Next time you are engaged in a heated discussion with a supplier, customer, or colleague—or your spouse or children—pause for a moment and ask yourself the quintessential question of the Higher Ground Leader: "How can I be kind, instead of right?"

Being right serves the ego; being kind serves the soul. Being right serves me; being kind serves us. Being kind inevitably leads us to the question, "How may I serve you?"

Serving others and practicing loving kindness is not the first business model that springs to mind when we think about corporate executives or leaders of organizations. This may be because we unconsciously train aggression into contemporary leaders. When Cornell University asked 250 business school students what traits they thought made a great leader, they put being "results-oriented" at the top of their list, and 60 percent said they admired slash-and-burn downsizers like "Chainsaw" Al Dunlap.[3] Jack Welch, the former CEO of General Electric Co., has been routinely ranked as the most admired and respected executive in America. He was voted "most respected" CEO in four out of five *Industry Week* annual CEO surveys.[4] At the same time, he was also notorious among those who knew him for his toughness and profanity. *Fortune* magazine reported that Jack Welch "conducts meetings so aggressively that people tremble. He attacks almost physically with his intellect—criticizing, demeaning, ridiculing, humiliating." During his 20-year reign as CEO, Welch, aka "Neutron Jack," re-engineered nearly 200,000 people out of their jobs in his relentless pursuit to be number one or two in every market segment in which General Electric operates, and he routinely fired the lowest performing 10 percent of teams. In Welch's biography, *At Any Cost: Jack Welch, General Electric and the Pursuit of Profit,* Thomas F. O'Boyle describes General Electric as a company "managed by threat and intimidation rather than encouragement."[5]

> Beginning today, treat everyone you meet as if they were going to be dead by midnight. Extend to them all the care, kindness, and understanding you can muster, and do so with no thought of any reward. Your life will never be the same again.
>
> Og Mandino

When we pay tribute to and celebrate the characteristics of violence and intimidation, holding them up to be the qualities of exemplary leaders, what message are we sending current and future leaders? What kind of model are we encouraging them to follow? In the case of many old story led organizations, the numerous labor disputes, financial woes, and corporate scandals they have endured suggest that old story leadership inevitably contributes to the paradox of our times—profits are up, but people are down.

Contrast this aggressive style with the Higher Ground Leadership practiced by Joe Calvaruso of Mount Carmel, who observes:

> I often wonder, how we can show more love, more servant-leadership, to the nurses and caregivers on the floor? They're so stretched, they're so tired, they have such a huge patient volume. Two of my colleagues said, "Let's have a

service where people volunteer their free time—lunch time, whatever—and use it to relieve the clinical workers, and we'll invite people to sign up for it." I've completed several shifts myself where I visit the Emergency Department for an hour. I say, "Okay, you go to lunch and take a break. I'm going to do some chores for you to help you catch up." Like cleaning up all the soiled laundry baskets, wrapping them up, and taking them down to the laundry chute, transporting patients, getting meals and taking them to patients, so that nurses don't have to make those trips, but instead can enjoy their own lunch. We restock the supplies in patient rooms, fill up their water bottles, and numerous other little chores to which nurses and caregivers dedicate so much of their time. We call this group of volunteers, who have full-time jobs elsewhere in the hospital, "Provide A Loving Service"—PALS for short, and it's called the PALS program. Last year, four thousand hours of volunteer time were given—people providing a loving service, a gesture of love to the caregivers—living our Cause of "Honoring Every Soul with Loving Service."

Sacred Listening

I have often marveled at the subtle messages that lie quietly in the construction of our language, just waiting to be discovered. Have you noticed, for example, that the words *sacred* and *scared* have the same letters? Does the word *sacred* scare you? What is the relationship between sacred and scared for you? It takes courage to move from the old paradigm and into a new one where we see the sacredness in everything—are we too scared to do this?

The words *listen* and *silent* are the same, too, save for the order of the letters. We cannot listen clearly until we are silent. Do you silence your mental chatter, your internal critics, and your distractions so that you may listen more deeply to others and yourself? We cannot hear until we are silent, until we suspend our opinions, arguments, and judgments and deeply drink from that to which we are listening. We cannot serve others until we have listened to them, so that we can learn how best to serve them. Our potential as inspiring servant-leaders rests on our willingness to be silent and listen and not be to scared of the sacredness that exists in every relationship, and to engage in what I call *sacred listening* with others in order to serve them.

I recently told an audience of nearly 1,500 people that if I ever had the use of a magic wand, I would abolish all performance appraisal systems, which are

> !
> The most important thing in communication is to hear what isn't being said.
>
> Peter F. Drucker
> !

universally reviled by both the appraisers and the appraisees. Often, their main purpose is to serve as instruments of power and control over others. I added that since organizational theorists have encouraged us to separate performance appraisals from salary reviews, this is a practice now followed by most organizations, yet few people are naïve enough to believe that a poor performance appraisal will not be reflected in a subsequent salary review. The audience erupted into spontaneous applause (a frequent reaction whenever I make this observation), which then swelled into a standing ovation. At the intermission, the managers of the organization pulled me aside for a private discussion. "This organization has just spent a small fortune on consultants who have overhauled our performance appraisal system and replaced it with a new one that we will be using for many years into the future, so we would appreciate it if you did not talk about new approaches and alternatives," they admonished me. It was clear that they did not listen to what they had just heard. I asked the manager if she realized that when 1,500 employees applaud, it represents empirical research—they were sending a message that they disagreed with her. She shrugged, citing the need to be competitive, to increase performance, to reduce costs, to focus greater effort toward customers, and to not make leaders look like they were out of touch (which, I pointedly observed, they were).

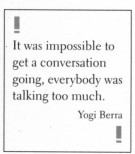

> ▌
> It was impossible to get a conversation going, everybody was talking too much.
>
> Yogi Berra
> ▌

We serve best by listening and then acting constructively on what we have heard. We alienate people when we believe that "we know better than they do." Higher Ground Leaders understand the wisdom I described earlier: employees are the customers of the leader—our job as Higher Ground Leaders is to meet the needs of our customer/followers, just as well as we have learned to meet the needs of our customer/buyers.

We can listen to ourselves, too, by asking ourselves questions and listening to the truth of our inner voices. We might ask: Is what I am doing inspiring others right now? If I were the other person, would I feel inspired by these words? If I say (or do) what I intend, will it inspire? Before I make my point, how can I be sure it inspires? Are my colleagues inspired? What inspires this person—how can I serve them? How will I live in order to inspire?

The Higher Ground Leader as Mystic

We are better able to serve when we view each other with a sense of wonder, not judgment, with the awareness that greater potential exists within us all that is not always apparent. Everyone is gifted and wondrous in their own special way, and Higher Ground Leaders trust in the potential of the Universe—which includes each other. Thus, Higher Ground Leaders are mystics, because inspiration and mysticism are handmaidens. If we fail to see the beauty in each other, we fail to honor each other, and where there is no honor, there can be no inspiration. Seeing the beauty in others is to love them, and from love flows inspiration. Every person who is inspired is a person who is loved.

How shall we define a *mystic?* A mystic is a person who sees the wonder in all of life, who looks at a flower and marvels at the colors, the sheen, the geometry, the fragrance, the radiance, the poetry, and the love within. The beauty of life continuously confounds the mystic. For the mystic, there is wonder and beauty in every boulder, in the hollow of a hill, in the symphony of a songbird, in the crouch of a cat, in the hocks of a horse, in the contours of a cloud, in the shimmer of a star, in the surge of the surf, in the rhythm of a river, in the flourish of a phrase, in the jest in a joke, in the laugh of a lover. When presented with a glorious sunset, a rapturous symphony, a ravishing sonnet, or brilliant artistry, a mystic loses all sense of space and time. A mystic sees the wonder in the shadow side of life, too—in the slums, war zones, places of pestilence, and in the suffering that surrounds us. When we effortlessly connect with the wonder of life, savoring the ceaseless beauty of the universe, then we fully engage our soul. When we watch the wonders of the world, we are watching God watch us. This is the moment when we become mystics. It is in this instant that we become woven seamlessly into the fabric of the universal consciousness. It is in this moment that we see the beauty, the potential, the marvel, and the soul of every person. This is the moment when we breathe with God—this is the divine moment when we become inspired and therefore are inspiring.

> There are two ways to live your life. One is as though nothing is a miracle. The other is as though everything is a miracle.
>
> Albert Einstein

The corporate mystic sees life as play, not work. Nature does not engage in work—it indulges in play. If we were to look upon the activities of nature as work, they would become dismal and boring, in the same way that work appears dismal and boring to a lot of people. But by looking at the activities of nature, or the activities of our work as play, as a mystic would, they become filled with wonder—mystical. This is a concept that corporate mystics carry into their work lives, and the difference in the energy they create around themselves is palpable as a result.

To be a mystic, we must accept others as they are, honoring them as sacred rather than assessing them from a place of judgment, or projecting our values onto them. We don't judge a rock or the sea—they simply are. If we view each other in this way, we will appreciate others as unique testimonies to the genius of God. God made no weeds, no runts, no losers, and no failures. We are all sacred, and if each of us stands in the light of another who views us this way, we will inspire and be inspired. When we are inspired, it is because we feel the unconditional love of another, hearing their advice as loving support, not criticism, and their teaching as healing wisdom. The Higher Ground Leader, that is, someone who loves and is loved, creates an inspired partner who loves and is loved.

Every set of circumstances and every relationship are an opportunity to give and receive that love, because everyone can be full of love and laughter; being able to see and draw it from all those around us allows us to stay in the stream of an inspired life. And, if you can see the sacredness in everybody, then you can't fail to respect everybody. Then you are a Higher Ground Leader who can *guide the contribution of brilliance from others*—which we will describe in the next chapter.

Being the Change You Seek in the World

Moral excellence, righteousness, goodness: these are the sweet sounds of virtue. She is the bond of all perfections and the heart of all life's satisfactions. Virtue makes men sensible, alert, understanding, wise, courageous, considerate, joyous, truthful, and visionary. Virtue is the sun of our lesser world, the sky of good conscience. She is so beautiful that she finds favor with both God and man. There is nothing lovely without her, for she is the essence of wisdom, and all else is folly. Greatness must be measured in terms of virtue, and not in terms of fortune. Virtue alone makes a man worth loving in life, and worth remembering after death.

—Baltasar Gracian

We must be the change we wish to see in the world.

Mahatma Gandhi

As leaders, when we talk of serving others, it is the intentions that count more than our words; what we do counts more than what we say. Followers are more interested in our integrity than our speeches about integrity, and their antennae are sensitive and efficient to any possible incongruities. People whose souls have been trampled at work yearn for leaders who are prepared to serve them. They want to know that when leaders have choices, the well-being of people comes before the bottom line. In any environment, we all value and love colleagues, friends, and family who value doing right more than doing things right, and being kind more than right.

Our intense and sometimes singular focus on meeting goals and targets—the ends—often clouds our judgment, causing us to overlook the lack of virtue in our means. The old story adage that the ends justify the means is seldom true. No ends are worthwhile if we must pursue shabby means to achieve them. Life is often a better measure than profit.

Being committed to serving others is a virtuous practice because it is nearly always a spiritual one, *and the most profitable practice in the long run.* In other words, for the Higher Ground Leader, the means *always* determines the ends. This raises a number of practical questions. First, how do we ensure that our strategy flows from our values, rather than the other way around? Old story leaders begin with strategy and then adopt the values that fit. Higher Ground Leaders develop their unshakable values first and then develop strategies that flow from them.

So, before we invite others to co-develop and implement strategy, we must be sure of our spiritual underpinnings. We need to ask difficult questions in order to test the mettle of our values: Are we pursuing noble values? Are we serving others at least as much,

> Pure goals can never justify impure or violent action . . . They say the means are after all just means. I would say means are after all everything. As the means, so the end. . . . If we take care of the means, we are bound to reach the end sooner or later.
>
> Mahatma Gandhi

if not more, than ourselves? Are we treading lightly on the planet and being kind to the environment? Are we ennobling the spirit? Are we doing all that we can to clarify the relationship between spirituality and our work and life? Are we leaving a noble legacy? Is what we are doing meaningful, just, and loving?

Research by Towers Perrin shows that five-year shareholder return improved significantly in organizations where employees felt strongly positive about their work—on average, companies saw a 150 percent improvement in shareholder return for a 95 percent increase in positive passionate emotions toward work, over five years.[6] Being a servant-leader and inspiring people is good for the bottom line.

Higher Ground Leaders invest just as much time encouraging deeper spiritual and metaphysical awareness among followers, introducing higher principles, and the wisdom teachings of history as they do coaching them to greater efficiency and effectiveness. David Overton, CEO of the wildly successful

Cheesecake Factory of Calabasas Hills, California, asks waiters and waitresses to send "a little love" to customers, along with their delicious desserts. In his restaurants, "Stream of Life" murals featuring Sufi and other spiritual motifs decorate the ceilings. Overton uses astrology and numerology to optimize each new restaurant's "birth date." Overton, who studied comparative religion while at college, is very open about, and committed to, his Sufi beliefs, even wearing a winged Sufi heart ring on his hand, a symbol that is also discreetly in evidence on every menu. But the impact of these philosophies is much deeper. It helps provide the underpinnings of Overton's "philosophy of treating people." At an employee training meeting, Executive Vice-President Linda Candioty told an audience of 30 new employees, "The customers come in to eat and pay and leave, but they deserve something more. It might just be some love."

> Example is not the main thing in influencing others. It is the only thing.
>
> Albert Einstein

It is a mistake to think that weaving spiritual underpinnings into business organizations might lead to distraction or poor performance. On the contrary, it helps them to become more focused. The Cheesecake Factory averages among the highest sales per unit and the fastest growth rates in the industry; it exports to many countries, has spun off a bakery sideline, and completed a successful IPO and is now listed on NASDAQ. Good servers earn over $40,000 a year, managers over $150,000—and a new leased BMW.[7]

A few years ago, I conducted a research project for one of the leading reinsurance companies in the world. Our goal was to determine the reasons for the sustained loyalty of their top 30 clients. The presidents and top executives of these VIP clients were flown in from around the world and invited to a roundtable session in which they were asked some 300 questions. Their responses were captured anonymously through the use of individual keypads connected directly to our proprietary computer systems. After the questions were answered, the findings were tallied instantly and then discussed frankly with the entire group. The company was one of the most sophisticated and technically advanced organizations in its field in the world, and justifiably proud of its huge investment in technical mastery. But when these major customers were asked why they continued to give the company so much business year after year, it was not the mastery they cited, but the relationships, the chemistry between key people in both organizations built up over time and nourished assiduously. The CEO of the company was passionate about servant-leadership and creating deep relationships of the highest quality, both internally and externally—and it showed. Employees, suppliers, and customers loved him and the standards of leadership he continually demonstrated and encouraged.

Since it is now possible for any organization with similar investments to achieve the same levels of mastery and technical prowess as any other, the only real distinguishing feature between different organizations will be the quality of their relationships, which means how well we serve employees, customers, suppliers, and the community. When I taught at the university, my MBA students would ask me which company would be the best for them to work for. I always gave the same advice: Find a great leader to work for, not a company. Working for Warren Buffett, whom some would consider to be the preeminent investor of our time, is not the same thing as working for Berkshire Hathaway. It's the same for suppliers, customers, and employees. Servant-leadership is the new (well, nothing is really new) differentiating advantage.

In her Ph.D. thesis for Florida State University, Bethany Goodier wrote about her research into Mount Carmel Health System's adoption of the Higher Ground Leadership principles and how the concept of servant-leadership touched people's lives:

> . . . participants reported a profound sense of personal change. In a presentation to the Mount Carmel Board, one participant explained that the transition toward a more spiritual model of organizing had been "the most important thing that ever happened" to him both "personally and professionally." He went on to explain how it had "transformed" his life, influencing his perceptions of himself, his work, and, most important, his relationships with his family.

Dr. Goodier also noted the impact of Higher Ground Leadership beyond the confines of the organization itself:

> . . . participants reported changes in the vendors with whom they most frequently worked, explaining that many had adopted some spiritual practices as a result of their interactions with Mount Carmel.[8]

As Joanne Gordon wrote in *Forbes*, "For those executives that still don't give a hoot how their employees feel, ask yourself this: If you needed a heart transplant, would you want the surgeon who feels good about his job or the one who complains about hospital policy while you're under anesthesia? Just asking."[9]

As the example of the Cheesecake Factory underscores, there is no need to trade off profit or performance for servant-leadership. We do not have to sacrifice bottom-line performance for a people-centered, caring, and sensitive leadership style that serves others. On the contrary, we can have it all. The more we focus on serving others, the more they will invent even better ways to enhance the bottom line. The one is the cause of the other—not a cost. The reverse is also true: the more we demand, more and more for less and less, the more we will sap people's spiritual energy and therefore limit their inspiration, contribution, and potential. The symphonies and sports teams that have been squeezed are the ones that are failing; those where there has been a concerted effort to serve members are thriving. The one is the obverse of the other. We cannot expect employees to serve customers if the employees are not served first—and at least as well as we wish them to serve others.

> Only a life lived in the service to others is worth living.
> Albert Einstein

We serve when we give. We serve best when we model the behavior we seek, by listening and then responding positively. This is greater than a mission, vision, or a values statement—it is our Destiny, Cause, and Calling.

Learning to Become a Servant-Leader

We were not born to spend our lives serving our own needs; we were born to serve the needs of others and, by doing so, realize our divine potential. The old story of leadership teaches us to set our goals and personal objectives in order to achieve success in life. This is an approach to living that is not entirely without merit, but it vastly underplays the cards we have been dealt as human beings because it is generally motivated by our egos. The New Story of leadership invites us to fulfill our *real*, fuller potential, to become aware of the more important reason we were born, which is to serve others by living our Destiny, Cause, and Calling. Remember our definition of leadership:

Leadership is a serving relationship with others that inspires their growth and makes the world a better place.

And too often at work, as in many other parts of our lives, we offer advice we seldom take ourselves. As Confucius, the great Chinese philosopher and teacher, wrote 500 years before Christ, "He does not preach what he practices till he has practiced what he preaches."

Life: All of It

Consider the concepts in Table 11.1 below. Which of these concepts applies only to your personal life, your work life, both, or neither?

TABLE 11.1
Applying Values to Life

Most Applicable in My:				
	Personal Life	Work Life	Both	Neither
Love				
Soul				
Grace				
Beauty				
Spirit				
Truthfulness				
Wisdom				
Bliss				
Happiness				
Virtue				
Joyfulness				
Sacredness				

> **❗**
> If we do not lay out ourselves in the service of mankind, whom should we serve?
>
> John Adams
> **❗**

I have (with the very best of intentions) led you into a trap. There can be no distinction. We have been misled into believing that work and life are separate and that different behaviors and values are expected from us in these two separate domains.

Let's consider this more closely. At what tender age did you first experience the delicious inspiration that can flow from such magical concepts as love, soul, grace, beauty, spirit, truthfulness, wisdom, bliss, happiness, virtue, joyfulness, or sacredness? Almost certainly you tasted many of these scrumptious emotional and spiritual delights to a greater or lesser degree before you were five years old, unless your early years were more barren than most.

But then someone told you that these concepts were inappropriate for the workplace. Do you remember who first taught you this acrid lesson? In doing so, they taught you to pave over the joyous wonders of your youth.

> **❗**
> I am in the present. I cannot know what tomorrow will bring forth. I can know only what the truth is for me today. That is what I am called upon to serve, and I serve it in all lucidity.
>
> Igor Stravinsky
> **❗**

As Martin Luther King Jr. put it, "Life's most urgent question is, 'What are you doing for others?'" When people are convinced that you value their dreams and aspirations, they will do everything it takes to help you to succeed. Throughout history, where leaders have dedicated their lives to serving their followers, the latter have readily even gone so far as to lay down their lives in pursuit of the leader's Cause.

Reflect for a moment on the questions in Table 11.2 on page 155. In what ways could you serve others better and therefore grow as a spiritual being, a more effective human, a servant-leader, therefore making a larger contribution to the universe by serving more?

TABLE 11.2
How Will I Serve and Grow?

How Do I Serve?	How Might I Serve More?	How I Will Grow:
Does my Calling *serve* others?	How can I dedicate my Calling to the service of others?	
Do I truly *listen* to others?	How can I become a better *listener*?	
Do I *inspire* others most of the time?	How can I ensure that I am *inspiring* others *all the time*?	
When I interact with others, whose agenda has the greatest priority?	How will I ensure that I fully honor the priorities of others?	
Do others feel more alive and honored because of my interaction with them?	How can I practice my Calling in a way that honors the sacredness in others?	

Step Six: Guiding the Contribution of Brilliance

The glory of friendship is not in the outstretched hand, nor the kindly smile, nor the joy of companionship; it is in the spiritual inspiration that comes to one when he discovers that someone else believes in him and is willing to trust him.

Ralph Waldo Emerson

Thirty years ago, Frederick Herzberg was one of the most popular business writers and organizational theorists of his day. A psychologist who believed poor mental health posed the greatest of all threats to Americans, Herzberg developed a keen interest in corporate life and studied the reasons why so many people were unhappy at work, and the reasons why so few others were happy.

After achieving pure clarity about their Destiny, defining and living the Cause, reaffirming their commitment to their own Calling, and coaching others to find and master theirs, aligning that Calling with the Cause, and asking the follower "How may I serve you?" the Higher Ground Leader guides the follower's contribution of brilliance.

One of Herzberg's most important contributions was what he called "Motivation-Hygiene Theory,"[1] in which he postulated the notion that people are motivated by certain factors (which he called "motivational factors"), while the *absence* of other factors resulted in employee demotivation. Flying directly in the face of the prevailing wisdom of the time, he reasoned that salary, status, and security did not motivate people, and thus these factors were not motivators, *but their absence*

157

nearly always proved to be demotivational, leading to poor mental hygiene. Thus, he called these "hygiene factors," and among them he included company policies and administration, supervision, working conditions, and interpersonal relations with colleagues and leaders. None of these, Herzberg argued, could be used effectively to motivate people, but their absence or inappropriateness was nearly always demotivational for employees. The leader's task, he believed, was to ensure that all hygiene factors were at least neutral in relation to those being led.

On the other hand, Herzberg reasoned, employees tend to be motivated when presented with opportunities for achievement, when they are recognized for their accomplishments, when they are interested in, and engaged by their work, when they feel stretched as a result of extra responsibilities or enlarged tasks, and when they are encouraged to grow and accept higher levels of responsibility. Thus, he called these "motivational factors."

Herzberg argued that the role of the leader was to keep both of these balls—hygiene factors *and* motivational factors—in the air at all times.

Now let's fast-forward to our contemporary workplace. So much has changed, and so many of these assumptions seem less valid now. Yet, we might be wise to rework Herzberg's theories and bring them up to date for our times.

Today, as I wrote in the Introduction, we have a greater need than motivation—we want to be *inspired*. We are not looking to leaders to *motivate* us so much as we want them to lift our spirits. The real issue has become inspiration. The question for us all today has become, "Am I doing everything I can to inspire every person with whom I interact—*all the time*?"

In a world where great contributors continue to be in short supply, our responsibility is to find the right colleagues to fill these roles and then inspire them so much that they wouldn't even think about leaving the team, but instead, use their imagination to entice their friends to join them, thus filling out our team's full complement and potential. This is one of the most important and distinguishing features of any inspired group—at work or at home.

The Myth of Strategic Leadership

Another myth about the great historic inspirers is that they were all great strategists. Some of them were, but many were not. More important than anything else, they found brilliant people and inspired them—they focused on guiding the contribution of brilliance from others. It was the brilliant people they attracted who developed and implemented the strategies necessary to achieve the Cause. The Higher Ground Leader is therefore largely responsible for developing, nurturing, and building the *relationships* inside and outside their group that will move everyone closer to the Cause, and followers are responsible for everything else. I am simplifying here to make my point—in reality, the distinctions cannot be this extreme—though it is accurate to say that the leader builds relationships that lead to the attainment of the Cause and others design and implement strategy. Each, of course, is involved in all aspects of both. As Viacom CEO Mel Karmazin puts it, "Viacom has 137,000 employees, and it's usually, 'Mel Karmazin did this or that.' We get far more credit than we deserve when things go right, and too much blame when they don't."[2]

Generally speaking, however, great organizations, groups, teams, and communities have two distinct leadership activities:

1. Developing the Cause and fanning its flame—the role of the Higher Ground Leader.
2. Implementing the actions that make the Cause a reality—the role of the follower.

Heart-Lifting

Higher Ground Leaders understand that these two tasks depend on the concept of heart-lifting. Heart-lifting is the practice of deferring to those who have found their true Calling, to those with the ability, passion, and talent to implement successfully. When we are heart-lifting, we inspire others, sometimes by doing, but more often by refraining from doing. Heart-lifting inspires others by encouraging them to fully utilize their own power and talents. In the symphony, the Higher Ground Leader defines the Cause—the opus being played—and becomes its guide and steward. The violinists implement the strategy that will make the Cause happen. The orchestra leader is the heart-lifter who refrains from personal implementation, focusing instead on the relationships among the team, and guiding their brilliance toward completion of the opus—the Cause.

In addition to the great myth that successful leaders always devise brilliant strategies is the accompanying myth that they must execute them brilliantly as well. This confines the roles of strategy formulation and implementation to the leader. This often results in a stifling, sycophantic culture, where the leader functions as Helios, the sun god, and all other moons must remain in its shadow. When egos dominate so forcefully, too big a shadow is created, and thus not enough light is permitted to shine in order that people may grow.

Our real purpose with others is to lift their hearts, to make it easy for them to develop and implement a brilliant strategy. The first violinist of a symphony will generally know more about playing the violin than the conductor will ever be able to learn during his or her entire lifetime. However, the conductor is the keeper of the Cause — the opus he or she wishes to offer, how it is to be presented, and the magic spell the symphony will weave over the audience. The orchestra leader has defined his or her own Destiny, defined the Cause, followed a Calling, and then aligned the Calling of the first violinist to the Cause, so that the violinist's gifts contribute to its achievement. Now it is time for the Higher Ground Leader (the conductor) to become a heart-lifter, to offer to serve the violinist by providing any personal and professional support required, to help him or her grow and excel. This is the role of coach, mentor, leader, and guide. Now the Higher Ground Leader is able to do the most important thing — get out of the way — to guide the brilliance that is in every other person. The Higher Ground Leader empowers and enables the violinist to do what he or she knows how to do best — to play magnificently, as a virtuoso and as a member of an ensemble, in order to manifest the Cause. In other words, the leader guides the implementation of strategy, but the follower does the implementing. The leader's role is to guide the contribution of brilliance that lies waiting to be released from within the first violinist — like the contribution of brilliance that lies within us all. We are all yearning for *infusion, not intrusion*.

Inspiring People to Greatness . . .

We have long been urged to "concentrate on core competencies." Tom Peters and Bob Waterman told us that the successful organizations in search of excellence "stick to their knitting," focusing on what they do best and outsourcing functions where they are weak.[3] A succession of management gurus has put their own spin onto this notion, but it all comes down to a simple general theory of core competencies: If we focus on what we do best, we will get better at it, which leads to mastery. The corollary is that organizations should stop doing those things where there is a perceived weakness. The intent of this is to encourage corporate strategists to guide their organizations to higher performance, and corporate leaders have paid attention. The result has been a boom in the practice of subcontracting, outsourcing, and forging strategic alliances with others whose strengths complement the weaknesses of their outsourcing customers.

But there is a paradox at work here. If it works so well with organizations, and if we buy the core competency idea so completely, why don't we apply the same principle to people? Guiding followers to brilliance depends on our playing to their strengths, not their weaknesses—outsourcing, as it were, to them.

. . . By Working on Their Strengths, Not Their Weaknesses

When I was the president of Manpower Limited, we had a franchisee called John Harold. To this day, I have not met his equal as a marketer. He was absolutely brilliant. But if he was the Leonardo da Vinci of sales and marketing, he was the super-klutz of administration—he couldn't submit a form to save his life, let alone complete it accurately. I would visit his operations in a trance about his sales, rhapsodizing about his commercial achievements, and then I would say something like, "John, I haven't had a monthly sales summary report from you for 18 months. Would you please start sending them?" He would assure me he would, then I would go home—and nothing would happen. My visits started to take on a similar pattern: ecstasy over his sales, despair about his forms. Once, after applauding another record-breaking sales performance that set a stratospheric standard for the rest of the company to follow, I gamely asked him if he would consider sending me a monthly summary once a quarter. He agreed (but nothing happened!).

I was the CEO, and I was supposed to be the teacher and coach, but I began to realize it was John Harold who was giving the lessons. Finally, he reached me, and I got it—I needed to be a heart-lifter. I went down to his office one day and I said, "John, whenever I visit you, I always compliment you on your brilliant sales performance and then I complain about your sales summaries. I am here to promise you that the last time I did this was the last time I will ever do so. I have hired someone on my payroll to complete your monthly summaries. I will never nag you again about your sales summaries. Now, how can I help you with your sales? How can I serve you?" We never looked back.

Whatever gave me the idea that I could turn one of the finest marketers I had ever met in my entire life into—at best—a mediocre form-filler? And why would I want to? Why was I so arrogant? Why would I try to reduce him to a multicompetencied clone? Here was a certified, one-of-a-kind genius, and I was about to squander his gifts and extinguish the flames of his inspiration. We cannot guide the brilliance of others by getting everyone to do something the same way; we guide the brilliance from others by playing to their strengths, teasing greatness from them by honoring their gifts, and making it as easy as possible for them to be brilliant at what they do. Dilberts are intimidated into doing everything the same way, and thus perform in the margins; Einsteins do everything in a way that plays to their strengths, and thus perform brilliantly. Sameness and conformity are easier to manage, but their price is mediocrity and demotivation. On the other hand, even though guiding brilliance sometimes feels like putting socks on an octopus, it is a gift to the soul—inspiration.

Marcel Proust said, "The real voyage of discovery comes not in seeking new landscapes, but in having new eyes." If we wish to inspire others, we will need to work on their strengths instead of complaining about their weaknesses. We need to know that the principle of focusing on our core competencies—working on building each other's strengths rather than picking at each other's weaknesses—is as sound for individuals as it is for organizations. We can work on the strengths of others and outsource their weaknesses to those for whom these weaknesses are strengths. This is a key to illuminating people, nourishing their souls, and inspiring them to greatness.

Brilliance and the Balance-Point

The two Chinese characters that make up the word *busy* are the symbols for "heart" and "death." In guiding the brilliance of others, we need to restore some semblance of balance to their lives. As the pace of home and work life spins faster and faster, we will not be able to expect consistency of brilliance from harried followers. It is unfair and illogical. The Higher Ground
Leader works hard to remove clutter from people's lives, rather than add to it.

Powered by indefatigable confidence, humans have spent centuries attempting to roll back the natural world, to disturb the natural balance-point. We have striven to tame nature, often successfully, in a million different ways. But the laws of nature are immutable and will only yield temporarily to humans. Everything seeks to find its balance-point, and in the end, everything does.

Where I live, the stone walls of farms built a hundred years ago are barely visible today beneath the tangles of brambles and accumulating earth. An abandoned hydroelectric dam that once powered mills, hotels, and homes has now fallen into disrepair as the river restores the site to its original state with humbling inevitableness. We used to be a thriving community with a railroad station and three hotels. Now we are a quiet hamlet of less than a hundred people.

The changes we impose on nature are illusory, because the underlying laws remain active and in force, even when they are not apparent. In the end, the Natural Laws always prevail. Meanwhile, if we challenge them, the energy of those laws will oppose us. The overarching principle behind the Laws of Nature is the need to seek a balance-point—for every action there is a corresponding and opposing action. This yin and yang of nature is the Law of Life.

> Simplicity is the ultimate sophistication.
> Leonardo da Vinci

These same Natural Laws apply in our own lives and especially in our relationships. Negative energy (emotions, ideas, actions, and communications) attracts similar energy. If we seek paths that attempt to disturb the balance in our lives, the immutable Natural Laws work to return our lives to their original balance-points. The rate of pain, suffering, and stress we experience will tend to be matched by the degree to which we stray from this balance-point. Though the matching energy may not always occur in the same time frame, it will eventually return to the balance-point. This is as inevitable as the erosion of the stone walls of the farm or the river's will to submerge the abandoned hydroelectric dam.

Just as surely, acts of loving kindness and inspiration will attract similar forces. Where there can be imbalances between negative and positive energy, the balance-point is a place of perfect energy. The Natural Laws of the universe are loving laws. Introducing negative energy that disturbs this balance-point attracts a correcting, negative force. On the other hand, positive energy—that is energy that respects the balance-point—reinforces the equilibrium of the Natural Laws and needs no correcting energy field.

The secret to achieving the balance-point in our lives—essential for inspiration and therefore brilliant achievement—is to respect the Natural Laws of the universe. If we complain about the lack of balance in our lives while creating the very negative energy that creates the imbalance, we should not be surprised. We can't have it both ways; the Natural Laws will not allow it.

When we push against the balance-points of life—by acquiring too much, by using more than our share of resources, by seeking to dominate or control markets, customers, employees, family, and friends, by destroying competitors, by pushing people beyond their limits, by demanding performance of which people are not capable—we set up an inevitable cycle of reciprocal negative energy—what is sometimes referred to as "push-back."

In a commencement address at Georgia Tech several years ago, Brian Dyson, then CEO of Coca-Cola Enterprises, spoke of the relationship between work and one's other commitments: "Imagine life as a game in which you are juggling some five balls in the air. You name them—work, family, health, friends, and spirit—and you're keeping all of these in the air. You will soon understand that work is a rubber ball. If you drop it, it will bounce back. But the other four balls—family, health, friends, and spirit—are made of glass. If you drop one of these, they will be irrevocably scuffed, marked, nicked, damaged, or even shattered. They will never be the same. You must understand that and strive for balance in your life."

Perfect equilibrium in our lives is achieved by finding our balance-point, and this is arrived at when there is alignment of our Destiny, Cause, and Calling.

The Balance of Yin and Yang

Soul Food

Everybody on earth knowing
That beauty is beautiful
Makes ugliness.

Everybody knowing
That goodness is good
Makes wickedness.

For being and nonbeing
Arise together;
Hard and easy
Complete each other;

Long and short
Shape each other
High and low
Depend on each other;

Note and voice
Make the music together;
Before and after
Follow each other.

That's why the wise soul
Does without doing,
Teaches without talking.

The things of this world
Exist, they are;
You can't refuse them.

To bear and not to own;
To act and not lay claim;
To do the work and let it go:
For just letting it go
Is what makes it stay.
—Tao Te Ching[4]

The exquisite rhythms of life are dependent on perfect balance—yin and yang, the warp and woof of life—light and dark, beautiful and ugly, loving and fearsome, accepting and judgmental, masculine and feminine. Life cannot exist and unfold without this balance.

Like everyone else, I have the intention to live (that is, think, act, and communicate), with love, compassion, kindness, truth, and grace. On the other hand, like many others, I sometimes find myself thinking, acting, or communicating from a place of anger, hostility, or judgment. I sense that I am growing here, but I still detect the presence of a trickster, the wily character of Native American folklore, lurking somewhere in my inner space. This trickster confounds my good intentions from time to time.

When we match the negative energy of those with whom we communicate, we give away our power to them. These are the moments when we are less than inspiring, when we may project or behave out of our shadow. The dynamics would be different if we reacted with balancing energy. Thus, we need both, even though yang energy may frustrate or disappoint us from time to time. It helps to view yang energy as a great teacher, offering lessons about the issues in our lives that we need to address. Buddha said that our enemies have been sent to us so that we can learn from them. When presented with yang energy, we have choices—we can invite the trickster to dance, or ask the question, "What am I being asked to learn by this yang energy?"

Like most of us, my behavior falls into two types—*yang*: assertive, decisive, focused, and directed, and *yin*: loving, graceful, compassionate, kind, and truthful. A search of our relationship patterns will reveal that when we generate yang energy, we cause others to generate more of the same, and when we generate yin energy, we receive more of the same. Although we are all a combination of yin and yang energies, certain people tend to trigger more yang reactions and responses, while others gently coax more yin behavior from those around them.

When we are uninspiring to others, it is because these energies are not balanced. If we are presented with aggression—an overload of yang energy, it can trip dormant aggression hiding in our own shadow—a response of more yang energy, and the resulting combination can result in a spiraling of yang energy, which, left unchecked, can destroy a relationship. Such exchanges lack the balance of yin energy necessary to restore equilibrium in dialogue and relationships and thus to enable us to be easily inspiring by contributing positive energy rather than depleting it. Only by introducing the right balance of energy can we inspire each other again—and we guide the contribution of brilliance from others by inspiring them—heart-lifting.

As we have discussed earlier, our conscious thought is influenced by our shadow, which is that unconscious part of us that contains our wishes, memories, fears, feelings, and ideas. Our shadow is too easily goaded into a yang response by people who address us with yang energy, and our yin energy is easily and willingly seduced when it is addressed by yin energy. It is as if visitors who show up at our door can choose to dance with yin or yang. If the visitor asks for yang, watch out, because that's who they will get; and if they ask for yin, a gentle soul will emerge as their partner. They both reside in the same house, and neither of them has any prior commitments on their dance card.

When we communicate, our role is to balance the energy we receive and to respond with the appropriate energy, or combination of energies, that the situation warrants. When we receive an excess of yang energy, we need to respond with an appropriate blend of yang and yin, bringing balance to the communication, thus making it whole, and creating a relationship infused with spirit. For some, the temptation to respond with more yang energy is powerful—the shadow behavior straining to show up as the trickster. But when we remember to balance the energy, it works like a charm!

Knowing this, we have another approach available to us: We can invite everyone with whom we interact to address our yin. Failure to do so risks offering a dance invitation to the trickster who lives within. This does not entitle us to hand over the responsibility for our communications and relationships to third parties. It simply means that you and I are always partners, seeking to achieve a spiritual connection, and in doing so, we must teach each other how to communicate effectively. The secret to building inspiring relationships and being a Higher Ground Leader in a yang world is to balance our energy from yang to yin whenever possible in our relationships and in our responses. By balancing this energy, we create a balance-point, and therefore partner with others to strengthen our dialogue and enrich our relationships. This leads to inspiration, and inspiration is the key to guiding the brilliant contribution that lies within everyone, ready, yet waiting to be released by the inspiring dialogue of the Higher Ground Leader.

"How Do We Get Them to Change?"

Guiding the contribution of brilliance of others requires us to relate with them at levels beyond the day-to-day, beyond the mundane with which we have become comfortable, beyond the data and the performance ratios, beyond the material and the physical. It requires us to relate with each other in a values-centered, heart-lifting, spiritual way. This requires us to reframe our approach to relationships and communications, by being brave and authentic, opening our hearts and maintaining a state of grace. In much of my work, I am told that this is simply too much to expect people to accomplish all at once. It is too big a leap; the change is too dramatic. Everyone knows that we need to change, but we need to do so in bite-sized chunks.

The question that I am most frequently asked in my work is, "How do we get *them* to change?" There is often a sense in people's minds that those who really need to hear this message of transformation are not in the audience. This is a classic case of projection. When we say that we really understand truth-telling, promise-keeping, integrity, trust, respect, values, and spirit and that it is everyone else who doesn't "get it," our shadow is really saying "I don't yet get it"—though this is sometimes an uncomfortable truth for us to hear. When we point a finger at someone else, three fingers point back at ourselves.

This is especially true when we consider the concept of critical mass reviewed in Chapter 2. There is a growing sense that more and more people are indeed "getting it," and that it has now become more important that we signal to others through our behavior that we now "get it," too.

This is not the easiest thing in the world to do, so the second most frequently asked question that I hear is, "How do I actually achieve this transformation?" It is done by practicing and living the following six vital values that are the underpinning ideas of Higher Ground Leadership—the CASTLE Principles.

The Keys to the CASTLE

CASTLE is an acronym that describes six very obvious concepts that distinguish the Higher Ground Leader from the old story leader and which, when fully lived, are profoundly inspiring to others. These are concepts that are within us already, but yearn to be recalled. It is through the CASTLE Principles that we guide the contribution of brilliance from followers.

The Higher Ground Leader is guided, in life and work, by these six principles:

1. *Courage:* Nothing happens until we become brave enough to reach outside our existing paradigms. When we are gripped by fear, we become ineffective and our performance is diminished—at work and at home. It all starts here. To leave our old story paradigm and strike out on the journey toward Higher Ground Leadership requires great courage, but courage overcomes fear and provides new, bold lenses with which to see life at home and at work;
2. A commitment to *Authenticity:* Showing up and being present in all aspects of life, removing the mask and becoming a real, vulnerable, and intimate human being, a person who is genuine and emotionally and spiritually connected to others;
3. A desire to *Serve:* Departing from an old story, self-focused, fear-based mode, and instead focusing on the needs of others by listening to them, identifying their needs and meeting them—and thus inspiring them;
4. A passion for and commitment to the *Truth:* The refusal to compromise integrity or to deny universal truths—even though in these testing times, avoiding the truth might, on the face of it, seem easier;
5. The capacity to *Love:* The source of a Higher Ground Leader's ability to inspire others, and the spiritual and psychological antidote to fear, stress, and anger, which, when freely given, results in people who are;
6. *Effective* in all aspects of life.

Courage

The easy part of life is telling others what they need to do. The hard part is being brave enough to reinvent ourselves and reframe what we thought we knew about life and then practice it. This takes enormous courage. In fact, no progress can be made toward the transformational practice of Higher Ground Leadership until we take a deep breath, center ourselves, and resolve to be different—

regardless of how much we may be criticized, how bruised our egos may become, or how dangerous it may at first appear, or how much people will tell us that performance and metrics will suffer along the early part of the journey (which nearly always turns out to be untrue). These are all part of the necessary investment in greatness. There is no other way.

As Higher Ground Leaders, we must model how we wish others to be. We all know that we should love one another, and tell the truth—the essential way of life for the Higher Ground Leader—and most of us know how to do both, we just need someone we respect to actually say the words in practice, in real life situations—in other words, to model the way. Until then, these concepts remain ideals, little more than nice theories better suited to a different kind of world than the one most of us believe we live in.

> !
> Courage is the power to let go of the familiar.
> Raymond Lindquist
> !

Without courage, though, we cannot take even the first steps because they contain so much perceived risk. We are afraid of how we will be judged and that our personalities might be diminished by the criticism of others. The soul understands the need and the desire to take the appropriate action to change culture and actions at home and work, but the ego stands in the way.

Courage is the fire that energizes the clarity, choice, and commitment that we described in Chapter 7. Until we listen to our inner voices, to our souls, inviting our egos to take a secondary role, courage will not be present, but when we do, courage will emerge and give us the one thing that we lack—will. It is the will to make change that starts the process; it is the will that invests fire into our passion, fanning the flames in our soul, so that we each become instruments of change.

Courage gives us the will to do what is necessary to make change, to rise above the intimidation that our personalities experience from the personalities of others. Without courage, we are unlikely to discover our Destiny, Cause, and Calling, let alone live them.

Authenticity

It is not until we become courageous that we can become authentic. It takes courage to be real, because being real requires us to be brave enough to reveal, to own—and sometimes share—our truth, our fears, our emotions, and our vulnerabilities. This is how we become authentic. William Shed said, "A ship in harbor is safe, but that is not what ships are built for."

As soon as we see someone else displaying compassion, love, and grace at work, our hearts are given permission to open, and we embrace the authentic person for their courage and genuineness. This is the practice of the Higher Ground Leader.

Most of us know inauthentic people—people who say one thing and do another; people who feel one thing but say another; people who think one thing, but do another. Authenticity is the opposite of this. When we are authentic, we align our minds, our mouths, our hearts, and our feet—in other words, we think, say, feel, and do the same thing with complete congruence. This is how we become real: by ensuring that what our minds think, what our hearts feel, what our voices speak, and where our feet walk are identical. Until we have the courage to think, say, feel, and do the same thing, in other words, until we are in alignment, we remain inauthentic. Thus, alignment of our thoughts, words, feelings, and deeds results in our becoming authentic humans.

Authenticity, as much as anything, generates love in the hearts of others because our souls are crying out for authenticity. What followers yearn for are leaders who are authentic and can therefore be trusted. Children yearn for the same in their parents, and we all yearn for the same in our friends. Authenticity is the basis for building relationships and inspiring each other and our families, friends, partners, communities, customers, and suppliers. The implications for increased performance are obvious. What a gift—a way of being that inspires the soul and gratifies the personality.

Service

Old story leaders emulate warriors, but we are all depleted by and afraid of the violence in the world. We yearn for human intimacy and sensitivity—for people who serve. We are exhausted from fear and competition. We are all searching for a new story of leadership, characterized by love and truth, meaning and fulfillment—qualities of the spirit. The New Story Leader will change the world by introducing a more demanding criterion: "Does it feed the soul as well as the pocketbook?" Servant-leadership embodies sharing, cooperation, consideration, and consciousness. The servant-leader honors the sacredness in others and in all of life. The servant-leader is a loving leader. Recall Mount Carmel's Cause: *Honoring*

The capacity to care is the thing that gives life its deepest meaning and significance.

Pablo Casals

every soul with loving service. To those who see their most important responsibility as being of service to others, life is not a continuous improvement project in which we strive endlessly toward greater and greater personal achievements. Instead, servant-leaders ask others, "How may I serve you?"

Truthfulness

We are suffering from truth decay: Boards who know in their hearts that it is time for a new CEO, but are afraid speak their truth and so fudge the facts; salespeople who accept outrageously unrealistic quotas, but deny this truth and lie by accepting them; brokers who advise their clients to buy while they themselves are selling; physicians who withhold the truth from their patients; companies who know their products are defective, dangerous, or damaging, but deny it and mislead regulators and the public; old story leaders who intend to limit the potential of an employee, but promise unwarranted opportunities; exec-

> Whoever is careless with the truth in small matters cannot be trusted with the important matters.
>
> Albert Einstein

utives who sand-bag their budgets. The strangest irony is that we have been teaching a myth about all this: The misguided notion that strong human relationships can be built on a flimsy footing of deceit. How can we build harmony, respect, integrity, honesty, inspiration, leadership, or love on a foundation of lies? There is no logical argument that can support the idea that we can build consensus, community, ethics, teamwork, high performance, organizational and personal transformation, personal and family relationships, or outstanding customer service and quality without first building the necessary foundation of integrity on which to place them. Why do we expect to become Higher Ground Leaders from a base of dishonesty? After all, if we can't even trust or tell the truth to each other, what are the grounds for expecting employees, customers, or suppliers to do any better? Walter Scott wrote, "Oh, what a tangled web we weave, when first we practice to deceive."

> After the grand jury session, he [Vernon Jordan] told reporters that he answered the questions truthfully and to the best of his ability. Well, come on, which is it?
>
> David Letterman

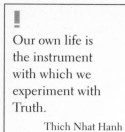
Our own life is the instrument with which we experiment with Truth.

Thich Nhat Hanh

Joseph Swedish of Centura Health puts it this way, "I'm better able to speak publicly now about our Destiny, Cause, and Calling based on foundational pieces I don't think I ever had, or they may have been there but not assembled correctly. So today, I am much more authentic, and maybe part of being authentic is being truthful. In fact, an attribute that I uncovered in this journey is that integrity and truthfulness are of the highest importance to me. I never really understood that, and why I was so demanding of the 'real story,' and now I know this is always who I have been. I'm able to take that expectation and translate it to the ability to speak with people about truth and how I can be so passionate about it, because I know it's a very important matter for me."

Love

Where did we learn the myth that we can get our way more effectively with petulance or through aggression and violence than with love? All human communications are transmitted and received on a continuum ranging between negative

There is more hunger for love and appreciation in this world than for bread.

Mother Theresa

and positive, between fear and love. Our brains release different biochemicals depending on whether we are experiencing pain and fear or love and inspiration. When we experience pain and fear, the brain puts the body into "stress mode," triggering the release of stress hormones by the limbic system. When we experience love and inspiration, the brain releases the body's natural "uppers" that lower blood pressure, heart-rate, and oxygen consumption.[5] Since the soul and the body are one, our experiences of love or fear directly influence us to the core of our being—emotionally, spiritually and, as we can see, physically.

Love and fear determines whether our relationships with others will be inspiring or not. Violence and love are at opposite ends of a continuum, with selfishness at one end and service at the other. One builds. The other destroys.

Love is when my heart touches your heart and adds to who you are as a person. We know that we all yearn for more love in our lives. But we delude ourselves when we think this is only true of our personal lives and is not just as vital to our work environments. We all want more love in *all* of our lives—at home *and* at work.

Effectiveness

In organizational and home life, the requirement to achieve high levels of performance is ever present. In fact, this is the reality of life in all its dimensions. Being a Higher Ground Leader is not about turning our attention away from these realities; it is the way in which we achieve them. Bottom line performance is our economic permission to continue leading the business as stewards for the owners of the enterprise. But too often we trade the short-term metrics in exchange for the greatness that can only come from consistent and patient investment in courage, authenticity, service, truth-telling, and love. According to the Towers Perrin/Gang and Gang study referred to in the Introduction ". . . negative emotion about work not only relates to higher turnover rates, but contributes to the kind of workplace malaise that can materially diminish productivity and performance. Conversely, strong positive emotion correlates with better financial results for an organization, as measured by five-year total shareholder return." The study also reveals that, while employers are aware of the widespread discontent in their workplaces, they misjudge some of the root causes and risk taking inappropriate actions as a result. "Right now, there is an enormous gap between employees' current and ideal work experience. People know what they want and need to feel intensely positive about their work, but unfortunately many are not getting it," said Mark Mactas, Chairman and CEO of Towers Perrin.[6]

It is common for our clients to see bottom line improvements of $50 million or more as a result of a couple of years of intensive work with their leaders to instill Higher Ground Leadership throughout their organization. When leaders rediscover their spiritual compass and use it to guide their organizations, it transforms their culture and helps them to focus their lives in service of those they lead. The result is inspiration for employees, customers, and suppliers, which generates increased effectiveness.

Says Joseph Swedish:

> The leader has to be practical and a realist, yet must talk the language of the visionary and the idealist.
>
> Eric Hoffer

What's interesting about our journey to becoming a Higher Ground organization is how we're now able to explore difficult issues more effectively and truthfully. As an example, one of our hospitals was facing serious and consistent customer service challenges as measured by a national research organization. Because we spoke with them in terms of the CASTLE Principles, our common language, they have set their sights on getting better. Prior to our Higher Ground journey, this would have been a much more difficult, defensive conversation. The CASTLE Principles have given us permission to put away our defensiveness and work together to be the most effective healthcare organization we can be. Whether it's a hospital's associates embracing their customer satisfaction challenges, committing to excel in customer service and turning things around, or one associate authentically expressing her appreciation for another, this journey is changing our organization one person at a time.

Our role as leaders is to treat each other as sacred and thus inspire each other so that we become effective humans. These are not mutually exclusive ideas. Indeed, the reason why Higher Ground Leaders are effective is *because* they treat others as sacred and inspire them all the time.

The practice of the CASTLE Principles leads to consciousness. The world is yearning for Higher Ground Leaders. The unconscious mind sees the world as a collection of individual objects, and Western science uses this intellectual framework to analyze, survive, and make sense of the universe. The Higher Ground Leader starts from the perspective of seeing the wholeness of the universe, and makes sense of life by appreciating the interconnectedness of everything and everyone with the whole. Consciousness is the awareness that we are simply part of a magical, flowing whole—like individual molecules of water in the river of life. Consciousness is being awake to the mystical and ineffable aspects of being alive, recognizing a higher power, an inner knowing that life is bigger than any, or even all, of us. The unconscious mind sees a world of scarcity and responds with fear. The conscious mind sees a world of abundance and responds with love. The unconscious mind describes compassion and caring for people as "touchy-feely," "lovey-dovey," "soft-stuff." The conscious mind sees compassion and caring for people as the juice—even the purpose and necessity—of life. The unconscious mind reasons that an imbalance between work and life is the means that is justified

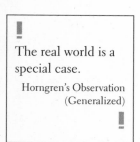

The real world is a special case.

Horngren's Observation
(Generalized)

by the ends. The conscious mind understands that everything in the universe, including work and life, must be integrated and that there is a season for everything. This is heart-lifting, and in this way, we change the world.

Escape

When we get out of the glass bottles of our ego,
and we escape like squirrels turning in the cages of our personality
and get into the forests again,
we shall shiver with cold and fright
but things will happen to us
so that we don't know ourselves.

Cool, unlying life will rush in,
and passion will make our bodies taught with power,
we shall stamp our feet with new power
and old things will fall down,
we shall laugh, and institutions will curl up like burnt paper.
—D. H. Lawrence

Step Seven: Magic Ingredient X— Creating the Environment That Inspires Others to Inspire Us

In everyone's life, at some time, our inner fire goes out. It is then burst into flame by an encounter with another human being. We should all be thankful for those people who rekindle the inner spirit.

—Albert Schweitzer

Over the past 30 or 40 years of practicing, researching, and teaching, it confounds me that none of the literature or the leading theorists have asked the question, "Who inspires the inspirer?" Much is written about how we should inspire—how to put it out—but not much about how to receive it. There is a scarcity of advice about how to inspire the inspirer. Leaders, for example, are commonly supposed to possess bottomless reservoirs of energy and resilience, like the Energizer bunny whose batteries outlast those of everyone else. Many act out this myth, pretending that they are invulnerable and capable of regenerating themselves without any input from others.

We all know, whether we admit it or not, that we need to be inspired just like anyone else, because we are just

> Finally, after achieving pure clarity about their Destiny, defining and living the Cause, reaffirming their commitment to their own Calling, and coaching others to find and master theirs, aligning the Calling with the Cause, asking the follower "How may I serve you?" and guiding others' contribution of brilliance, the Higher Ground Leader creates the environment that encourages followers to inspire the leader. All leaders need to be inspired, and their followers are a vital source of inspiration.

like everyone else—we are human. The most important source of this inspiration is from those whom we inspire. We cannot demand inspiration from others; we must create the environment that encourages such inspiration. I call this *Magic Ingredient X* because it is a missing component in almost all leadership and community theory.

Not Everything Can Be Measured

Inspiration is often simply unexplainable. This is very perplexing and frustrating for analysts so anxious to reduce the concept of inspiration to a finite science made of quantifiable parts. But some things cannot be quantified. The energy of Higher Ground Leaders emanates from an inspired place. Sometimes, our inquiring scientific minds are not up to the task of analysis, and in those situations, it is best if we simply trust in the ineffable.

The intuitive mind is a sacred gift and the rational mind is a faithful servant. We have created a society that honors the servant and has forgotten the gift.

Albert Einstein

Performance metrics and measures are an ever-present fact of life. The old adage, "What gets done gets measured" stands guard over our lives at work and home. Prevailing wisdom for many people is that what we do not analyze and measure with some form of quantitative calipers, is not real or experienced. Meg Whitman, who has powered eBay to a billion dollar Internet juggernaut with over 60 million users says, "If you can't measure it, you can't control it. Being metrics-driven is an important part of scaling to be a very large company. In the early days you could feel it, you could touch it. Now that's more difficult, so it has to be measured."[1] Measurement is a vital part of work and life and a necessary part of success—eBay is testimony to this mastery. But life is in two parts—that which can be measured, and that which cannot.

In the movie, *Dead Poet's Society*, Robin Williams plays the part of John Keating, the newly appointed English teacher at a private boys' school. In his first English class, he invites one of his students to read from a book entitled *Understanding Poetry* by Dr. J. Evans Pritchard. The student describes the theories of Dr. Pritchard, who asserts that one may evaluate poetry with the use of a matrix, with "perfection" being measured on the vertical scale, and "importance" on the horizontal scale, the total area being equal to "greatness." Thus, a poem by Byron, Pritchard suggests, might rate highly on the vertical but poorly on the horizontal, while a Shakespearean sonnet might rate highly on both the vertical and the horizontal. When the student finishes, Keating turns to his class and exclaims, "Excrement! That's what I think of Dr. J. Evans Pritchard! We're not laying pipe—we're talking about poetry. How can you describe poetry like American Bandstand—'Oh, I like Byron, I'll give him a forty-two, but I can't dance to it'?" To the amazement of his entire class, he underscores his view by asking them to rip out the chapter from their poetry textbook containing Dr. J. Evans Pritchard's theories, and toss it in the wastepaper basket. The startled students complete this ritual as Keating warns them of the dangers of measuring the unmeasurable in life. "The casualties could be your hearts and souls," he exclaims. "Armies of academics going forward measuring poetry! No! We'll not have that here . . . Now in my class, you will learn to think for yourselves again; you will learn to savor words and language. No matter what anyone tells you, words and ideas can change the world." Suspecting that some of his students believe that nineteenth-century literature has nothing to do with completing business or medical school, Keating continues, "We don't read and write poetry because it's cute, we read and write poetry because we are members of the human race, and the human race is filled with passion. Medicine, law, business, engineering— these are noble pursuits, and necessary to sustain life. But poetry, beauty, romance, love—these are what we stay alive for." Then borrowing from Walt Whitman, Keating points out, "You are here, that life exists . . . that the powerful play goes on, and you may contribute a verse." Peering intently into the faces of each student, he asks them, "And what will your verse be?"*

There are other ways, in addition to analysis, to measure the realities and experiences of life, and other ways to achieve our dreams. There are many aspects of our lives that will simply not yield to conventional metrics. How do you measure the way a glorious sunset touches your soul? What stirs inside you when you hear beautiful music or poetry? Or the juicy inner sensations when you walk barefoot in the soft sand along the ocean's edge? What criteria would you use to measure the visceral experience of holding a newborn baby? How do you measure the magic of a full moon, the beauty of the Mona Lisa, or the rush of a Rocky Mountain high? What is the financial or quantitative measurement of being "in flow," or being transported to a different plane when lost in the practice of doing something you love, of doing it as well as you know how— mastery? How does one plot a chart or create a graph of being deeply in love? Is there a 10-point scale for measuring a profound sense of gratitude? How do you define the moment when you feel at one with the universe? Or when you are

---

* Chapter 4 begins with the full poem.

passionately engaged in your faith? These are moments that touch your soul and are as real, perhaps even more so, than many other so-called measurable experiences in life.

A four-kilometer-wide corridor separating North and South Korea, known as the Demilitarized Zone (DMZ), has been a no-go zone for people since it was mined and rimmed with razor wire at the end of the Korean War in 1953. South of the DMZ in South Korea, economic development has helped to extinguish all mammals larger than a mouse. But within the DMZ, where people do not tread for fear of becoming extinct themselves, leopards, tigers, and many endangered plants thrive and diversify. Where people have banished themselves, numinous inspiration has prevailed for the other life with which we share our planet. The buildings destroyed in Hiroshima by nuclear bombs were built from bricks formed from the clays of the mountains above. The dormant seeds of trumpet flowers captured in these building materials were released by the clash of atoms, and from the ensuing rubble sprouted a new floral beauty. In Canada, the Jack Pine can only release its seeds when the heat of a forest fire opens its cones, thus enabling the seeds to fall on fertile soil. The acorn is an example of inspiration— inside rests the beauty of a majestic oak tree, waiting to be unlocked by love. No doubt there are scientific explanations for all of these marvels—but there is much more mystery than science behind them.

All this makes the subject of inspiration such a difficult concept for old story leaders to grasp—we simply cannot measure it with quantitative, scientific tools. We can easily gauge the achievement of sales figures, budgets, revenues and profits, business metrics, finishing lines, and political campaigns. It is less easy to create the metrics for happiness, joy, beauty, love, loyalty, truth, dignity, respect, or bliss. We need to understand that there are some things that simply cannot be measured by conventional management metrics. And yet we know, and can produce endless research to confirm, that inspired people achieve extraordinary results. We long for heightened spiritual experiences in our working and personal lives, most of which are measured only by the spirit. Inspiration of the soul goes beyond motivation and mathematics, and though we are forced by convention to reduce many things to a bar chart, identifying additional ways to gauge a soulful experience can be truly inspiring. Higher Ground Leaders know how to find fresh, instinctive, emotional, visceral measures to gauge our level of connectedness with the universe—at work and at home.

> !
>
> You can use all the quantitative data you can get, but you still have to distrust it and use your own intelligence and judgment.
>
> Alvin Toffler
>
> !

The questions we need to ask about our preoccupation with linear analysis is, "Does it matter?" and, "Is it the best way to determine value?"

Why do we feel so compelled to measure *everything*? And why are we only prepared to accept as real, those things that are finite, linear, and measurable, by old story definitions—what is "concrete"? Why do we dismiss the ineffable as "touchy-feely" or "fluff"? Are we afraid of the mystery? Why are the greatest and most inspiring events and experiences of humanity immeasurable by conventional, "scientific" means? Could it be that only the mundane yields to measurement?

> Not everything that can be counted counts, and not everything that counts can be counted.
>
> Albert Einstein

Jim Paquette, CEO of Providence Health in Kansas City, tells the story of the difficult times he was having setting up a heart unit at St. Vincent's Hospital and also dealing with the crash of a helicopter in which the pilot and patient were both killed. As he was leaving to go home one Friday evening, his phone rang. It was his director, the president of the Health Service Corporation, Sister Macrina Ryan from Kansas. She asked how Jim was doing and inquired about his family. Then she asked how things were going at the hospital. Jim walked her through the financial trials and challenges he was facing. Sister Macrina said she was aware of all the issues. Then she continued, "I want you to know that we are praying for you and keeping you in our thoughts." Sister Macrina wasn't asking about the metrics. She had heard about the other issues and was asking how Jim was *feeling*. Jim Paquette reflected recently on this experience: "I was pretty confident that the president of General Electric rarely, if ever, got a call like that from the chair of his board. This is a caring organization, and that caring starts at the very top." This is inspiration—unmeasureable and magical—at work.

Jim lives his own life the same way—he is well known in the healthcare industry as an outstanding Higher Ground Leader who inspires and serves others. The golden thread that runs from his Destiny through his Cause and to his Calling is his desire to serve. That's why Jim's followers love him.

At a conference in October 1994 organized by *CIO Magazine*, Peter Drucker dryly observed to participants that an orchestra managed like General Motors would have a conductor, an executive conductor, several associate conductors, and 32 vice-president conductors.

Subjecting the mystery of inspiration to the rigors of management science may not always serve the needs of the soul, nor be the most heart-lifting thing to do for others or ourselves.

Being on a Dream-Team

None of us can completely insulate ourselves from the social and emotional turbulence of the world. Sometimes we are too heavy to take off. Change and chaos are an unavoidable fact of life. However, we all have the power to select the kinds of teams we belong to—and that is what most of us try to do. It makes sense to be on a team that is potent and fun, rather than one that is dysfunctional. Then we can take flight and navigate these changes safely. Dream-teams are light enough to fly.

Finding a dream-team that meets our spiritual aspirations is vital for the soul and essential for our inspiration. Without it, we become spiritually adrift, and this alienation wounds the spirit at work, just as much as failure to find a Calling. In fact, though it may not be an inspiring experience, many people can subsist with relative comfort on a dream-team, even while they are unsure of their Calling. The sense of community temporarily offsets the emptiness that comes from not being passionately engaged with a vocation.

I described the concept of the sanctuary in Chapter 2. The word comes from the Latin *sanctus*, "sacred, holy place"; it is a place of refuge or protection, a shelter, as a soulful workplace, a safe environment.[2] A dream-team is a sanctuary. We each have the tools and the opportunity to bring our own influence upon our team, shaping its character with our own, and adding and strengthening its values and spiritual fiber. It is because of this spiritual energy that a team becomes a sanctuary—a team that stands together on higher ground. The power of a dream-team to inspire is extraordinary. Anyone who has been part of one will tell you that few things can match the sense of joy that comes from being with a masterful team of colleagues whom one loves and by whom one is inspired—or being married to a partner with whom one has created a dream-team. In our personal lives, perhaps our greatest wish is for a life-partner with whom we form a marital dream-team. Leaders are inspired by dream-teams.

Enhancing the Spiritual Quotient (SQ) of Teams

Have you ever noticed how some people steal power from a team? Energy vampires I call them, and they are present in many teams, draining the collective energy from them and causing a shift from being inspired to tired. The soul wilts in these conditions and the energy barometer plummets. Think about the people with whom you work, your family, the members of teams to which you belong— what is their SQ?

We may not be part of a dream-team all the time, and even when we are, all teams encounter difficulties—life is a mystery and a puzzle. Events do not always unfold as our egos would wish, and this may cause us to gossip, vent, and complain about things, and very often about each other.

The soul views these events with equanimity, but the personality is less forgiving. In a team that has become a sanctuary, where we have raised our spiritual awareness, these ego-based forms of communication give way to a more loving style of communication. We each have choices for communicating and resolving our frustrations. In a sanctuary, *we are loyal to each other behind our backs.*

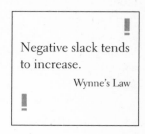

Negative slack tends to increase.

Wynne's Law

There is simply no excuse for displaying dysfunctional behavior—ranting, rage, anger, violence, rudeness, shouting, heated arguments, cursing, sarcasm, storming out of meetings, hanging up the phone on someone, throwing things, and so on. Nor is there any excuse for any of us to be copyfrogs. Yet, I hear about behavior of this kind all the time in my work—among grown-up adults! There is much we can do that will move us from our copyfrog status and engage us in changing this behavior, including telling each other the truth about how it causes us to feel, offering and seeking professional advice, maintaining a daily state of grace with one another, loving each other, making a promise to heal each other, accepting responsibility for the pain our behavior causes, and inviting the friendship and support of our colleagues. What is not acceptable is to continue to drain energy from the team and destroy the possibility of building a team that is inspired; nor is it acceptable for us to be copyfrogs when we observe these behaviors. We must do our inner work, accept responsibility for our behavior, and recognize that there is only one reason why teams become dysfunctional—it is because we (that usually means I) feed dysfunctional behavior into them.

The responsibility of the Higher Ground Leader is to name these dysfunctional behaviors and invite healing around them. What I see so often in uninspiring teams, is what Jerry B. Harvey described in his book by the same name as *The Abilene Paradox.*[3] This is the story of a family of copyfrogs who are playing cards on a terrace on a hot sunny afternoon. One of the family members thinks they should drive to Abilene for dinner. He does not want to do this himself, but he thinks the others do. The car overheats, no one has any fun, and the food is bad—and everyone suffers in silence until one of them admits they would have preferred to stay home. It turns out that everyone else felt the same way, but were afraid or too lazy to say so while there was still time to enjoy the afternoon. We all tend to do the same—we know when there is uninspiring behavior in teams, we are simply afraid or too lazy to own up to it, deal with it, and heal it. This calls for Courage—the first letter of the CASTLE Principles.

The Spiritual Quotient (SQ) is a casual litmus test that you might apply to people whom you do not know well. When you think about these people, how does their spiritual energy feel for you? Is this person spiritually aware and contributing SQ to the team, or are they draining spiritual energy from the team? Are they spiritually awakened, *conscious*, as I have described it earlier, or do they remain spiritually asleep and far from embarking on a path of spiritual renewal and discovery? Are they givers or takers? Do they plunder the energy of the team or augment it? Do you feel better or worse from having been in their company? Do they inspire or deflate? Do they practice the CASTLE Principles? This is not meant to be a prescriptive formula, nor is it intended to be judgmental or quantitative, but rather to make us aware of what we are looking for in teams. It is important for us to always ask the question so that we remain aware of each other's spiritual development, choosing to contribute to the spiritual energy of a team, and to work with people who are on the same journey as ourselves, even if we may be on different roads and at different stages. We are interested in ensuring that spirit and values are showing up on a person's radar and that they are growing as spiritual beings. As leaders and followers, we want to be clear about others and whether they are depositing spiritual energy into the team's bank or withdrawing it—whether they are enhancing or depleting the collective SQ of the team. It is from followers with a high SQ that leaders draw much of their own inspiration.

All team members, including leaders, have a critical responsibility: to contribute energy to the group and to build the SQ of the entire team. In short, the role of the Higher Ground Leader is to inspire all of the time—*all of the time*. We all know this is a standard that is almost impossible to maintain, but the question we each need to ask is: "Will everyone else be inspired as a result of what I am about to say?" If we cannot answer "yes," we should pause, because it is the responsibility of every team member to strive to inspire all of the others *all of the time*—even when it seems that our will or capacity to do so may have been depleted. We know Higher Ground Leaders by this ability. They have the knack and the inner resources needed to inspire others, even when they are imparting information that may be challenging or unpleasant. *All* our exchanges within teams must energize each other—

> !
> In saying what I have in mind, will I really improve on the silence?
>
> Robert Greenleaf
> !

in every direction and in every communication within the team. It is not some-one else's responsibility—*it is our responsibility.*

When We Must Part

Often, though, we are faced with some tough choices. The team we belong to or the organization or community with whom we are associated becomes one with which we can no longer align ourselves because of its values or practices, or the values it represents. Spiritual liberation and inspiration will not be ours until this dilemma is addressed—either the team changes or we do, because we cannot be inspired by an uninspiring team, or by uninspiring team members. If we cannot change the energy in this way, we may be left with only one practical option: to seek another team. This, sadly, is sometimes the only route to authenticity, to en-sure that we stop living the lie of a career, or a relationship, where the material benefits are good, but the spiritual rewards are nonexistent. To remain in these circumstances is an affront to the soul because behavior that does not inspire hurts at a deep level. In this situation, others are not inspired, and therefore can-not inspire us.

New Story Leaders deal with these situations with grace, ensuring that the needs of the soul are always appropriately addressed. Old story leaders, on the other hand, invoke euphemisms such as layoffs, furloughs, separation, reengi-neering, rightsizing, and downsizing. In a recent ex-ample of old story practices, Accident Group, a personal-injury company owned by Luxemburg-based Amulet, sent text messages to the mobile phones of their 2,500 employees advising them to call a number. There, a message from the company's in-solvency administrators informed them that, "All staff who are being retained will be contacted today. If you have not been spoken to, you are therefore being made redundant."[4] We all have the option of ap-proaching this and similar situations in ways that are inspiring instead of demoralizing by simply reframing our relationship with oth-ers, by being heart-lifting, and being courageous, authentic, serving, loving, and truthful—and therefore effective—the CASTLE Principles.

> ❗
>
> Warning to All Personnel:
> Firings will
> continue until
> morale improves.
>
> ❗

If there really are no options left but separation, that is, if elegant and inspir-ing options are eluding us, then the most heart-lifting path is to separate in a graceful, caring, and friendly way that honors the souls of those affected and treats them as sacred beings—the CASTLE principles of Courage, Authenticity, Service, Truthfulness, Love, and Effectiveness.

Beyond Therapy: Accepting Personal Responsibility in Teams

Healing is a necessary transition for all of us, but not a permanent way station. We must honor each other's needs to heal with patience, understanding, and compassion. Wounds that took time to accumulate will also take time to heal. Though we all need to visit a place of healing to repair our inherited and incurred wounds, we cannot park there forever. After overcoming the denial and repression of our past injuries, we must undertake the work of completion, bring closure to past painful experiences, and begin following our own true path to our Destiny, Cause, and Calling as loving humans. After we have worked through our necessary therapies, we must begin the greatest therapy of all, which is to serve others. In doing so, we will be served, healed, and therefore inspired. This is the special gift of the Higher Ground Leader and the enlightened and inspired follower. Helping others to heal and move on to new lives of fulfillment and meaning is how the Higher Ground Leader becomes inspired.

Sow good services; sweet remembrances will grow them.

Madame de Stael

The dynamics of teams show that we need to mature and move on. When we sit in teams revisiting our wounds—what medical intuitive Caroline Myss calls "woundology" behavior—we drain power from each other, build resentment among members, and weaken the team.[5] As a result, we lower the SQ by leaching toxins that pollute team chemistry, goad each other's egos, and create dysfunctional battles among members. In these environments, the copyfrog prevails. If we shift our energy from victim behavior to inspiring behavior, we will dramatically change the energy and the SQ of the entire team. This is one of the hallmarks of Higher Ground Leadership. Jerry Chamales, whose story is told in Chapter 3, told me, "I stuffed my emotions and pain away for years, not even recognizing that I had a shadow. My life changed when I came to terms with my shadow and its associated behavior. This was the beginning of my journey towards authenticity." If we raise the SQ of others on the team, even when it is the last thing in the world we are moved to do at that time, it will lift their souls, and they in turn will respond by lifting ours. If we need to be healed, we can start by healing others, even when our own needs are greater. Others will be inspired to heal us in response. In other words, *we get what we give.* This is a powerful way to serve others and therefore create behavior that is inspiring.

When we choose to serve, we inspire—remember that the meaning of inspire is to breathe, "the breath of God." First, we inspire each other, then we will conspire. The resulting healing of our wounds is the gift that teams bestow on members who serve. We are not put on this planet just to follow our bliss—we are here to create bliss—and healing, serving, and inspiring others is how we follow our bliss.

When we see these transformations taking place, everyone becomes inspired. Watching a team grow, heal, and learn to inspire each other is a marvel to experience—this is another of the ways we can be inspired by others. Each of us can give light—if we stay bright. People inspired this way experience a mystical urge to inspire others. They are joyful, and joyful people cannot resist sharing their joy.

The Courage to Heal

Imagine that an employee's performance is deteriorating. You have had several performance reviews with him or her and have recommended additional training, but no improvement has been forthcoming. You are becoming desperate; none of your warnings and proposed solutions seem to lead to improved results. Suppose that we now change tactics altogether. Suppose we ask the employee this question: "How can I serve and inspire you?" Note the language—we are asking questions, instead of prescribing plans or solutions; we are offering to serve, without judgment, and we are making it clear that we mean to listen to, and then act on, the response, whatever it might be.

Perhaps the employee might respond, "I recently remarried and my youngest daughter is making life very difficult for my new spouse. I am feeling sad about this, and I would dearly love to heal this relationship. This is what would truly inspire me."

Note that although the conditions that lead to inspiration may be work-related, very often, they are not. The astute Higher Ground Leader knows weak on-the-job performance has its roots in personal stresses at least as often as in work-related stresses.

As a Higher Ground Leader, we might respond to this employee in this way, "We are a very well-connected organization in our community. We know people who are professionals in this field, and if you would agree to it, I will make arrangements for you to find a professional of your choice who will work with you to help heal this relationship. We will help to pay for the service and arrange your work schedule so that you can invest the time required."

Suppose that in time the *relationship* improves, even heals—isn't it entirely likely that an emotional and spiritual burden will be lifted from this employee, which in turn will transform their attitude, leading to renewed engagement with their work and colleagues, which might, in turn, result in improved productivity, increased loyalty, and greater effectiveness? Healing this broken relationship would enable this employee to shed the distraction of it, and thus divert the consuming negative energy into a greater commitment to the Cause of the leader and the organization. None of this would be achieved with more job training, reprimands, motivation, or threats.

Old story leaders will view such an approach with discomfort, believing that this sounds more like therapy than leadership. But in the evolved organization, our responsibility is to engage with people in ways that are important to them— serving *their* needs as whole persons—not just their work needs. The Higher Ground Leader is therapist, mentor, teacher, guide, friend, role model, and counselor all rolled into one. We are not just there to perform and represent functions, merely relating with other functions, but to remove the mask, to be real human beings who relate with other human beings at a level that really matters.

Most of us have no formal training in this area and might shrink from such a role, from becoming "personal." Yet, this is the level of engagement that inspires and, therefore, as Higher Ground Leaders, we have no choice—we must learn to focus on the needs of others because it is in everyone's interest. We must become involved in what has traditionally become an "out-of-bounds" domain: the personal life of colleagues and friends. In our hearts, we know this truth: A spouse who lives in an abusive relationship at home converts that abuse into dysfunctional behavior and brings it to work. This is costly, first to the human spirit because it is diminished, and second to the organization because it reduces the effectiveness of the employee. And when we ask questions—instead of offering advice and solutions—we will be amazed at how many effectiveness issues are rooted in personal, emotional, and relationship issues.

Joe Calvaruso describes how our philosophy affects our lives, becoming a worldview, because we are integrated human beings, not just employees, but also parents, children, friends, and partners:

> One of our executives went home and said to her family, "I want to teach you this method we use, called a *Truth-Telling Circle* that I learned in our Higher Ground Leadership Retreat." During this family application of a leadership

process used for work, she learned some important information from her oldest daughter, who was beginning the next phase of her education at college: She felt she had to be successful in sports to win her mother's love. Her mother was able to say, "That's not the case . . . I love you for who you are," and from that point their relationship dramatically transformed. They're very close. This is just one example of many. I hear of people having the courage to be Higher Ground Leaders at their church. Others have achieved extraordinary results in youth groups and with teenagers.

Our job as leaders is to do everything we can to inspire effectiveness and the human spirit. You don't need to be a rocket scientist to realize that an employee struggling with chemical dependency or domestic violence is, first, experiencing great spiritual and physical pain, to which we have a responsibility to bring relief, if we can, and second, cannot reach their full potential as an individual or team member—at home or at work—until these conditions improve. The Higher Ground Leader does not shrink from involvement with the messy, but real, issues of peoples' lives, no matter what the risks or barriers may be, because they know that if it will inspire just one soul to do so, it is worth it, and if there is a chance of just one success—the world becomes a better place and the Higher Ground Leader becomes inspired.

We Are All Leaders

This also raises the question, "Who is the leader?" The answer is everyone, because at some point or another, we all must assume a leadership responsibility. This is what every member of a great team does all of the time. In an earlier book of mine, a fable called *The Way of the Tiger*, Moose, the wise tiger, teaches values to his community and defines this shared responsibility for leadership in his inimitable way: *Moose's Law of Leadership: In a team of 100 people, there are 100 leaders.*[6] Leadership is not an activity for "them," nor is it limited to the person at "the top," or the eldest. It is the responsibility of every human who is present on this planet, regardless of age, function, race, material status, or any other condition. Everyone leads at some time. Siblings take turns leading; parents alternate with their children in leading and following. Spouses and partners practice leadership and followership responsibilities at different times; so do customers and suppliers, students, senior and junior team members, physicians and nurses, members of a cast, a band, or a sports team—all juggle the responsibilities of leading and following as appropriate. None of us is exempt from the responsibility, nor unworthy of the opportunities to lead.

Higher Ground Leadership is leadership that comes from the heart and soul. Its applicability as a leadership approach is not limited to corporations, but is equally relevant in families, churches, governments, healthcare, law enforcement agencies, educational organizations, and communities—anywhere where groups of people combine to advance the purpose of the human spirit. The Higher Ground Leader is constantly seeking opportunities to lead and inspire—in whatever circumstances he or she may be. We are all leaders, and our purpose is to inspire others. And we all need each other in order to do this well.

To paraphrase Pierre Teilhard de Chardin, we are spiritual beings enjoying a human experience. We need to ask, all the time, "Am I behaving in a way that affirms not just the personalities of team members, but their souls, too?" In other words, are we Higher Ground Leaders?

The Art of Followership

We hear a great deal about leadership and how leaders should lead, but we hear much less about followership: how followers can best serve each other, their leader, and their community. In building relationships, the roles of leader and follower are part of a hologram; they are all part of the same relationship, just seen from different perspectives.

> Remember that it is far better to follow well than to lead indifferently.
>
> John G. Vance

As I have found out all too often, a speech, for example, can be made or broken by the quality of the introduction—the way the speaker is "set up." Similarly, leadership often depends on the quality of the followership. The Higher Ground Leader teaches followers how to follow, and part of the art of followership is knowing when and how to lead. The more followers know about, understand, and practice the dynamics of leadership and followership, the more effective the relationships between colleagues and within teams can be. The Higher Ground Leader encourages the sharing of power in this way, recognizing the need to maximize material and spiritual power in both leader and followers.

Followers contribute greatly to the leadership process by:

- Being clear about their Destiny.
- Promoting, protecting, and supporting the Cause.
- Being passionate about their Calling.

- Telling the truth and keeping promises to each other and the leader (and everyone else).
- Inspiring each other and the leader—*all of the time.*
- Being open and willing to learn and change.
- Refusing to be copyfrogs.
- Teaching each other and learning together.
- Earning the respect of colleagues through personal mastery, thus enhancing team mastery.
- Always remaining alert to "helicopter pilots" and bringing them onto the team.
- Being adaptable and capable of leading when appropriate.
- Contributing to the team energy and augmenting the spiritual richness of the team (SQ).
- Following the CASTLE Principles.

One of the most important roles of followers is to give emotional and spiritual support to Higher Ground Leaders—all the time, but especially in moments of stress, crisis, or loneliness—inspiring the inspirer. Higher Ground Leaders are frequently subject to frailties, just like the rest of us, because, just like the rest of us, they are human. Incredible leader though he was, Martin Luther King Jr. had his shadow side, too. He was frequently plagued with doubts about what to do next in the civil liberties movement. Over many years, the FBI wiretapped King's home and office, putting listening devices into his hotel rooms, where they recorded his numerous sexual liaisons. He suffered from depression and despair. Although he enjoyed the loyalty of many, he also endured constant opposition from many of his colleagues.[7] Despite all this, he was one of the greatest leaders of the twentieth century, and this could not have happened without the strong support of those who loved and followed him, were passionate about his Cause, and sustained and encouraged him, especially in the bleakest of periods. Inspiring followership contributes to inspired leadership.

I developed a pledge for our clients (see box on page 192). It has been used in many organizations and can help to guide groups toward supporting each other and maintaining a high level of SQ.

From Theory to Practice: Modeling the Behavior

Ernest Hemingway once defined courage as "grace under fire." We learn as much, often more, about others from what they do, rather than what they say.

A Pledge to Honor Others

I Pledge to:

- See the sacredness in others at all times.
- Refrain from using negative or insulting comments when describing anyone else, including sarcasm, snide remarks, criticism, and judgment, or making observations about others that would dismiss or diminish them, rather than honor and inspire them.
- Refrain from indulging in gossip.
- Ask before speaking: "Will what I am about to say really improve on the silence?"
- Not say anything that does not inspire.
- Remember the words of St. Francis, who said, "Always preach the gospel, and where necessary, use words."

I ask you to join me in this commitment, to call me on my behavior whenever I am not adhering to this pledge, and to be open to a way of communicating in which all of us do the same for each other. Let us model the behavior we teach and BE the change we are seeking in the world.*

When leaders are under pressure or operating in unfamiliar conditions, followers watch their reactions with a heightened sensitivity, searching for displays of courage—grace under fire. In these situations, they look to leaders for clear signals about their inner qualities, about whether he or she is a true Higher Ground Leader. They learn in these circumstances about the leader's values and inner compass, and use what they see to shape their assessment of how the leader might act with them in the future. Such events, of varying magnitude, occur each day, and each of them is a test of grace.

Traveling as much as I do, delays inevitably occur, and the reactions of travelers vary. Some are charming and philosophical, while others take their rage out on harassed airline employees.

A few years ago, a rainstorm shut down the Pittsburgh airport. I was stranded for 14 hours. With the entire airfield gridlocked, nothing was going

*I thank my friends at Mount Carmel Health System, who took my original writing and improved upon it.

anywhere. Soon, the airport was transformed into an ugly showcase for old story corporate warriors displaying their frayed tempers—working with old paradigms and projecting their aggression onto others.

Whenever I encounter these situations, I amuse myself by observing *homo executivus* responding to stress. Frequently, when the airfield becomes socked in and all the aircraft are unable to leave their gates, some old story executives switch to warrior mode, berating airline company staff with invective, abuse, anger, rage, and bombast. They reason that it seems to work at the office—so why not here?

On this day in Pittsburgh, a typical example of homo executivus was berating the airline's customer service staff, pounding them with insults, and venting his frustration. After a string of shrill sarcasm and insulting comments, he paused, unsure about his effectiveness. Catching his breath and collecting his thoughts, he prepared to unleash another wave of invective. Slowly and very deliberately, he puffed up to his full executiveness, determined to impress. "Don't you know who I am?" he spluttered. The customer service agent, doing an impressive imitation of a swan—serene on the surface, but paddling like crazy below—reached for the microphone and announced calmly to those in the long line-up, "Excuse me for a moment, ladies and gentlemen; I have a man here who apparently doesn't know who he is."

> If you have to tell people how important you are, you're better off in the long run having it printed on a T-shirt.
>
> Joe Martin

More recently, weather caused me to become stranded in the Toronto airport. My flight had been cancelled and my fellow travelers and I were bumped to the next flight, delaying our departure by more than three hours. The airport had by now been reduced to an uncivilized bedlam, and the frazzled airline employees were showing signs of wear and tear. The friendly customer service representative booked me onto the next flight and handed me my boarding pass. I thanked her, and then said, "Boy! This is a mess! You are having a really bad day. Is there anything I can do to make this a little less stressful for you? Could I, for example, get you a bottle of water, or a coffee? Since, thanks to you, I now have all this extra time to spare, perhaps I can do something to brighten your day?"

> Do not weep; do not wax indignant. Understand.
>
> Baruch Spinoza

She looked at me in stunned amazement for a moment. And then she said, "No, it's quite okay. Thank you for asking, though. I'm fine. But, you know,

I'll tell you what I can do for you. I can bump you up to first class. I have all these extra people from your flight squished into the economy cabin, and I need to move some of you into the first class cabin—it may just as well be you!"

So which system works best? My mother used to say more flies can be caught with honey than vinegar. What makes anyone think he can unplug an airport that is in a ground-stop situation by screaming abuse at the staff? Why do we think that intimidation and fear will cause others to bend in our favor? Surely it is not a great intellectual leap to understand my mother's wisdom—not just at the airport, but throughout life—at home and at work? When we charm and inspire others, they will do remarkable things for us and inspire us—when we intimidate them, we create fear and resentment.

As I observe those passengers haranguing airline employees who are struggling to deal with the complexities of travel, I wonder, "Do you really think that you will achieve your goals with your hostile, aggressive, insulting, and demeaning behavior?" This is old story leadership at its very worst. Where did we learn the myth that we can get our way more effectively with petulance or through aggression than with love and truth? In our hearts, we know that we will achieve more by serving others than by berating them. Try this experiment: Next time you find yourself in an exasperating and frustrating situation, ask the person who has the power to resolve your frustration, "Is there anything I can do to make your day go a little more smoothly? How can I serve you?" Then watch the frustration melt and the employee's helpfulness grow. At the very least, even if your service snag cannot be resolved, the entire encounter will be more inspiring and less stressful for you. This is the magic of service. When we serve others, we inspire them—the essence of servant-leadership.

There is a widely held view that we can "motivate" high performance from others by intimidating them into the results we hope for. But the great leaders in history knew that servant-leadership—serving the needs of others before our own—was the failsafe method of serving oneself. It doesn't matter if the reason for doing this is enlightened self-interest or a genuine caring and love for others; either way, giving in order to receive always creates good karma. The key to inspiring others to high performance is serving and loving them, and telling them the truth—a lesson from the ages.

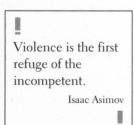

Violence is the first refuge of the incompetent.

Isaac Asimov

It may appear to be different in the short term, but in the end, the universe does not reward bullies.

The Physical Setting for Inspiration:
The Soulspace for Our Calling

Beauty is crucial to our well-being because it nourishes the soul and therefore inspires. Without beauty, our soul withers, yet many of us immerse ourselves in ugliness every day. Even if we are fortunate enough to have found our Calling, we cannot inspire our souls if we practice it in hideous surroundings.

A recent Steelcase Workplace Index Survey revealed how critical physical comfort is to the levels of satisfaction and productivity of employees:

- An overwhelming 79 percent of respondents believe that physical comfort has a serious impact on worker satisfaction.
- Over half (53 percent) of those surveyed thought their organizations had minimal information regarding the level of satisfaction people have with their physical work environment.[8]

When Jamie Dimon was CEO of Bank One Corp. (now merged with J.P. Morgan Chase & Co.), he said he saved $2 million in annual expenses by eliminating all of the live plants from the company's Chicago headquarters and 1,800 branches. Explaining his decision to employees, Dimon said, "You're not there to make people feel warm and fuzzy with trees." But before making decisions of this kind, we need to ask:

- Does a decision like this serve and inspire followers?
- Will it increase their commitment and therefore their productivity?
- Or will it, in fact, cost more than it saves because it will demoralize them and lead to depleted energy and performance?
- Can the goal be achieved in a consultative way that inspires and meets the needs of others?

Visual aggression surrounds us, and it grates on the soul. The daily assaults made on our senses by self-centered commercialism, violence, and ugliness first penetrate our personalities, distressing our emotional selves, and then seep into our soul, where they have the same, only more profound, effect. Some of the efficient and economical, but ugly, buildings in which people find themselves working are a case in point. But we can achieve efficiency and economy

> Flowers always make people better, happier, and more helpful; they are sunshine, food, and medicine to the soul.
>
> Luther Burbank

just as well through the opposites: service, love, and beauty. Indeed, we might ask ourselves what could be achieved through self-centered, cost-focused, ugly approaches that cannot be better achieved through service, love, and beauty? The former may take us to our short-term, personal goals, but the latter will take us to higher ground and help us to be more effective and productive, while at the same time rewarding our souls. This is the difference between motivating others and inspiring them.

Nor is the mundane, the boring, the utilitarian or the conventional necessarily the cheapest or most effective form of physical space. In fact, creating beautiful surroundings may pay handsome dividends, beyond even those reaped

> **!**
>
> Respect the masterpiece. It is true reverence to man. There is no quality so great, none so much needed now.
>
> Frank Lloyd Wright
>
> **!**

by the soul. Ford Motor Co. is creating the world's largest living roof by covering it with 10 acres of drought-resistant sedum plant costing $3.6 million. Though this is double the cost of regular roofing, it will last twice as long, and the company will therefore break even on its investment. But there are additional benefits: It will reduce polluted storm-water run-off and act as an insulating blanket in warm and cold weather by absorbing and reducing rainfall. The air quality around the plant will be improved because the roof will absorb and trap carbon dioxide, and release oxygen into the environment. And the company will save $35 million that it will not need to spend on storm sewers and storm-water treatment systems because the roof acts as a natural filtration system, sending excess storm-water to retention ponds before being released into the Rouge River.[9]

Many leaders are realizing that our physical environment, our soulspace, must be more than functional; it must be fun, playful, and entertaining, with textures, sounds, colors, and smells that charm the senses, entrance the emotions, and speak to the soul. It must relate with our environment in a safe and friendly way. It is part of the message we send announcing who we are—our "voice." It must resemble life as it is richly lived, connecting us with the reality of human relationships and our yearning for community.

A visitor to the head office of British Airways, five miles west of London's Heathrow airport, is greeted by receptionists who flank the lobby as if they were checking you onto a flight, before passing between two giant wheels from the undercarriage of a jumbo jet. A corridor designed as a street, complete with cobblestones and sidewalk trees, links six small office blocks within the complex. The center of the complex mimics an English village square. Employees emerging from the basement car park cross the village square, as they would in a real village community, greeting and chatting with neighbors along the way. Employees are no longer tethered to their desks by telephone cords—having been liberated by digital wireless phones that double as their desk phone and can be carried anywhere. Employees can even order groceries online from a local supermarket and have them delivered to their cars before their daily commute. Such care and attention nurtures the soul. Many companies are beginning to see the wisdom in making their offices more like the soulspaces that people—*not functions*—enjoy. Other companies are introducing streets, cafés, restaurants, meditation rooms, chapels, quiet areas, daycare, pet facilities, indoor parks, and gardens.

W. L. Gore & Associates tries to locate its premises in natural environments. Its medical-products division is located south of the Grand Canyon in Flagstaff, Arizona, and the company acquired 150 acres of land in Glasgow, Delaware, for a new facility, to which the State of Delaware added 200 acres to be set aside as protected woods and wetlands and another 100 acres for the creation of a regional park.

Joe Calvaruso of Mount Carmel Health System says:

> We have a "Time Out Room," a room in the hospital where we bring a massage therapist to do chair massages, we offer aromatherapy and provide soft music and food and refreshments. People can take a 15-minute pause—nurses can go up there and enjoy a peaceful moment, a breath of inspiration, and a little pause that breaks up their day. Obviously, this is an initiative that's generated from love. We tell people, "We want you to be inspired. We want you to do the most inspiring work of your life. We want this organization to be one where you're inspired about work and look forward to coming here every day, and we want you to do it in physical places that are inspiring to you—your work environment." One of our employees invited an artist friend of hers to paint the walls of the operating rooms—some appear to be mountains, another is a beach, another is an environmental seascape. The patients' comments have been phenomenal. Instead of a sterile, institutional environment, they experience the beauty of a mural. Another person, who just returned from their Higher Ground Leadership Retreat, arranged for a fish aquarium to be placed in the registration lobby of one of our hospitals. This has a very calming effect on patients and their families during this very tense time as they register for their hospital stay or procedure.

> Art washes away
> from the soul the
> dust of everyday life.
> Pablo Picasso

Mark Scott is the former CEO of Mid-Columbia Medical Center in The Dalles, Oregon. As a Higher Ground Leader, he built an outstanding healthcare center, rated by the Joint Commission on Accreditation of Healthcare Organizations (JCAHO) as one of the top 10 percent in the nation, and, during the past seven years alone, 1,100 healthcare professionals have made the trip to Oregon to see how this marvelous place works. Scott describes the critical role of a soul-space in the healing process in healthcare:

> The arts play a very important part in the healing process. There's no question that we have grown immune to such things as music, relaxation, massage therapy, artwork, story telling, and videos. These are all critical factors in creating an environment that encourages patient recovery and wellness. Our patient rooms are healing environments, and they are sacred healing spaces for us. Our hallways are elegant—they are frequently straightened up, nothing is ever allowed to litter the hallways. This is where most of our patients experience their first freedom of leaving the bed, therefore our hallways should not be cluttered with IV stands, laundry bags, trash bags, wheelchairs, dietary carts, pharmacy carts, and so on. We strive to maintain our environments as sacred healing spaces in order to fully reach the inner souls of our patients and our staff, and therefore accelerate the pace of healing. The physical environment can enhance the well-being of both patients and staff. The focus is not just to make our healthcare institutions nicer, prettier, and less institutional looking, but to acknowledge that the physical environment must change in order to enable a change in philosophy, to encourage a values-centered approach, and inculcate behavior changes that lead to patient-centered, humanistic care. We need to be aware of the real and symbolic messages of our environment. We must give the message to our patients that this is a caring, safe place; that "you are important here." We want patients to get well and stay well. We want them to know they are part of this community, that we encourage their mobility. We believe that art and beauty have important healing qualities.

> Form follows function—that has been misunderstood. Form and function should be one, joined in a spiritual union.
>
> Frank Lloyd Wright

Over the years, my own organization has evolved in a similar way. Our offices are located in a converted log house, perched at the edge of a cliff overlooking a seven-hundred-acre wilderness that unfolds into the valley four hundred feet below. The offices are wrapped in six-by-eight-foot windows that enable colleagues and visitors to connect with the spectacular views, which change with each magical season and weather pattern. The panorama is breathtaking and the silence extraordinary. Visitors arriving for the first time are astounded by the awe-inspiring views; even regular visitors return to their favorite spot to stand and gaze for a few moments to enjoy the pristine tranquility before settling into the business that brought them to our soulspace. Hummingbirds feed near all of the office windows during the summer, and songbirds visit the many feeders placed strategically for everyone to enjoy. Deer often cross the property, pausing to watch us as we watch them. In the native tradition, the deer is the symbol of gentleness, reminding us that we have created a gentle environment and of our intent to be gentle with each other. Skiing is five minutes away, a swimming pool beckons outside, and trails through the woods offer opportunities for exercise, reflection, and conversation.

We hold regular Wisdom Circles in the main office, warmed by the airtight stove in the colder months, and in the warmer times, we gather at the end of the thirty-foot cantilevered deck that thrusts out over the cliff edge. Any team member may read an inspiring poem, quote, or essay to precede and end each meeting. Breaking bread together is an important ritual for our team. Members bring the components of lunch and prepare it together in the kitchen, which is fully stocked with refreshments and snacks. Team members frequently bring treats to share: homemade cookies, cakes, soups, even wine. On one occasion, we made grape jelly together from wild grapes collected from the local area, turning the event into a collaborative project. The entire team shares the responsibility for growing tomatoes, which we eat during our communal lunches. We have a surround-sound stereo system with hundreds of CDs and a library with several thousand books. We have raised five babies in the last five years in our offices, where we have vied for the opportunity to carry them around while talking on our portable phones. And we have Spirit, the wonder dog, to entertain us each day. Though we may be pastoral and romantic, cutting-edge technology connects our global team of colleagues and faculty, thousands of members of the Higher Ground Community, and our clients and suppliers. Our soulspace is a means for building a greater sense of community in our team.

> Space and light and order. Those are the things that men need just as much as they need bread or a place to sleep.
>
> Le Corbusier

You may be reading this and thinking, "This guy isn't in the real world. He should come and smell the coffee and see the awful place where I work." But you and I are the same—we have choices. I have always wanted to work with inspired teams, and I've always known this is not possible in uninspiring physical environments. Consequently, I have always refused to pay rents to landlords for efficient but ugly buildings. Even when we founded the head offices of Manpower Limited, we refused to locate in the city, choosing instead a rural town that offered convenient commuting for our team members. We studied maps and the home addresses of all of our employees and located our new head office exactly in the place that represented the average shortest commuting distance for all of them. We were one of the first companies to hire an architect to design office landscaping; we were one of Herman Miller's first customers, outfitting our entire offices with modular, custom-designed, and personally chosen furniture. We built a meditation room, we abandoned dress codes, installed kitchens, loaded the health insurance, disability, and retirement plans—in short, we went out of our way to create a soulspace for our team. We wanted to create the conditions in which they would be inspired, so that they would, in turn, inspire their leaders. We wanted to be Higher Ground Leaders—we all have the choice.

Our physical workspace must connect us with nature—we cannot attain extraordinary levels of achievement when we are disconnected from the Earth. Our association with the Earth is not only a natural need, but also vital to our souls. The Earth represents our very physical essence: we are made of earth and, ultimately, we are returned to Earth. For reasons that are not always obvious, therefore, we all experience a connection with landscape and the natural world. A numinous voice calls to us from the rocks and streams, from the birds and fishes, from the stars and storms. A mystical beauty speaks to our souls, reminding us where we belong and that we share the life force of the universe. Plastic plants and fake trees are no substitute for the real thing. If we are surrounded by plastic and fakery, our thoughts will become the same.

If you work in a dismal environment, ask yourself what is holding you back from changing it, making it better, converting it into a soulspace. In addition to tradition and inertia, what real reasons are in your way? If you love the people you work with and you want to inspire them, why aren't you spoiling them, making them feel special and indulging their needs, feeding their soul with physical beauty?

Christopher Morley wrote, "Truth is the strong compost in which beauty may sometimes germinate." Perhaps the inverse is also true: Beauty is the compost, which may sometimes germinate truth. Who can nurture the urge to violence or deceit when beauty and love are cradling them? What matters to Higher Ground Leaders is that they attempt to meet the needs of *all* the members of the team sharing the soulspace, whether they are on the payroll or are partners, suppliers, and customers. Higher Ground Leaders want them all to be inspired to produce their finest work on their behalf. A soulspace, the physical beauty with which we surround ourselves at work, is essential for our inspiration. Beauty is holiness. Beauty is grace. Beauty is sacred. As Josiah Gilbert Holland said, "The soul, like the body, lives by what it feeds on." If we want to inspire people, let's feed their souls by making their surroundings inspiring.

Throwing a Curve to the Soul

Try this experiment: Find the ugliest piece of furniture in your office or home and study it for a few moments. Walk around it and really experience the extreme hideousness of the offending piece. Then make some notes about what you noticed or experienced about it and why it affronted you so. Now find the most elegant and beautiful piece of furniture in your office or home and study it carefully, too. Note what engages you; what attracts you about it, and why you find it exquisite. Compare notes between the two.

One of the striking differences between the two pieces, perhaps not obvious at first, may be the lines: the ugly will tend to be more rectangular or right-angular and regular, and the beautiful will be more curved, irregular, and sensuous.

Right angles are hard to find in the natural world. Even trees do not grow at right angles to the Earth. Animals, reptiles, fish, flowers, clouds, rivers, trails—not an obvious right angle between them. Even the Earth itself is curved. The right angle is the result of the combination of the lack of human imagination and our urge to be cost-efficient and utilitarian—only meeting the needs of the personality, while ignoring the soul. In creating our physical environments, our default behavior often leads us to create right angles. But where an object or an environment has been divinely fashioned, it will curve sensually, enrapturing the eye and the imagination, engaging the soul. In short, our DNA has been programmed for curves, and this is why it, and therefore we, reject right angles—unless they are fashioned by a genius like Frank Lloyd Wright, who famously said, "First throw out the box!"

When we create "efficient" but ugly working environments, we challenge our natural will and affront the soul. Humans cannot work or play at their best in linear and therefore ugly places. Simone Weil said, "Beauty captivates the flesh in order to obtain permission to pass right through to the soul." We cannot expect people to do amazing, creative work, and thus fulfill their potential, in uninspiring environments.

I often ask audiences to imagine that they have been asked to do the most creative work of their lives, an assignment that will be their legacy on this planet. Then I ask in what physical location they would choose to work to best access their genius and cause their creative juices to flow. They usually describe places like the mountains, the forest, the desert, the beach, or exotic islands. Some-

> ❗
> Organic buildings are the strength and lightness of the spiders' spinning, buildings qualified by light, bred by native character to environment, married to the ground.
>
> Frank Lloyd Wright
> ❗

times, they will name a place—Yosemite, the Rockies, the Napa Valley, Mount Rainier, Hawaii, or the Grand Canyon. They never suggest the office!

Suppose though, that we designed our work-spaces with curves—not right angles—with round windows, curved walls, and irregular shaped doors and rooms (think Herman Miller furniture). Suppose we inserted tables and chairs that were fluid and nonconformist; made abundant use of natural, not plastic, plants; ensured that the delicious curves of water and sound were evident; that we invited the sky and the stars through curvilinear skylights, and that visual rhapsodies replaced linear environments. Then we would access our imagination and lessen our linear thinking and, once again, creativity and brilliance would feel invited to flourish among our

employees. Creative environments romance creative work from people. Inspiring workspaces—what I call soulspaces—inspire luminous results and leadership. It is not an accident that Apple computers are nearly always preferred, at least from a design point of view, to any other computer maker's boring square putty-colored boxes. Name your favorite item, and it will have curves, not straight lines—and you may have noticed that this also applies to people. "In life, as in art, beauty moves in curves," said Edward G. Bulwer-Lytton.

> ❗
> I have learned the novice can often see things that the expert overlooks. All that is necessary is not to be afraid of making mistakes, or of appearing naive.
>
> Abraham Maslow
> ❗

By dramatically changing the lines of our working environments and the artifacts with which we fill the spaces, we can dramatically enhance personal and therefore organizational performance. My company has helped clients rethink the original designs of their office buildings and influenced the structures and decors and been able to achieve remarkable changes in the performance, inspiration, and attitudes of all of the people who enjoy the space. Want to prove it yourself? Give similar tasks to two different teams of equal talent, but put one in their traditional Dilbert cubicles and the other in a cathedral, forest, park, or gorgeous building, and watch the difference in output.

Somerset Maugham once observed, "The ideal has many names, and beauty is but one of them." Who says the old story way of designing workspaces is efficient and cost-effective? It costs money to be "efficient," and investing in beauty in our surroundings makes money—the opposite of traditional, utilitarian thinking. Why? Because it nourishes the soul, and when the soul is nourished, the world wins.

The Path of Inspiration

There is a natural Law of Inspiration—"To be inspired by others, you must first inspire." We innately understand this logic, but often forget to apply it; if we inspire others, they will inspire us. Consider Figure 13.1.

The purpose of the healthy, soul-guided ego is to serve others, and when the ego does this effectively, it does something even greater—it serves the soul. This is the diagonal path in Figure 13.1, which I call "The Path of Inspiration," because when we do this, we are always an inspiration to others and ourselves. But when our egos seek to serve ourselves more than others, we descend into the

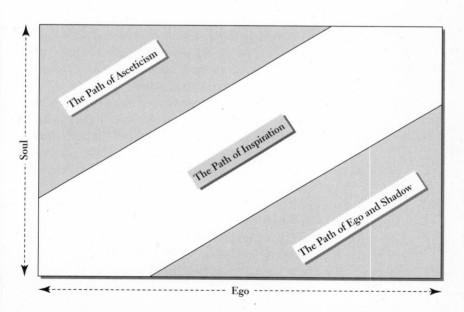

Figure 13.1 The Path of inspiration.

lower part of the diagram, egocentricity, and it is here that we spend much time in our shadow. When we behave this way, we may display the hubris and arrogance that comes from the self-serving, shadow-dominated, unhealthy ego. But if, on the other hand, we abandon or suppress our egos, failing to take sufficient care of our own needs as we sacrifice them on behalf of others, we become ascetic (the practice of rigidly denying ourselves) and therefore we can be of little value to ourselves or to others. As we discussed in Chapter 8, this is when service is stretched into sacrifice—the Path of Asceticism.

It is ironic that so many people feel that, although they have dedicated themselves so fully to their families and work, they nevertheless experience the "Rodney Dangerfield effect"—they feel they "don't get no respect." Often, this perception is real and caused by their persistently manipulative behavior, masquerading as a desire to serve others, but in reality, it is a means to better serve themselves. You know the type: They can't seem to do anything for someone else without first attaching strings or harboring some ulterior motive. This is the Path of Ego that is serving self—not servant-leadership.

The Higher Ground Leader inspires by coming to terms with his or her own ego, warts and all, naming and taking responsibility for the less attractive attributes that arise from their shadow and using this learning to adapt their behavior by living in service to others. Think about it—all of the greatest leaders in history have been servant-leaders and in doing so have become an inspiration to others, as well as themselves, not just for their lifetimes, but in many cases, for many subsequent generations.

> ❚
> The man who lives for himself is a failure; the man who lives for others has achieved true success.
>
> Norman Vincent Peale
> ❚

A question we might keep in our hearts is this: Who is leading—the ego or the soul? If the ego is out front, the priority becomes oneself—self-absorption, and this can lead to selfishness, arrogance, aggression, and the need to dominate and control. This is the behavior that others find *uninspiring*. If the soul is an equal, or even principal, guide in our lives, the priority changes to serving *others*, and this causes us to become people who serve and inspire.

Larry Bird, the basketball great, said, "First, master the fundamentals."

This is the power of knowledge and learning, but after becoming aware of technique through learning, it is time for us to let this learning go, to place less emphasis on the ego and more on the soul. The ego-lessons will not be soon forgotten, but they can now rest comfortably in our subconscious mind, no longer being top-of-mind. Understanding the intricacies of the persona and how we relate to each other and how we can grow and improve our relational chemistry is a vital part of the human experience. But once we have mastered the fundamentals, we need to leave the learned approach behind us in order to transcend this knowledge. This is the journey to Higher Ground. Michael Jordan, perhaps the greatest basketball legend, summed it up beautifully when he said. "Just play. Have fun. Enjoy the game."

Emptying the Mind

The degree to which we inspire others is a direct result of how much we love them unconditionally—and *unconditionally* is the operative word. When we suspect another of hateful characteristics and uncharitable behavior, attributing blame and responsibility for the pain they cause us, finding their achievements to be inadequate, assuming that they are capable of hurtful and dishonest practices, or being critical of their appearance, heritage, beliefs, actions, values, or idiosyncrasies, then we cannot be fully loving toward them and therefore cannot inspire them, or inspire them so much that they inspire us—the seventh step for the Higher Ground Leader. These critical and judgmental behaviors are generally examples of projection, which we described in Chapter 1. To create the energetic space where love can flourish, and therefore where we can inspire and in turn be inspired, we must first empty our minds of our preconceptions about people—our judgments and our suspicions—our tendency to project.

In meditation, particularly Zen meditation, there is a concept known as "beginner's mind," *shoshin* in Japanese. A beginner's mind is empty. Miles Davis, the great jazz musician, said, "I always listen for what I can leave out." We may have opinions and baggage, but our challenge is to set them aside, empty the mind by assuming the beginner's mind, just for this moment, knowing that our prejudices and preconceptions will still be there for us to collect later—if we still feel we really need them. If we can empty our mind, then we will become open—and then we will be able to love each other without inhibitions. The Japanese word *mushin* (from *mu*, which means "no" or "non," and *shin*, which means "heart," "mind," "feeling," or "intention") is a word that roughly translates into "no mind." It describes the complete absence of intellectual or discursive thought; a state in which the ego is forgotten and the individual is free to perform without concern for dualistic notions of good or bad, success or failure. Mushin is a gentle heart and an open, ready mind.

One of the techniques in meditation is to empty the mind and then to keep it empty for as long as possible, so that our souls are able to invite and embrace

> !
> If your mind is empty, it is always ready for anything; it is open to everything. In the beginner's mind there are many possibilities, but in the expert's, there are few.
>
> Shunryu Suzuki
> !

the essence of the universe. Approaching others with an open, beginner's mind, a mind free of assumptions and projections, invites a soulful response. This is the preparation of the mind that is offered by meditation. Meditation is only one of many methods of emptying the mind, but it is a very effective way as I described earlier in Chapter 5. Meditation is a good starting place for inspiring others by loving them — the essence of soul-to-soul communication. And it is a good place to return to when we temporarily bring a relationship to a close — almost like bookends for relationships.

To inspire others so much that they inspire us, we must move beyond perpetual analysis — to loving acceptance. Daisetz T. Suzuki wrote, "Man is a thinking reed, but his great works are done when he is not calculating and thinking. Childlikeness has to be restored with long years of training in the art of self-forgetfulness. When this is attained, man thinks, yet he does not think. He thinks like the showers coming down from the sky; he thinks like the waves rolling on the ocean."

Thus, inspiring others so completely that they always *want* to inspire us, is achieved by letting go of our personality-based models, techniques, theories,

> !
> We cannot change anything unless we accept it.
>
> Carl Gustav Jung
> !

processes, tests, assumptions, and other left-brained paraphernalia, and doing a simple, although not easy, thing: loving others without judgment, seeing the sacredness in them, searching for their gifts, and nourishing them — building on their strengths, not focusing on their weaknesses.

Here are eight helpful steps to go beyond the personality-based behavior in order to communicate soul-to-soul:

1. Meditate.
2. Name the behaviors of which you are aware — that are not in your shadow, but in the light — that do not inspire others.
3. Through questioning, therapy, coaching, soulwork, or inquiry, identify, name, and own the behaviors of which you are *un*aware — that are in your shadow — that do not inspire others, sometimes called the disavowed self.
4. Bring these shadow behaviors into the light by understanding their source.
5. Forgive the source of the hurt and bring this experience to a healthy closure.

6. Adjust your behavior, avoid projecting, and refrain from judging others.
7. Perfect the "technology of the personality" and then let it go.
8. While embracing the healthy personality, empty the mind (*mushin*), and communicate soul-to-soul.
9. Meditate.

This process involves calming the mind and emptying it of preconceptions and "technique." Over time, it can serve us well to be analysts of behavior and the personality, but once we have mastered this, it is time for us to go past this, to widen our capacity to relate with others, by making connections that are less from personality to personality, and more from soul to soul.

The opportunity is available to us all to resolve to become Higher Ground Leaders who first learn how to bring the shadow behaviors we all own into the light, and then move past all of this so that we are leading from the soul. At this stage of our personal growth, we become the kind of leaders that others admire because we are being courageous, authentic, serving, truthful, loving, and effective—that is to say, *living* the CASTLE Principles—as Higher Ground Leaders, and this is what others see in us, experience of us, and therefore find so inspiring. In this way, we become Higher Ground Leaders because our behavior inspires others to inspire us.

The Higher Ground Leader, then, is a servant-leader who discovers the exquisite space between self-sacrifice and self-indulgence, the magic space that becomes a legend like Martin Luther King or Gandhi—and if you and I serve and inspire others enough—perhaps like you and me.

By inspiring others, we cause them to become so inspired that they become a constant source of inspiration for us—inspirers inspiring inspirers.

Outing the Closet Human

The ego is like the moon. Though it can be bright at times, and often full, the moon always depends on the sun for its light. Like the ego, it has a shadow side, which will remain dark as long as it is not exposed to the warmth and light of the sun. The soul is like the sun. It is the source of its own energy and light. It shines its light freely and consistently. It shares and warms. It heals and nourishes. It even adds light to the ego-moon, which otherwise would be permanently cold and dark. By turning our egos to the warmth and light of the soul and inviting its healing and loving power, we will grow and be bright and warm—even though parts of us will remain in the shadow.

The Aspen Institute asked 1,978 MBA students who graduated from thirteen leading business schools, including Carnegie Mellon, Columbia, Northwestern, and the University of Pennsylvania, what a company's top priorities should be. Some 75 percent cited maximizing value for shareholders, 71 percent said satisfying customers, and 33 percent put a high priority on producing high-quality goods and services. Only 5 percent thought the top goals should include improving the environment, and just 25 percent said creating value for their local communities was a priority. Two years earlier, when these students started B-school, 68 percent had opted for shareholder value, 75 percent cited customer satisfaction, and 43 percent voted for producing quality goods and services.[10]

We abandon our values in an effort to adapt to external norms that will win approval, and this process begins, as we can see, early in our lives. At work, the pattern is accelerated, causing our souls to be in the shadow of our personalities: we think of one another as "functions" (executive, teacher, parent, pilot, physician, letter-carrier), instead of what we really are: spiritual beings sharing an earthly experience. We wear an ego mask, pretending that we are strong, potent, invulnerable heroes and, at work in particular, we often labor under the delusion that it is unseemly to permit our true feelings to be visible, let alone that our feelings should infuse our decisions. As the data above confirms, our conditioning causes us to falsely believe that showing our emotions, being vulnerable and authentic, is weak, unprofessional, or "nonbusinesslike."

But this is not real life—it is a lie. We become masks locked in arid conversations with other masks. And when we behave like this, we are closet humans. And this is not inspiring for others, who are therefore not inspired to inspire us—because they feel we are not *real*.

We need to "come out"; to own up to being human, to being vulnerable and fragile, to owning pain, needing love, compassion, and forgiveness, to wanting more from life than profit improvement, a paycheck, or a promotion. In short, we need to come out by declaring ourselves to be real humans. We need to conduct communications with each other that are authentic, truthful, and deep, instead of pretending to be the fictitious macho characters we have taught our personalities to idolize. We need to discuss matters that serve a higher purpose as well as the data, the metrics, the tasks at hand, and the bottom line, because if we limit our dialogue to the secular and the material, our relationships will be brittle and barren, and it is difficult to feel inspired from this place. We need to reveal ourselves to each other for what we really are—spiritual beings and whole people who are parents, spouses, lovers, teachers, and

> !
> That's all a man can hope for during his lifetime—to set an example—and when he is dead, to be an inspiration for history.
>
> William McKinley
> !

learners, who laugh and cry, hurt and heal, but above all, have loving intent and are here to serve each other. The nine steps outlined on pages 206–207 are a path to becoming secure enough in ourselves to be real with others.

When we "come out" by revealing our true, emotional, and spiritual selves, a remarkable thing will happen. For the first time, our masks will fall, and others will recognize us for who we truly are. As a result, they in turn will be emboldened to reveal their humanness with us, and we will come to know each other for the first time. Others will join with us and thus create the beginnings of a sanctuary—a community of people who share the same values. In time, others will notice the extraordinary sense of teamwork and the personal effectiveness and energy flowing from this sanctuary. They will be drawn to it, and they will want to join. Others will want to come out, too, and some will want to form their own sanctuaries. This spontaneous rejuvenation of authenticity works like an immune system that has been spurred into new vigor. Sanctuaries will sprout in disparate parts of the organization, replacing the unproductive relationships that existed before, and healing the souls trapped within corporate walls. This magic produces a bonus—because organizations, families, and communities are simply collections of individual spirits—and when these spirits heal one at a time, the sum of all of them eventually heals, too. This results in greater organizational, family, and community effectiveness and performance. Then, we will become inspired.

> The world is round and the place which may seem like the end, may also be only the beginning.
>
> Ivy Baker Priest

This is the way of the enlightened changemaker, the Higher Ground Leader. Demanding change from others seldom works.

We get commitment by making a commitment.

In my research into the greatest leaders in history, the ones we now revere most dearly, the ones that continue to inspire us most, the ones that we each know and love at a personal level today—they were the ones who had the greatest capacity to *love*. Higher Ground Leaders inspire us for one major reason: they love us. Higher Ground Leaders have a love affair with humanity; an intense affair of the heart, and this is what fuels their capacity for inspiring others. Inspiration can only come from love—it cannot come from any other place. Every Higher Ground Leader makes a soul connection with followers at a level that captivates us both—leader and follower.

As Kahlil Gibran might have written, Higher Ground Leadership is love made visible.

In Summary:
The Seven Key Questions

The Higher Ground Leader asks the following seven key questions and then dedicates his or her life's work to finding the answers:

1. What is my Destiny? Why am I here on Earth? How does my life make a difference?
2. What is my Cause? How will I *be* while I am here? What will I stand for? Are my aspirations a magnet for passion?
3. What is my Calling? What will I do, and how will I use my talents and passion to serve? What is your Calling, and how can I help you to achieve greater mastery?
4. Are my Destiny, Cause, and Calling aligned? Is my Calling aligned with the Cause of our organization? Is it the same for you?
5. How may I serve you?
6. How can I guide your contribution of brilliance and help you to grow and become fulfilled?
7. Am I inspiring others in everything I say and do? Am I creating the conditions that will inspire me?

Inspiring others is an act of service that flows from love. Motivational leaders also love others, of course, but others are not their primary focus; Higher Ground Leaders make a loving connection with others. We can all see and feel the difference in a heartbeat. We sense the presence of a motivator—their manipulative and self-focused agendas are often so transparent. So, too, is the commitment to ego and personality, to the superficial and to the material. Higher Ground Leaders love others so genuinely, they cannot resist serving them—and followers are at once inspired by this congruence. The result is a connection of souls, of people doing soulwork, and of the creation of a sanctuary. These are magical moments and magical places in which to live and work because Higher Ground Leaders are fully present. In these exhilarating states, we become inspired. And to the great joy of those around us, we are inspired to offer our greatest gifts—we are called to release *all* of the music within us.

We all need to work through our "stuff," understanding the journeys we have traveled and the events and experiences that have shaped our lives and made us who we are. With this understanding, we can become masters of the finer aspects of the technology of the personality. But then it is time for us to move on, to go beyond the narcissistic and self-absorbed world of the personality, so that we can become free to learn as much about the soul as we have learned about the personality. The Higher Ground Leader matures to this place, relying less on the technology of relationships and more on the natural grace of soul-to-soul connections. And thus begins the transition from old story to New Story Leadership. This is the person who becomes so inspiring to others, that they become inspired by their capacity to inspire. This is the magic ingredient X of the Higher Ground Leader.

Blessing for a Higher Ground Leader

Thank you for being clear about your Destiny
And following your Calling.
Thank you for being a caring Listener,
For inviting me to bare my Soul and share my dreams with you,
And for hearing my story and asking about the path that I am on;
For being interested in my LIFE as well as my work.
Thank you for not wearing a mask, for being a *real* human,
And revealing the genuine article, when I ask;
For being vulnerable, not invincible,
For owning your fears and learning about mine.
Thank you for understanding the difference between motivation and
    Inspiration
And for knowing the right time and place for each one.
Thank you for being a Mentor, generously sharing your wisdom with me,
Including the little secrets and special tricks that really make a difference.
I pay tribute to your courageous heart that so invigorates you and others,
Causing you to keep trying even when the world has no ears for you;
Lesser beings would have given up long ago.
I recognize you for telling the Truth and keeping your Promises—
I offer you, in return, my complete trust and loyalty.
Thank you for having faith in me, patiently encouraging my potential,
And helping me to discover my greatness.
Thank you for running interference through the "system" on my behalf,
Promoting my Cause, being fair and even-handed and defending me when
    appropriate.
Thank you for having vision, always seeing the bigger picture,
Dreaming in Technicolor while others settle for a world of gray.
Thank you for getting out of my way and encouraging me to do my job
So that we can both excel at what we each do best.
I celebrate your creativity, the muse within you who asks "Why"
And the divine being within you who thinks more about solutions than
    problems.
I admire your grace, your peaceful intent, your search for balance and
    friendship and
The way you calm disagreements,
Always focusing on what unites us, not what divides us,
Playing to strengths, not weaknesses.
Thank you for growing and encouraging me to do the same.
Thank you for Serving, for putting me first and yourself next.
I honor you for balancing the energies of your personality with those of
    your Soul,
Always considering both—in yourself and others.
Thank you for being a beautiful leader, for loving me and others and
    yourself.

Thanks to Higher Ground Leader Caroline Martin for inspiring this poem.

The Higher Ground Leadership Commitment

As corporate leaders, we steward a sacred opportunity to change the world by leading others as we would be led ourselves. You can support these Leadership Principles by signing them at

http://www.secretan.com/hglcommitment

and inviting others to do the same.

Sign the Higher Ground Leadership Commitment now!

Yes, I will sign the Higher Ground Leadership Commitment and help change myself, others, and the world. I commit to practicing these Principles more and more every day and to guiding others to do the same:

Courage – I pledge to be courageous and to stand for and defend high values;

Authenticity – I commit to being transparent and true;

Service – I will lead others by serving them;

Truth-telling – I will tell the truth in all relationships;

Love – I will love and honor all people;

Effectiveness – I will strive to be truly effective in all endeavors.

Notes

Introduction

1. *What the World Thinks in 2002: How Global Publics View Their Lives, Their Countries, the World, America,* Pew Research Center for the People and the Press, December 4, 2002.
2. Rushworth M. Kidder, "From a Dark Present, a Brighter Future," *Ethics Newsline,* December 23, 2002.
3. "Johnny PayCheck Weighs In," *Fortune,* February 7, 2000.
4. "Working Today: Exploring Employees' Emotional Connection to Their Jobs," Towers Perrin/Gang and Gang, January 2003.
5. *The Q12 Survey,* The Gallup Organization, 2002.
6. Nina Munk, "My Life Is Miserable. You've made a BIG difference," *Forbes,* March 24, 1997, p. 40.

Chapter 1

1. "I Did What, Dick?" *Maclean's,* November 13, 2000.
2. "Uncertain Times, Abundant Opportunities," PricewaterhouseCoopers' Fifth Annual Global CEO Survey, conducted in conjunction with the World Economic Forum.
3. Rushworth Kidder, Institute for Global Ethics, *Newsline,* August 12, 2002.
4. Rainer Maria Rilke, *Letters to a Young Poet,* "Letter Four, Worpswede, Near Bremen," July 16, 1903.
5. Thomas S. Kuhn, *The Structure of Scientific Revolutions,* 3rd ed., Chicago: University of Chicago Press, 1996; see also, Lance H. K. Secretan, *Managerial Moxie: The 8 Proven Steps to Empowering Employees and Supercharging Your Company,* Rocklin, CA: Prima Publishing, 1993, pp. 5–6.
6. Leslie A. Perlow, *When You Say Yes But Mean No: How Silencing Conflict Wrecks Relationships and Companies . . . and What You Can Do About It,* New York: Crown

Publishing, 2003; Irving Janis described this pattern in his book, *Groupthink: Psychological Studies of Policy Decisions and Fiascoes*, 2nd ed., Boston: Houghton Mifflin, 1982, a classic of social psychology based on the idea that people in groups tend to think differently, and by implication, less effectively than they would have thought as individuals on the same issue at the same time.

Chapter 2

1. Carol J. Loomis, "EDS Executives Don't Suffer," *Fortune*, April 14, 2003, p. 56.
2. Peter Coy, "High Turnover, High Risk," *BusinessWeek*, spring 2002.
3. Chris Argyris, "Empowerment: The Emperor's New Clothes," *Harvard Business Review*, May–June, 1998, pp. 98–105.
4. Stephanie Armour, *Tucson Citizen*, Gannett News Service, January 31, 2003.
5. U.S. Department of Labor, Bureau of Labor Statistics, Bureau of Labor Statistics Data, January 2003.
6. Lou Harris and Associates, "The Annual Work and Leisure Poll #49," September 25, 2002.
7. Michael A. Verespej, "Uninspiring Leadership," *Industry Week*, February 1, 1999, p. 11.
8. Rita Koselka, "For Whom the Bell Tolls," *Forbes*, December 2, 1996, pp. 127–128.
9. "The Columbia Seven," *The Economist*, February 8, 2003, p. 76.
10. Frank White, *The Overview Effect: Space Exploration and Human Evolution*, Boston: Houghton Mifflin Company, 1987, p. 38.
11. Lance H. K. Secretan, *Reclaiming Higher Ground: Creating Organizations That Inspire the Soul*, Alton: The Secretan Center Inc., 2003.
12. See note 10.
13. Personal interviews with John Dornan, SAS Institute, February 12, 2003.
14. Joel Stein, "Bosses from Hell," *Time*, December 7, 1998, p. 153.
15. Wendy Zellner, "How American Execs Covered the Bases," *BusinessWeek*, April 28, 2003, p. 40 and "What Was Don Carty Thinking?" *BusinessWeek*, May 5, 2003, p. 32.
16. Ben McConnell and Jackie Huba, *Creating Customer Evangelists*, Deaborn Trade Publishing, December, 2002.
17. Rushworth Kidder, Institute for Global Ethics, *Newsline*, February 17, 2003, Volume 6, Number 7.
18. Paul H. Ray, Ph.D. and Sherry Ruth Anderson, Ph.D., *The Cultural Creatives: How 50 Million People Are Changing the World*, New York: Harmony Books, 2000.
19. Pierre Teilhard de Chardin, *The Phenomenon of Man*, Bernard Wall (trans.), New York: Harper & Row, 1959.
20. James Redfield, *The Celestine Prophesy*, New York: Warner Books, 1994.
21. Paul Thurott, "Windows Market Share Rises, But PC Sales Flatten," *WinInfo*, September 10, 2002.

22. Janice Maloney, "The Mighty Finn," *Time*, October 26, 1998, p. 69; Scott McCormack and Cecile Daurat, "Icons of the Net," *Forbes*, September 7, 1998, p. 216; "Revenge of the Hackers," *The Economist*, July 11, 1998, p. 63; Linus Torvalds and David Diamond, *Just For Fun: The Story of an Accidental Revolutionary*, New York: HarperBusiness, 2001.

23. Lance H. K. Secretan, *Managerial Moxie: The 8 Proven Steps to Empowering Your Employees and Supercharging Your Company*, Toronto: Prima Publishing, 1993.

Chapter 3

1. Caroline Myss, *Sacred Contracts: Awakening Your Divine Potential*, New York: Random House, 2001, p. 33.

2. To see a video of Joe Calvaruso discussing Higher Ground Leadership and current developments at Mount Carmel Health System, please go to http://www.secretan.com /inspire.

3. Media Advisory, 10/15/01, Fossil Rim Wildlife Center, Glen Rose, Texas.

4. An inner or attendant spirit or inspiring force, *The New Oxford Dictionary of English*, New York: Oxford University Press, 1998.

5. James Hillman, *The Soul's Code: In Search of Character and Calling*, New York: Random House, 1996, p. 8.

Chapter 5

1. "The Evolving Role of Executive Leadership," *Accenture*,1999.

2. Dawn Schauble, *Survey on Employment Benefit Preferences*, New York: William M. Mercer.

3. The rough draft of the Declaration of Independence written by Jefferson reads, "We hold these truths to be sacred and undeniable; that all men are created equal and independent, that from that equal creation they derive rights inherent and inalienable, among which are the preservation of life, and liberty, and the pursuit of happiness. . . ." (in Walter Isaacson, *Benjamin Franklin: An American Life*, New York: Simon & Schuster, 2003).

4. One in 20 American men has had a prison experience (one in six African Americans); the number of cons and ex-cons has doubled from 1974 to 2003 from 1.3 percent to 2.7 percent of the adult population; 11.3 percent of boys born in 2001 will go to jail in their lifetimes (one in three for African Americans); two-thirds of prisoners will be rearrested within three years. (*Source:* U.S. Bureau of Justice Statistics.)

5. John P. Kotter, *Matsushita Leadership*, New York: Free Press, 1997.

6. To see a video of Joe Swedish discussing Higher Ground Leadership and current developments at Centura Health, please go to http://www.secretan.com/inspire.

Chapter 7

1. Carlos Castaneda, *The Teachings of Don Juan: A Yaqui Way of Knowledge*, New York: Washington Square Press, 1985.
2. Reprinted with permission from *Touching Peace: Practicing the Art of Mindful Living*, by Thich Nhat Hanh, Berkeley, CA: Parallax Press, 1992.
3. Biography of Scott Adams 1, http://www.unitedmedia.com.
4. *USA Today*, October, 1998; see also http://www.wildsanctuary.com.
5. See, for example, C. Schwartz, J. B. Meisenhelder, Y. Ma, and G. Reed, "Altruistic Social Interest Behaviors Are Associated with Better Mental Health," *Psychosomatic Medicine*, September–October 2003, 65(5), pp. 778–785.
6. Leslie R. Crutchfield, "Teaching Jazz: Creating Community," *Stone Soup for the World*, edited by Marianne Larned, Berkeley, CA: Conari Press, 1998, p. 21.
7. "*Numbers*," *Time*, November 4, 2002; p. 13.

Chapter 8

1. Lance H. K. Secretan, *The Way of the Tiger: Gentle Wisdom for Turbulent Times*, Alton: The Secretan Center Inc., 1990.
2. Gregg Michael Levoy, *Callings: Finding and Following an Authentic Life*, Three Rivers Press, 1998.
3. Thomas Moore, *Care of the Soul: A Guide for Cultivating Depth and Sacredness in Everyday Life*, New York: HarperCollins, 1993.
4. If you would like to listen to an audio version of this meditation, please go to the Secretan Center web site at http://www.secretan.com/inspire.
5. Joel Stein, "Just Say Om," *Time*, August 4, 2003, pp. 38–46.
6. Mara Der Hovanesian, "Zen and the Art of Corporate Productivity," *BusinessWeek*, July 28, 2003, p. 56.
7. Steve Hamm, "Who says CEOs Can't Find Inner Peace?" *BusinessWeek*, September 1, 2003; Erick Schonfeld, "The Biggest Mouth in Silicon Valley," *Business 2.0*, September 2003.
8. James Hillman, *The Soul's Code: In Search of Character and Calling*, New York: Random House, 1996, p. 8.
9. "The Placebo Effect: All in the Mind," *The Economist*, February 23, 2002, p. 83.
10. Theresa Perry, Claude Steele, and Asa Hilliard, "Young, Gifted, and Black: Promoting High Achievement Among African American Students," Boston, MA: Beacon Press.
11. See note 9.
12. See note 4.

Chapter 9

1. "Tobacco's Death Benefits," *USA Today*, July 23, 2001.
2. http://www.organicconsumers.org/Monsanto/droptt.cfm; see also, Jeffrey Kluger, "The Suicide Seeds," *Time*, February 1, 1999, p. 43.
3. See note 2.
4. Lance H. K. Secretan, *Reclaiming Higher Ground: Creating Organizations That Inspire the Soul*, Alton: The Secretan Center Inc., 2003.
5. "The Game of Risk: How the Best Golfer in the World Got Even Better," *Time*, August 14, 200, pp. 38–45.

Chapter 10

1. To download your own personal Destiny, Cause, and Calling Workbook, please go to http://www.secretan.com/inspire.

Chapter 11

1. This is sometimes attributed to Mohammed Ali as, "The service you do for others is the rent you pay for the time you spend on earth."
2. Robert K. Greenleaf, "The Servant as Leader," essay, 1970.
3. *Fortune*, February 17, 1997, p. 127.
4. Tim Stevens, "Chief Among U.S.," *Industry Week*, November 16, 1998, p. 33.
5. Thomas F. O'Boyle, *At Any Cost: Jack Welch, General Electric, and the Pursuit of Profit*, New York: Vintage Books, 1999.
6. "Working Today: Exploring Employees' Emotional Connection to Their Jobs," Towers Perrin/Gang and Gang, January 2003.
7. 40 Ann Marsh, "Slice of Life," *Forbes*, April 22, 1997, pp. 64–65.
8. Crandell Bethany Goodier, Ph.D., "Sustaining the Spirit: Creating a Sanctuary for Living, Working, and Healing," Doctoral Dissertation, University of South Florida.
9. Joanne Gordon, "My Job, Myself, My Problem?" *Forbes*, January 24, 2003.

Chapter 12

1. Frederick Herzberg, *Work and the Nature of Man*, Cleveland, OH: World Publishing Company, 1966.
2. Marc Gunther, "The Kid Stays in the Picture," *Fortune*, April 14, 2003, p. 134.
3. Thomas J. Peters and Robert H. Waterman, *In Search of Excellence: Lessons from America's Best-Run Companies*, New York: Harper & Row, 1982.

4. Ursula K. Le Guin, *Lao-Tzu, Tao Te Ching: A Book About the Way and the Power of the Way*, Boston: Shambhala, 1997.

5. For a detailed description of the biochemical effects of love and fear, see Lance H. K. Secretan, *Reclaiming Higher Ground: Creating Organizations That Inspire the Soul*, Alton: The Secretan Center Inc., 2003, Chapter 5, "The Alchemy of the Soul."

6. "Working Today: Exploring Employees' Emotional Connection to Their Jobs," Towers Perrin/Gang and Gang, January 2003.

Chapter 13

1. Adam Lashinsky, "Meg and the Machine," *Fortune*, September 1, 2003.

2. Lance H. K. Secretan, *Reclaiming Higher Ground: Creating Organizations that Inspire the Soul*, Alton: The Secretan Center Inc., 2003.

3. Jerry B. Harvey, *The Abilene Paradox and Other Meditations on Management*, San Francisco: Jossey-Bass, 1996.

4. "How to Fire People: U R Sacked," *The Economist*, June 7, 2003, p. 54.

5. Caroline Myss, *Anatomy of the Spirit: The Seven Stages of Power and Healing*, New York: Random House/Value Publishing, 1997.

6. Lance H. K. Secretan, *The Way of the Tiger: Gentle Wisdom for Turbulent Times*, Toronto: The Secretan Center Inc., 1990.

7. Taylor Branch, *America in the King Years, 1963–1965*, New York: Simon & Schuster, 1999.

8. *Steelcase Workplace Index Survey*, Grand Rapids, MI: Steelcase Inc., December 11, 2002.

9. "Outfront," *Forbes*, February 3, 2003, p. 44.

10. "Where Will They Lead? MBA Student Attitudes About Business & Society," Aspen Institute: Initiative for Social Innovation through Business (ISIB), March, 2002.

Index

Scott, Mark, 198
Scott, Walter, 171
Secret Life of Walter Mitty, The (movie), 82
Secretan Centre Inc., The:
  Cause of, 69
  as example of Soulspace, 198–200
  Wisdom Circles, 199
Secretan, Lance:
  Cause:
    corporate, 69
  Destiny, 55
  Destiny, Cause, and Calling, xiii
Secretan, Tricia:
  Destiny, Cause, and Calling, 76–77
  Destiny statement, 55
Selfishness:
  of ego, 204
September 11, 2001:
  effects of, 36
Servant-leader:
  Higher Ground Leader, as, 207
  ideal parent as ultimate servant-leader, 138
  learning to become, 152
Servant-leadership, 3
  described by Robert Greenleaf, 136
  inspiring others by serving them, 194
  parental model, 139–140
Service:
  as CASTLE Principle, 168, 170–171
  confusing with sacrifice, 96
  how to serve, 78
  loving service as foundation of Higher Ground Leadership, 135
  questions to ask, 78
ServiceMaster, 118
Shadow:
  easily goaded into yang energy response, 166
  Path of Ego and Shadow, 203
  projection from, 12–15

Shareholder return:
  improvement with employees' positive feelings about work, 149
Smith, Fred, 90
Soul:
  alignment with Calling, 86–87
  Calling as extension of, 85
  difficult to define, xxviii
  leading from, 207
  questions that stir, 2
  serving the soul by being kind vs. being right, 143
  soul-to-soul communication:
    meditation as agent for achieving, 206
    steps toward, 206–207
Soulspace, 4
  for Calling, 195–203
  crucial to well-being, 195
  curved lines in, 201
  essential for inspiration, 200
  importance of, in healing process, 198
  importance of nature to, 200
  The Secretan Center Inc., 199–200
  "Time Out Room" in hospital at Mount Carmel Health System, 197
Soulwork, 8, 211
Southwest Airlines, 119, 125
  Cause as beacon attracting people, 62
  example of "Voice," 35–36
  market capitalization of, 36
  marketing strategy of, 35–36
  unique culture of, 35–36
Spirituality vs. Religion, 6
Spiritual Quotient (SQ):
  enhancing the SQ of teams, 182–185
  in understanding power, 41
Staff turnover:
  high:
    reduced through Higher Ground Leadership, 48–50

Inspire! What Great Leaders Do

Books by Lance Secretan

Managerial Moxie: The 8 Proven Steps to Empowering Employees and Supercharging Your Company
The Masterclass: Modern Fables for Working and Living
The Way of the Tiger: Gentle Wisdom for Turbulent Times
Living the Moment: A Sacred Journey
Reclaiming Higher Ground: Creating Organizations That Inspire the Soul
Inspirational Leadership: Destiny, Calling, and Cause
Spirit@Work: Bringing Spirit and Values to Work

CDs by Lance Secretan

Inspire! What Great Leaders Do
Reclaiming Higher Ground: Creating Organizations That Inspire the Soul
Inspirational Leadership: Destiny, Calling, and Cause
The Keys to the CASTLE: The Magic of Higher Ground Leadership
The New Story of Leadership: Reclaiming Higher Ground
Values-Centered Leadership: A Model for Work and Life
Living the Moment: A Sacred Journey
The Calling Meditation
A Divine Conversation

Videos by Lance Secretan

Inspire! What Great Leaders Do
Values-Centered Leadership: A Model for Work and Life
Reclaiming Higher Ground: Creating Organizations That Inspire the Soul
Inspirational Leadership: Destiny, Calling, and Cause
The Keys to the CASTLE: The Magic of Higher Ground Leadership

If you would like to contact the author to order his books, videos, or CDs, please do so at the following address:

Dr. Lance H. K. Secretan
The Secretan Center Inc.
R.R. # 2 Alton
Ontario, L0N 1A0 Canada
Web: http://www.secretan.com
E-mail: info@secretan.com

For public speaking engagements, please contact:

W. Colston Leigh Inc. Advisory Services LLC
1065 U.S. Hwy 22
Bridgewater, NJ 08807
Phone: 908.253.8600
Fax: 908.253.8601
Web: http://www.Leighbureau.com
E-mail: info@Leighbureau.com

A Note to the Reader about
Additional Resources

If you would like to access additional resources that will enable you to enjoy *Inspire!* even more, you may find the following, and much more, at : http://www.secretan.com/inspire:

- *The Calling Meditation* conducted personally by Lance Secretan.
- A *Divine Conversation* read by Lance Secretan.
- A multimedia presentation titled *Leading from the Soul.*
- The *Inspire!* Workbook containing an expanded version of all the exercises described in this book.
- Excerpts from this book.
- Video clips of Lance, as well as many of the Higher Ground Leaders referred to in *Inspire!* Clips are added and updated frequently.
- PowerPoint presentations.
- Media about *Inspire!*
- A forum where you may post your own Destiny, Cause, and Calling and read the "Why-Be-Dos" of others.
- Videos, CDs, and other merchandise that will support your work in becoming a Higher Ground Leader.